T0328557

THE ASSAULT ON DEMOCRACY

THE ASSAULT ON DEMOCRACY

HOW WE UNDERMINE OUR OWN STRENGTH

GERHARD FALK

Algora Publishing
New York

Library of Congress Cataloging-in-Publication Data —
Names: Falk, Gerhard, 1924- author.
Title: The assault on American democracy / Gerhard Falk.
Description: New York: Algora Publishing, [2017] | Includes bibliographical
    references and index.
Identifiers: LCCN 2017011832 (print) | LCCN 2017019676 (ebook) | ISBN
    9781628942637 (pdf) | ISBN 9781628942613 (soft cover: alk. paper) | ISBN
    9781628942620 (hard cover: alk. paper)
Subjects: LCSH: United States—Politics and government. | Social
    problems—United States.
Classification: LCC JK274 (ebook) | LCC JK274 .F26 2017 (print) | DDC
    320.973—dc23
LC record available at https://lccn.loc.gov/2017011832

Printed in the United States

TABLE OF CONTENTS

Introduction

The Assault on American Democracy is mainly promoted by Americans themselves. This book demonstrates that almost all American institutions include people willing to undermine the democracy which is made this country unique in the history of mankind. The first chapter of this book provides a brief history of the long struggle to gain freedom and liberty for the individual as guaranteed by the American Constitution.

Two hundred and fifty years ago, our third president, Thomas Jefferson, predicted that the generation must fight for freedom again and again. American history proves him right. From the days of slavery, the Civil War, the feminist revolution, the voter registration drives and the wars against dictatorships of all kinds, Americans have always risked everything to maintain democracy in this country.

Nevertheless, there are unelected bureaucrats who seek to interfere in the private lives of Americans by going so far as to dictate which necessary rooms we may use. There are among us religious fanatics who claim to be pro-life but also kill abortion doctors. We are plagued by terrorists who, in the name of religion, commit mass murder on innocent Americans. We have employers and union bosses who deprive employees of the rights to free speech and we have voter fraud and a criminal justice system guilty of innumerable injustices perpetrated on the American people by members of the judiciary and ambitious prosecutors.

The country is faced with a drug problem that sometimes seems to overwhelm us and destroy our democracy.

Despite all these difficulties and threats, it is my contention that, in the words of the song "We will overcome," our democracy will be passed on to future generations despite those who assault it. I have concluded this book with the words of the great British Prime Minister Winston Churchill that: "democracy is the worst form of government except for the others".

THE FOUNDATIONS OF WESTERN CIVILIZATION

Western civilization differs from all other civilizations in that it promotes the interests of the individual over the rights of government. This development took centuries to achieve and must be defended constantly against innumerable assaults by government, moneyed interests and others who seek to return citizens to the status of subjects conforming to a police state.

A second distinction between Western civilization and all others was the rise of capitalism, which has allowed anyone to gain wealth by accumulating money instead of inheriting land, which was for centuries the only source of income and social stratification.

In the course of the past 200+ years, democracy has steadily expanded in the Western world, even as centrally-controlled and authoritarian rulerships remained the fate of most of mankind.

The democratic developments were supported by the work ethic, which defeated inheritance and led to the Industrial Revolution and all its consequences.

Associated with the Industrial Revolution was the discovery of the Western hemisphere by European explorers and the assimilation of foreign customs into the belief system of the capitalist-industrial world.

These achievements depended on the Age of Reason and the creation of scientific knowledge, indeed derived in part from the most ancient sources. Thus science has altered the Western world by creating innumerable tools leading to a vast increase in longevity, a serious challenge to religion, and a decline in family and community.

Philosophy, which seeks to show mankind the way to a "good" life, has been reduced in recent years to analyzing language and creating computer models. Its huge tomes, written by scholars from Philo to Kant, have little meaning to industrial man and, together with religion, have been assigned a "back seat" among the industrial democracies of the Western world.

We begin then with a discussion of the rise of the individual in Western civilization.

CHAPTER 1. THE EVOLUTION OF THE INDIVIDUAL

The Crusades and the Liberation of the Peasants

When Pope Urban II preached the First Crusade in 1095, he unknowingly laid the seeds for the liberation of Western man from his enslavement in the medieval feudal system.

The Pope traveled to his homeland, France, and then to Germany to raise a force of Catholic men for a holy war against Muslims in the Middle East. He told the serfs, or feudal peasants, that their oath of allegiance to the landlords who owned them was null and void if they participated in a crusade to take the Holy Land from the Muslims and bring it under Christian control. Over 100,000 peasants followed that directive. The First Crusade succeeded in capturing Jerusalem in 1099. A second Crusade collapsed, but in 1190, the Third Crusade became popular in England, leading to another war. The fervor against non-Christians also stimulated deadly attacks against Jews in Europe, and in a breath-taking cynical move the Fourth Crusade was directed to sack and essentially destroy the Orthodox Christian city of Constantinople, center of the Byzantine Empire, looting and pillaging it.

When the former serfs returned from the Crusades, they generally did not go back to their feudal lords but moved into fortified cities which men on horseback could not penetrate. This led to an acute shortage of farm labor and the gradual rise of urbanization and democracy, as money earned in commerce began to replace land ownership as another means of establishing wealth. Eventually, some citizens were able to lend money to the aristocrats (an activity that had been dominated by Jews, who were occupied in trade and commerce and therefore had gold or money, rather than land). In return, such cities were given charters conferring special privileges on them. The word "citizen" has its origins in the word for city.

The Crusades also stimulated shipbuilding, because the Crusaders sailed from Genoa and Venice to the Holy Land. Shipbuilding in turn led to increased commerce and to the exploration of Africa and, later, Asia and America. Furthermore, the products of great cities in the East were imported to Europe, increasing and diversifying the food supply and other sectors. In addition, rare luxuries like silk, jewelry, perfume, and tapestry were sent to Europe together with innumerable other goods and inventions.

Custom may be divided into material, behavioral, and ideational. Material custom consists of physical objects, behavioral custom deals with human conduct, and ideational custom consists of beliefs.

The Age of Exploration

The travels of Marco Polo (1254–1324) were the beginning of the Age of Exploration. Marco Polo did not travel alone. When he was 17 he traveled with his father, Niccolò Polo, and his uncle, Maffeo Polo, to China, India, and other parts of Asia. They returned to their home in Venice after an absence of 24 years. The Polos were not the first to reach China. However, Marco Polo was the first to write a book about these travels. It was this book and numerous oral accounts by other travelers which provoked Vasco da Gama, Christopher Columbus, and others to explore the world and thereby end the feudal age in favor of the age of enlightenment and the rise of science.[1]

Vasco da Gama (1460–1524) was the most successful explorer of the 15th and 16th centuries. At a time when his native land, Portugal, was a major sea power, da Gama sailed around the Cape of Good Hope and reached India in 1498. Da Gama's voyage was possible because Bartolomeo Dias had found the way to the Indian Ocean in 1488. Da Gama had traveled along the Atlantic side of Africa but did not land on African soil until he reached an area just north of the Cape of Good Hope, where he remained for one week in November 1497. The expedition then sailed north after rounding the cape and landed once more at what was later named Cowher's Bay on the eastern coast. Thereafter da Gama and his followers reached Natal, continuing up the eastern coast of Africa. Subsequently, other Portuguese expeditions followed, and in the name of the Christian religion subjected the African natives to pillage, slaughter and destruction.[2]

One of the consequences of this aggressive stance by the Portuguese and other Europeans was the spread of Christianity on the African continent.

The Portuguese were of course aware that they would profit from increased commerce and colonization of Africa if they could succeed in converting the natives to Christianity. Their efforts had mixed results. Nevertheless, by the end of the 17th century there was a "network" of Catholic rulers in Africa.[3]

In the 17th century, Portuguese was the leading European language in use in Africa, although the Dutch invaded South Africa, so that their language later became one of the eleven official languages of the South African Republic. The English were the most successful colonizers of Africa, only slightly ahead of the French. English colonizers established schools for African children and also accepted a number of Africans in their homeland so that these Africans could learn the English language. In addition, the da Gama expedition had the effect of fostering the slave trade, so that by 1800 there were 4.5 million African slaves in the Americas.[4]

The most famous of European explorers in the 15th century was Christopher Columbus, who re-discovered "The New World" in 1492 after Leif Erikson had already been in the Western Hemisphere in 1000 CE and several million "natives" had lived in the Americas for 20,000 years. Columbus' mistake was his belief that the earth is smaller than it is. This led him to erroneously conclude that he had found India. Columbus was a student of ancient and medieval science and therefore was well aware that the earth is a sphere. This was already known to the most Ancient peoples, including the Greek mathematicians.

Columbus had a good deal of experience sailing as a deckhand with a Genoese fleet to England and Flanders, and later sailed to Iceland on Italian and other ships. These voyages were made in the interests of businessmen seeking to profit from the ever increasing commerce between the Mediterranean lands and the then known world. These voyages also included the Madeira Islands and the Azores, all in the interests of Italian investors. This meant that Columbus had over fifteen years of experience at sea as a sailor and a captain when he left Europe for America in 1492, seeking profits for himself and his investors.

Thus Columbus, like Polo and da Gama, became a major catalyst in the development of capitalism, which is the foundation of democracy as we know it. Capitalism allows anyone to make a profit and to become wealthy, unlike feudalism, which freezes the social classes into a state of permanence, depending on land ownership and inheritance alone.[5]

In the late Middle Ages, Europe experienced a growth of its population which outgrew its production of goods. From the 11th to the 14th century, an advancing material civilization was built up, leading to an ever increasing demand for commodities and promoting the voyages of Columbus.[6]

It is significant that in 1503 "The House of Trade" was set up in Seville, Spain, to organize the royal enterprise for two hundred years. This "House of Trade" kept all records of cargoes and markets and chronicles of sea voyages. It literally became the Wall Street of its time.[7]

An Age of Opening

Intellectually, Europe benefitted from the Crusades and the explorers and their voyages, as mathematics, such as algebra, geometry, the zero, and other improvements in arithmetic became known to the Europeans. Science and architecture as well as many arts not known in Europe became part of European civilization. The Europeans returned from the Crusades with at least a minimal knowledge of science and literature learned in the East. Many former Crusaders adopted a greater understanding of other cultures different from the narrow feudal confines which had governed medieval thought for centuries. Europeans also imitated the manners and polite conduct they observed abroad, which was hardly known in the West until the twelfth and thirteenth centuries. All of this led to more and more intellectual activity.

The importation of foreign opinions and attitudes finally led to the rebirth of scholarship, the Renaissance, which propelled Europe to the forefront of intellectual achievement and made the discovery of America the culminating achievement of the Age of Exploration.

All that led to an increase in the independence of the individual and the decline in feudal rule. Not only were the peasants moving to the cities, many of the aristocracy never returned while others wasted their fortunes on the expenses associated with the Crusades. Thousands of knights and barons mortgaged their castles and lands, further leading to a decline in the nobility and the aristocracy. Consequently, kings and people became more and more independent of the feudal lords. At first this greatly increased the power of the kings, and then revolts overthrew a number of them, so that democracy was born out of the ashes of feudalism.

In the end the Crusades failed, but the peasants never returned to their slave status in Europe. Instead they built fortified cities and resisted the nobility seeking to return them to their former role. This led to the eventual creation of the "Western man" who values the individual before the state and who gradually created democracy and all the rights enshrined in the Constitution of the United States.

The medieval Crusaders knew none of this. They believed that force would succeed in driving the Turks from the holy sites valued by Christians. Instead, the Crusades weakened the Byzantine Empire, permanently deforested many islands in the Mediterranean, eliminated serfdom, gave cities a new importance, rewarded capitalist enterprises, and promoted travel, leading to exploration of the world and to the assimilation of more broad-minded values and the growth of secular societies.[8]

I. Individual Rights Begin to Gain the Upper Hand over Absolute Rulers

In the thirteenth century the English nobility contributed significantly to the eventual advent of democracy when they forced King John to sign the "Magna Carta," limiting the power of the monarchy. This document, now eight hundred years old, became a foundation of British democratic living and was influential in producing the "Bill of Rights" as included in the U.S. Constitution. Indeed, that great charter was limited to the nobility of 1215 but nevertheless became a cornerstone of British and American recognition of the rights of every man.[9]

The English Bill of Rights

When the English Parliament secured a Bill of Rights in 1689, they laid the foundation for the American Bill of Rights as found in the first ten amendments to the U.S. Constitution. The English Bill of Rights included the right to freedom of speech in parliament, and limited the powers of the monarch, William of Orange and Queen Mary, who ruled jointly. As this document was reaffirmed by subsequent British monarchs, it strengthened the development of democracy in England, America, and other Western countries whose citizens were greatly influenced by these events.[10]

In 1789 the French Assembly issued a "Declaration of the Rights of Man," which immediately preceded the influential pamphlet of a similar name by the American Thomas Paine. This declaration is indeed the source of French democracy, although the Dreyfus trial. As we will see, however, documents officially enshrining citizens' rights are one thing, while the conduct of the government, and the public, may be another. Thus in the 21st century we see episodes of violence against many different groups even in the heart of liberalism, in Europe.[11]

The new understanding of rights is best understood by listing some of the seventeen articles constituting that Declaration (the French original is longer than this overview).

These articles include:

1. "Men are born and remain free and equal in rights."

2. These rights are liberty, property, security, and resistance to oppression.

3. All authority "proceeds directly from the nation."

4. Men are free to do anything that does not injure others as defined by law.

5. Law can only prohibit injuries to society and no one may be forced to do anything not prohibited by law.

6. Law expresses the general will and must be the same for all.

7. No person shall be arrested or imprisoned except by law.

8. Punishment shall only be that inflicted by law.

9. Everyone is innocent unless proved guilty by law.

10. Freedom of opinion and religion is supported.

11. Everyone has the right to write or print any opinion but shall be responsible for abuses as defined by law.

12. Military force shall be used for the good of all and not only for those in command.

13. The cost of administration should be equally distributed among all citizens.

14. All citizens have the right to know how and for what taxes should be assessed.

15. All public administrators must be accountable to the citizens.

16. Laws must be observed and a separation of powers must be assured.

17. Property must not be seized unless there is a clear public need to do so and the owner has been indemnified.

This declaration was a great contribution to the eventual development of democracy in our day. This is a major step forward, while at the same time man-made laws can still be used to pull society backward. Evidently, restrictive laws can be implemented as well as liberating ones, as seen in Sharia law as practiced in certain Muslim states or the racial laws imposed in America at various times in the last 400 years.

The French Declaration of the Rights of Man

The French version of the Declaration of the Rights of Man was carried all over Europe by Napoleon and his armies. Ironically, despite Napoleon's absolute rule as emperor, he carried the message of human liberation as viewed by the French National Assembly all over Europe, and it became the catalyst for revolutions even after Napoleon's defeat at Waterloo on the 8th of June 1815.

The efforts of Europeans to free themselves from ancient tyrannies were only sporadic and not always successful. European history records a constant movement from freedom to tyranny by kings, princes, and dictators of all kinds of political orientation, which always supported the subjection of the European population to dictatorships by a variety of names.

France is a colorful example. It had become a republic in 1792, but this republic lasted only until 1799, when Napoleon made himself emperor.

After Napoleon's defeat in 1815, the monarchy was restored, until a second republic was established in 1848, only to be ended by Napoleon III, nephew of Napoleon I. Napoleon II remained emperor until Germany defeated France in 1870, leading to the establishment of the third republic. Then, during the German occupation of France in 1941–1944, France became a dictatorship ruled by the Nazi collaborator Pierre Laval until the end of the Second World War, when France once more became a republic.[12]

It is evident that the metamorphosis to political systems supporting the rights of the individual is a difficult one and is not a linear process, but may go back and forth as powerful individuals and interests groups vie for control.

The US Bill of Rights

These rights are also found in the US. Constitution, although displayed in a different manner. It is important to recognize that these rights were promoted at a time when absolute power in European monarchies still existed, although it was beginning to be questioned.[13]

In fact, the belated inclusion of a bill of rights into the American Constitution occurred even as European monarchs continued to tyrannize their subjects. The first ten Amendments to the Constitution were therefore most revolutionary in the 18th century. Unfortunately these guarantees of individual liberty have been gradually eroded since 1789 by means of legal interpretations designed to undermine their original intent.

The First Amendment demands that "Congress shall make no law respecting an establishment of religion," etc. Further, this amendment prohibits "abridging" freedom of speech, or of the press or the right of the people to peaceably assemble," etc. These "rights" have been circumscribed to such an extent that they are almost extinct in 2017. This is also true of the second amendment, which supports the right to bear arms.

The American experience concerning the rights of the individual deviated from its European counterpart in that the founding fathers viewed human rights as derived from the dictates of nature and not from human laws. This means that the rights of each person are permanent and impervious to government. Rights that are thought to come from God, that is, rights that are inherent in humanity and not dependent upon the generous whim of those in power, are not subject to human revocation. Paradoxically, even at the time when this concept was being formulated, slavery was a common practice in many parts of the world, and we are still dealing with its fallout.

Despite the inevitable pendulum swings for and against liberty, Americans have extended constitutional rights to anyone present in the country, whether citizen or not. As a consequence of these beliefs, innumerable immigrants have enjoyed the rights of individuals on arriving in the United States

The U.S. Supreme Court has sometimes prevented the erosion of the rights of the individual by a number of decisions in favor of individual liberty. One such example is the Gault Decision, which deals with the rights of a person accused of a crime.

II. Individualism

Individualism is central to American expectations. This means that Americans support the Declaration of Independence and the Constitution, which are both based on the assumption that every human being has "inalienable" rights that are not given by government or any other human source. Related to this belief is the promotion of democracy, including the right to vote, to hold any opinion, to write or say anything, and to accumulate wealth. Most important in this connection is the right and the duty to work at any task, as all work is viewed as honorable, as it is considered a "calling" in the sense that Providence has called some to work at construction while other are bankers or teachers.

Attitudes towards Work

This is of course a theoretical picture of the American work ethic, which diverges in reality from this and other formulations of Weber's Protestant Ethic. No doubt, Puritan New England in the 17th century lived according to these tenets which became the basis of the American republic. Included in this work ethic is the additional view that luxuries are sinful and a waste, and that profit from work or business should be reinvested in later enterprises rather than spent on temporary enjoyments. These views are generally known as the American work ethic.

In the decades of the 21st century and for some years before, this attitude towards work has changed a good deal. More recently, work has been seen as a means of achieving personal growth, and individuals regard opportunities for personal development on the job as important. Heretofore productivity was the only criterion of success, defined by those only interested in profit. The humanistic view of work seeks to make work meaningful and not only a matter of routine.[14]

Another view of work is based mainly on economics. Since people cannot exist without work (as already announced in Genesis 3:19), work is seen as a necessary evil which benefits mainly those who, as Karl Marx phrased it, own the means of production.[15]

There are those who view work as a meaningful enterprise only if it benefits a group or organization. From that point of view, success is not measured by individual satisfaction but the ability to conform to the group's demands rather than individual achievements.

There is also the belief by some observers that work is nothing more than a necessity and that leisure is the only worthwhile activity.

All of these beliefs are superseded by the work ethic to the effect that work bestows dignity on anyone who works at any task. This view holds all work in esteem, whether simple or difficult, whether highly paid or modestly compensated.[16]

Those who conform to the work ethic believe that by working hard, one can overcome all obstacles and succeed. Success, according that view, can be measured by the accumulation of material wealth, which is not to be spent on foolish nonsense but reinvested for yet more gain.[17]

The outcome of these beliefs, despite the Puritan dictatorship, was and is the view that the individual is paramount and that government is the servant of the people. Included in these Puritan beliefs is the dogma of self-reliance, which holds that those who seek government assistance are irresponsible in that they violate individualism and hard work, the two cornerstones of the American experience. These doctrines were taught by Luther and Calvin, who claimed that each person has a direct relationship to God without needing the intercession of any church or clergy. This concept of self-reliance has been largely eroded because much work these days is related to collectivities such as labor unions, large government agencies, corporations, and numerous means of gaining benefits from Social Security and other group insurers.[18]

III. Capitalism and Political Democracy

A considerable literature has been published which supports the view that capitalism furnishes the foundation of modern democracy in a way that feudalism did not. The reason for this argument is that, in theory, anyone can become wealthy in a free capitalist society. In feudalism, monarchies including today's Gulf States, and many other forms of society, wealth and power are limited to those who have seized, inherited or been granted political power, while the majority has no voice. Capitalism can foster political democracy. Political democracy depends on voluntary political participation.[19]

Democracy, which implies individual liberty, is threatened most by government — including various forms of police. That threat becomes real when governments legitimize the status of monopolies in the form of large corporations and financial firms who finance political candidates, who in turn limit freedom of expression and other liberties in favor of their benefactors, partners and associates.

Those who opposed the decision of the Supreme Court in April of 2014 to allow unlimited contributions to political candidates by corporations (or anyone else) pointed out that that decision would reduce the influence of individuals on the political process in favor of the rich, that is, those who control corporations. Yet, the majority of the Justices held that the First Amendment applies to the right to make contributions of any size to politicians, and that "corporations" are legal "persons."[20] Some have taken this to be the epitome of a government/corporate collusion against the interests of the average citizen.

In capitalist societies, economic power is translated into government power and the reverse is also true. This means that, generally speaking, the legal structure in capitalist societies protects private property. These characteristics of capitalism were achieved by American investors at the beginning of the 20th century. By that time the Industrial Revolution had produced the McCormick reaper, the steam engine, the automobile, and numerous other labor saving devices which had a large part in ensuring the success of capitalism.

Wealth and income are closely associated with the capitalist system. In America, wealth and income were concentrated in the hands of relatively few families before capitalism became widespread. The economy of the South was largely based on a sort of feudal model, wherein plantations were run using slave labor; in the North, fortunes were made in shipping, trade and commerce. The United States had considerable natural resources, and it was increasingly possible to exploit these natural resources especially as railroads began expanding in the 1840s This helped make manufacturing worthwhile. In addition, foreign investments made America rich, or at least made some Americans rich, even as the poor sank lower and lower and the gap between the rich and the poor became greater and greater. It was then asserted that the fundamental function of government is the protection of the individual and his right to make money.[21]

Chapter 2. Domestic Attacks on Democracy

The Declaration of Independence includes numerous accusations against King George of Great Britain including the charge that, "He has erected a multitude of new offices, and sent hither swarms of officers to harass our people and eat out their substance."[22] There can be little doubt that the same accusation can now be made against the present U.S. government, that in 2017 also consists of "swarms of officers" who "harass our people and eat out their substance." The evidence for this development is overwhelming. Already in 1962 the executive branch of the U.S. government employed 2,585,000 bureaucrats. By 1972 this had increased to 2,823,000 bureaucrats. This number has continued with slight variations into the 21st century.[23]

Regulating Liberty

Therefore, two ominous trends threaten us. One is the monstrous growth of the regulatory state whereby independent agencies such as the EPA and the FCC are creating countless rules that carry the force of law. This means that the real lawmakers in this country are these agencies full of unelected bureaucrats and not Congress, which is charged under the Constitution to be our lawmaker. Operating from whim and without reason of any kind, these bureaucrats dictate in an ambiguous language all kinds of decrees which are plainly unconstitutional. Even the Treasury Department, which is part of the president's cabinet, has issued a rule whereby a company that changes its headquarters outside the United States to save on taxes can be penalized outside the law. The unelected bureaucrats also criminalize all kinds of normal behavior. For example, it is now a federal crime to walk a dog on federal land without a leash that is shorter than 6 feet. Violators can be sent to prison for six months. It is estimated that these bureaucratic offenses have increase the number of actions that are held to be crimes to over 5,000. These so-called crimes are nothing more than an effort by government agencies to turn this country into a police state — or a fee collection operation. Here are some additional examples.

A fisherman who threw back some undersized fish was hauled into court and convicted of violating the anti-shredding clause of the Sarbanes-Oxley Act.

A Maryland developer, James Wilson, was prosecuted and sentenced to prison for violating the Clean Water Act because he improved a piece of land the Army Corps of Engineers claimed as navigable water. This was despite the fact that the nearest river was 6 miles away.

An Alaska fishermen sold ten otters to a person he thought was an Alaska native. Selling otters to non-Alaska natives is a felony. The fisherman, who was hardly rich, pleaded guilty to a felony when it turned out the person was not an Alaska native.

A chief engineer at a retirement home diverted backup sewage to a storm drain. He did not know the drain was not connected to the city's sewage system but to a stream that emptied into the Potomac River. That river is a protected waterway, so that the engineer was convicted of a felony and put on probation.

Bureaucrats love to criminalize all kinds of ordinary conduct. They particularly like to target people without much money who cannot afford to hire expensive lawyers and therefore cannot fight the enormous resources of the government.

Now it is obvious that the nearly three million federal bureaucrats want to perpetuate their employment and therefore they invent innumerable rules, regulations and other directives which have the force of law, although these unelected bureaucrats act entirely outside of the U.S. Constitution, which requires that the laws are made by Congress and the legislatures of the several states. It is this usurpation of unconstitutional power which is the root of the dispute between American citizens and the U.S. government. No better example of this dispute can be exhibited than the Oregon land dispute in 2014.

The controversy between the citizens of Oregon and other bureaucrats originated with a decision to put in jail two ranchers for their good-faith effort to manage land in collaboration with the government. Dwight Hammond, 73, and his son Stephen, 46, were both convicted on arson charges related to a pair of fires they admit setting on their land in 2001 and 2006. The Hammond family has owned the land on which the fires were set for many generations. The Hammonds owned animals which grazed on their land and occasionally walked into government-owned land nearby. When lightning struck and burned some land owned by the Bureau of Land Management, the agency firefighters combatted the fire caused by the lightning. Because the Hammonds had admitted setting some earlier fires, the Hammonds were accused of also setting fires caused by lightning and were sentenced to three months of prison time by a district judge. Nevertheless, federal prosecutors managed to have the sentences increased to five years on the grounds that the Hammonds had damage public property. This interference of the federal government in a local dispute leading to unjustified and extreme prison sentences caused ranchers from around the Western United States to come to Oregon and protest the Hammonds' treatment by prosecutors.[24]

Double Jeopardy

There is hardly a schoolchild in the United States who does not know that the Fifth Amendment prohibits trying the same defendant for the same crime twice. Yet the Hammonds were tried two times for minor offenses, which were then escalated into a felony by prosecutors who seek to undermine the Fifth Amendment by a variety of legal hairsplitting designed to eventually abolish the Bill of Rights entirely. Indeed, clever lawyers of the so-called liberal view have for years re-interpreted the Constitution so as to emasculate it completely. These legal maneuvers serve to turn to the United States into a police state until "the land of the free and the home of the brave" will become nothing more than a phrase in a song.[25]

Many Americans actively seek to preserve the rights of citizens guaranteed by the U.S. Constitution, and hundreds of supporters of the Hammonds traveled to Oregon and rallied in the town of Burns to defend not only the Hammonds but all American citizens against this apparent tyranny. Among these out-of-state arrivals was a subgroup of protesters who entered a US Fish and Wildlife Service building on a wildlife preserve about 30 miles from Burns. These militants were led by a Nevada rancher, Ammon Bundy, who claimed that 150 armed people were gathered at the facility. Ammon Bundy is the son of Cliven Bundy, whose ranch was the site of a much larger standoff between armed militiamen and federal agents over cattle grazing rights in 2014.

The 2016 occupation of the headquarters of the Malheur National Wildlife Refuge by a group of ranchers was mainly symbolic and served as means of demonstrating that local citizens wanted to maintain democracy and the rights of individuals. This effort was supported by some politicians who sought to roll back federal authority over public lands. These politicians are also supported by capitalists who would like state lawmakers to distribute mining and drilling permits in wilderness areas.

In any event, the government forces aggravated and escalated the dispute between the occupiers of the wildlife refuge and the Bureau of Land Management when the Oregon state police officer shot and killed LaVoy Finicum, a 54-year-old father of eleven children, who had participated in the protest against government ownership of most of Oregon's land. At his funeral, his widow said: "The day my husband LaVoy was murdered, assassinated by our government, he had been invited to speak to the citizens of his country." She called him a fallen hero and a "patriot" murdered in the fight for freedom.[26]

The murder of Finicum did succeed in causing the occupiers of the wildlife refuge to surrender and to leave those premises on January 29, 2016. The murder, however, also convinced many citizens that the US government was willing to kill its own citizens. In the end the protesters were all jailed, even as these protests demonstrated that many citizens in the West resent that the government acts in the interest of a few bureaucrats and against the will of the people who live there. Those who were arrested were charged with conspiracy to prevent officers of the United States from discharging their official duties, even at the expense of killing an American citizen for protesting their actions.[27]

Then, on October 27, 2016 a jury found Ammon Bundy, his brother Ryan and five co-defendants not guilty. Nevertheless, the judge would not release the Bundy brothers, on the grounds that the Bundys would be tried a second time in Nevada. When their lawyer protested their continued incarceration and asked that the Bundys be released, the judge had the police Taser him.[28]

The "not guilty" verdict was interpreted by many observers as a long overdue victory for American liberty. Opponents of the vindicated citizens claim that this verdict invites the militants to oppose the rule of law. Yet it was obvious from the start that those who occupied the wildlife refuge did so peacefully and had threatened no one. Whatever view the various contestants in this dispute may support, the overriding consequence of this jury verdict is the assertion that the people of the United States government this country and not some unelected bureaucrats. Many years ago our third President, Thomas Jefferson wrote: "When government fears the people there is liberty, when the people fear the government there is tyranny." [29]

There are also those who seek to demonstrate their displeasure with the federal bureaucracy by failing to pay grazing fees of $1.69 per animal per month.

Those who oppose the federal government's Bureau of Land Management are convinced that federal authority over public land is illegitimate and that the constant interference of government in the affairs of citizens is only a forerunner of the time when the government would turn its guns on its own citizens, against its own people.[30]

It needs to be remembered that the Oregon standoff was initially provoked by the unfair and unjustified sentences leading to five years in federal prison for Dwight and Stephen Hammond, who had been originally sentenced to a far lesser amount of jail time.

The Laws Apply Equally

In April 2014 *The American Catholic* summed up the dispute between The Bureau of Land Management and the ranchers opposing them in an article written by Judge Jeanine Pirro. Here she correctly shows "that the underlying assumption of all is the belief that we are talking about law and the American tradition that obligates everyone equally and that are enforced dispassionately. Speaking of President Obama she further writes, "The rule of law is not the way of a man who himself serially violates the laws he finds inconvenient and who, under the distortion of the prosecutorial discretion doctrine, gives a pass to his favorite constituencies while punishing his opposition."

No better example of this distortion of the law is the support which the Democratic Party has given to illegal immigration into the United States. It needs to be understood that when the laws are enforced arbitrarily or ignored because an administration finds them inconvenient, then all law is viewed with disdain by the citizens. This means that all laws must be equally enforced lest all laws come into disrepute.

I. The Tension between Diversity and Social Cohesion

Since 1924, the United States has adopted immigration laws which have been changed and amended several times, but which nevertheless were designed to designate those who could be legally admitted to the United States and those who were not to be admitted.

Section 211 (8 U.S.C. 1181) part (c) plainly states: "[N]o immigrant shall be admitted into the United States unless at the time of application for admission he has a valid unexpired immigrant visa."

It is therefore as illegal to violate this law as it is to fail to pay income tax. Nevertheless, the Obama administration ordered immigration officials in 2012 to give legal status to an estimated 800,000 to 1.76 million illegal immigrants.

In Europe, a number of politicians have recognized the mistake they made by allowing millions of so-called guest workers to enter their countries from societies in which democracy is unknown. The former prime minister or Chancellor of Germany Helmut Schmidt wrote in *Die Zeit*, a Hamburg newspaper, "The concept of multiculturalism is difficult to make fit within a democratic society." Schmidt, who was Chancellor from 1974 to 1982, further wrote: "The problems resulting from the influx of mostly Turkish guest workers has been neglected in Germany and the rest of Europe. These problems could be overcome only by authoritarian governments," naming Singapore as an example.[31]

It is true that the Roman Empire, the Byzantine Empire, the Ottoman Empire and the Austro-Hungarian all included a large and diverse population speaking numerous languages and exhibiting a variety of cultures. These empires were held together by the vast power of the emperors and dynasties who ruled them. Such authoritarian rule has generally been absent from the United States and Western Europe in recent times.

It is a common culture, a common history, beliefs and values which hold together the United States from the Pacific to the Atlantic. Evidently millions of immigrants who know are not used to — and who perhaps do not value democracy and the freedom of religion, freedom of speech, and freedom of the press — will dilute the rights of citizens as expressed in the first Ten Amendments to our Constitution. This ignorance or even disdain of democracy and differences of opinion means that such newcomers do not know or care about their rights and the rights of their neighbors, do not see the need to defend these rights, and are susceptible to abuse by authorities who will infringe their rights.

II. Repression is not Security: Illegal Immigration

Numerous terrorist attacks have been carried out on the United States, by Islamists or forces using Islamists and others, some mentally unstable, as "weaponized" disgruntled individuals. These shocking disasters have led to a marked drift towards an American police state, to which much of the population will acquiesce out of fear. The evidence for this is the Patriot Act, which allows random searches of law-abiding citizens and government spying on conversations between Americans by means of various electronic devices. In addition, government agents have attempted to ask librarians to tell them who is reading which books, even as local police and sheriffs are also spying on our population. Instead of restricting the influx of potential terrorists in the United States, with this Act the George W. Bush administration suppressed freedom for all Americans.

That being said, protecting its citizens from external and internal enemies is the most important role of government. This means that a responsible government on the federal, state, or local level will prevent violent attacks on Americans by illegal immigrants and others. Unfortunate for all Americans, some local governments as well as the federal government are unwilling to furnish Americans with the protection to which they are entitled.

One excellent example of this failure to give the safety of Americans priority over the demands of foreigners is the policy of allowing hundreds of Palestinians and Syrian Arabs into the United States because they fraudulently register as Honduran citizens. Using forged Honduran passports, these Arabs enter the United States with American visas. The Honduran newspaper *La Prensa* has revealed the sales of Honduran passports to Palestinian and Syrian citizens. Apparently there is an organized crime network with international ties to smugglers and officials who are able to illegally register at least several hundred Palestinians and Syrians with fraudulent documentation. Evidently the Honduran Embassy of the United States makes little or no effort to prevent the use of fraudulent documents.[32]

A second, better-known example, relates to our southern neighbors. A number of illegal immigrants have committed violent crimes in this country. The murder of Catherine Steinle is one example, although far from the only one. On July 1, 2015, the illegal immigrant Juan Francisco Lopez Sanchez indiscriminately fired three shots from a .40 caliber handgun in the Embarcadero district of San Francisco. One of the bullets struck Catherine Michelle Steinle in the chest and pierced her aorta. She collapsed to the floor while screaming for help from her father Jim, who was accompanying her at the pier. She died two hours after the bullet struck her.[33] Thereafter Sanchez was arrested and booked into San Francisco County Jail on suspicion of murder. It turned out that the gun Sanchez used was stolen from the Bureau of Land Management. Sanchez, a citizen of Mexico, had been convicted three times in Washington State for felonies and was deported. Nevertheless he returned to the United States within two years and was convicted again in Washington State. He was deported for a second time in 1997. Then in 1998 Sanchez was deported for a third time after reentering the United States through Arizona. He was therefore sentenced to five years and three months in federal prison for unauthorized reentry. In 2003 he was deported for a fourth time after he reentered the United States through the Texas border and then was deported for the fifth time in June 2009 four reentering yet again.

He was turned over to the San Francisco authorities for an outstanding drug warrant. However, the city of San Francisco did not honor the detainer requested by federal authorities. San Francisco government considers the municipality to be a sanctuary city and therefore refuses to arrest, jail, or deport foreign criminals. In sum, this policy places the physical safety of Americans behind that of illegal immigrants, even if such illegal immigrants commit murder. There are 300 sanctuary cities in the United States. These include Dallas, Texas, Philadelphia, Pennsylvania, and five Kentucky counties, the whole state of Massachusetts, and 292 others where federal law enforcement demands for information and access to jailed illegal immigrants will be denied. The cities and counties receive federal funding from the taxpayers but nevertheless are willing to put the lives of the same taxpayers at risk.[34]

There are about 11 million illegal immigrants in the United States. They are therefore no more than 3.5% of the United States population. Nevertheless, these immigrants account for about 14% of violent crime committed in the country. Nearly 12% of murder sentences are credited to illegal immigrants, and 20% of kidnapping sentences and 16% of drug trafficking sentences are also the result of crimes committed by illegal immigrants. In addition about 2,100,000 illegal immigrants are living free in this country although they have committed similar crimes. Each year about 900,000 legal and illegal immigrants are arrested, while another 700,000 are released from prison. In addition, according to Customs Enforcement, there are more than 1,200,000 illegal immigrant criminals still at large[35].

In Florida there were 5,061 illegal immigrant inmates in state prison facilities as of June 30, 2015. In Illinois, where state prisons house 46,993 inmates, there were 3,755 illegal immigrants according to the Illinois Department of Corrections. In Florida and in Illinois, state officials do not compile figures for county jails. In Arizona, the Arizona Department of Corrections shows that out of 42,758 prisoners held in state facilities, about 11% were illegal immigrants in July 2015.[36]

In California there were 128,543 inmates in custody on August 12, 2015. California does not keep track of the citizenship status of inmates. Nevertheless other sources have discovered that 18,000 foreign-born immigrants in California state prisons were part of the 133,000 inmates incarcerated. The last research conducted in 2011 showed that there were 55,000 illegal immigrants in federal prisons and 296,000 in state and local prisons. Experts say that these figures are much larger in 2016.[37]

In 2010, the *New York Times* reported that about four and half million illegal aliens in the United States drive on a regular basis without a license.[38] The Office of Immigration Statistics reported that of the 188,382 deportations of illegal aliens in 2011, 23% had committed criminal traffic offenses like driving under the influence or leaving the scene of an accident. Congressman Stephen King estimates that illegal alien drunk drivers kill 13 Americans every day (that is a death toll of 4,745 per year).[39]

According to the Center For Immigration Studies, 23%, or more than 43,000, illegal aliens were convicted of drug offenses in one year. Moreover, 12% of the violent crime categories of assault, robbery, sexual assault, and family offenses are committed by illegal aliens, although the proportion of illegal immigrants to the total American population is only about 3.5 %. The nonviolent crimes of illegal immigrants, larceny, fraud, and burglary, constitute 7% of the total.[40]

The sheriff of Pinal County, Arizona, Paul Babeau, revealed that most major crime statistics dropped during the past few years, except crimes tied to illegal immigrants. The sheriff said that high-speed vehicle pursuits have increased each year, from 142 in 2007 to 340 such incidents in 2010. He attributes the increase in arrests for illegal immigrants to drug use. According to Babeau, marijuana seizures have spiked from the low in 2008 of about 19,600 pounds to over 40,500 pounds in 2010. The United States Border Patrol reported 212,200 illegal aliens were caught in the Tucson area alone. The border patrol estimates that for every illegal alien captured at the border another three make it into the United States undetected. Of those apprehended, 30% already have a criminal record in the United States resulting from previous stays which ended with deportation. Evidently a good number of those once deported return again and again.

The liberal *Huntington Post* recently published that "this year more than 60% of all federal criminal convictions have been for immigration related crimes, federal data show." [41]

According to Trackimmigration.Com, illegal reentry under title eight section 1326 of the United States Code was the most commonly recorded lead charge brought by federal prosecutors in the first half of 2015. The average prison sentence for this offense is 14 months, at an estimated cost of $134 per day or $48,970 a year. That is more than most college tuitions cost for one year, even as many a poor college student cannot pay for his education because illegal offenders use up the taxpayers' money.

The Columbus Dispatch reported that "illegal reentry cases represent about a third of the caseload for the federal public defender's office." Gordon G Hobson, a senior litigator for the federal public defender's office, said, "10 years ago it was about 5%. Moreover not everyone who comes back illegally and comes back a second time is prosecuted."[42]

A study by The Migration Policy Institute and the Wilson Center discusses the passage of central Americans through Mexico. This is called transmigration. These findings show that arrests by the United States border patrol of individuals from countries other than Mexico have increased year after year.[43]

The United States Government Accountability Office has published information on the arrests of illegal aliens in the United States. In 2005, 55,322 illegal aliens were arrested at least a total of 459,614 times. 38% or about 21,000 had between two and five arrests. 32%, or about 18,000, had an average of 13 arrests. About 15% of arrests of illegal aliens were property related offenses such as burglary, larceny, or motor vehicle theft; 12% of arrests of illegal aliens were for violent offenses such as murder, robbery, assault, and sex-related crimes; 45% of these arrests were drug related, while others included forgery, jewelry theft, counterfeiting, weapons violations, and obstruction of justice.[44]

According to the FBI, 83% of warrants for murder in Phoenix are for illegal aliens. In Albuquerque, 86% of warrants for murder are for illegal aliens. On the most wanted list in Los Angeles, Phoenix, and Albuquerque, 75% of those are illegal aliens. In California detention centers, 25% of all inmates are Mexican nationals; 40.1% of all inmates in Arizona detention centers are Mexican nationals; 48.2% of all inmates in New Mexico detention centers are Mexican nationals. Our state and federal prisons hold 29%, or 630,000, convicted illegal alien felons, at a cost of $1.6 billion a year. Of all investigated burglaries reported in California, New Mexico, Nevada, Arizona, and Texas, 53% were perpetrated by illegal aliens. More than 50% of all gang members in Los Angeles are illegal aliens. 71% of all apprehended cars stolen in Texas, New Mexico, Arizona, Nevada, and California were stolen by illegal aliens. 47% of cited or stopped drivers in California have no license, no insurance, and no registration for the vehicle. 92% of these 47% are illegal aliens.[45]

In addition to the crimes committed by individual illegal aliens, the United States has also become subject to cross border crimes committed by gangs. These gang-related crimes include child sex trafficking, robbery, prostitution, homicide, alien smuggling, human trafficking, drug shipment protection, burglary, theft, assault, and drug sales. All of these crimes are heavily influenced by Mexican nationals on both sides of the United States-Mexican border.[46]

III. The IRS Overrides the Constitution Left and Right, Driving Law-Abiding Citizens to Leave the US

Public opinion surveys concerning federal agencies have repeatedly demonstrated that the Internal Revenue Service is the most hated agency of the United States government. This loathing for the IRS cannot be attributed to the duty of that agency to collect taxes imposed by Congress. Americans know that it is the Congress of the United States and not the IRS which determines how much citizens are expected to pay in taxes. The reason for the hatred of the IRS is the manner in which this collection agency holds the American public in contempt and consistently violates the law and the Constitution.[47]

No better example of this bureaucratic conduct can be cited then the case of *United States v. Troescher*, which was decided by the United States Court of Appeals ninth district on November 7, 1996. The Constitution of the United States famously protects Americans against self-incrimination. This requirement was originally inserted into the Fifth Amendment so as to prevent torture of those accused.

The 5th Amendment to the Constitution of the United States includes the phrase "No person... shall be compelled in any criminal case to be a witness against himself."

It is to be assumed that those who work for agencies of the United States government would adhere to the law and uphold the Constitution. This is unfortunately not the case among those employed by the Internal Revenue Service.

The *Troescher* case was an attempt by the IRS to circumvent the Constitution and deprive Leon C. Troescher of his constitutional rights. The IRS sought to compel Troescher to appear before the Internal Revenue Service to answer questions and produce documents. The IRS issued the summons after Troescher apparently failed to file income tax returns for several years. Troescher asserted that the Fifth Amendment protected him against self-incrimination. This assertion was rejected by the District Court, which sided with the IRS. The IRS claimed "that there is a tax crime exception to the Fifth Amendment." However, the Court of Appeals ruled that there is no tax crime exception to the Fifth Amendment. The court further held, "The case law in this circuit is clear that the Fifth Amendment may be validly invoked when the taxpayer fears prosecution for tax crimes."[48]

It is significant that federal employees seek to circumvent the Constitution which they have sworn to uphold.

Citizens not acquainted with methods used by the IRS to intimidate taxpayers would hardly believe that tax agents can seize the bank accounts of Americans at will and without accusing their victim of any offense. In 2014 *The New York Times* reported that the IRS had seized the checking account of $33,000 from Carol Hinders, the owner of a Mexican restaurant in Iowa. Hinders was not accused of any crime nor did she owe the IRS any money. Her assets were seized because she had made multiple bank deposits of less than $10,000 at one time. The IRS used a law intended to catch drug traffickers, racketeers, and terrorists by tracking their cash. Instead of doing that, the IRS goes after run-of-the-mill business owners and wage earners without any allegation of any crime committed. The IRS takes the money without ever filing a complaint and the owners are left to prove their innocence. This maneuver contradicts the constitutional requirement to the effect that in American jurisdiction someone accused of a crime is considered innocent unless proven guilty in a court of law. Yet here the IRS turns the Constitution upside down and forces the accused to prove his innocence. Banks are required to report to the IRS that someone has made multiple deposits under $10,000 to evade reporting requirements. The practice of seizing money from innocent citizens resembles similar practices followed in all dictatorships in which citizens have no rights at all. Seizure of bank accounts from innocent citizens has led to depriving students of college educations, businessmen of their inventories, and widows of their pensions. The IRS is not the only government agency which collects bank reports for accounts to seize. Under The Bank Secrecy Act, banks and other financial institutions must report cash deposits greater than $10,000. In addition, banks must also report any so-called suspicious transactions including deposits below $10,000. Since owners of these seized accounts are usually not wealthy enough to dispute these claims in court, these government agencies keep this stolen money for themselves. For example, in Long Island the police seized almost a year's worth of daily deposits by a business ranging from $5500 to $9910. The government seized $447,000 from that business, a cash intensive candy and cigarette distributor which had been run by one family for 27 years. The business was ruined and the family destitute. The government also requires the bank employees not tell depositors anything about the government's seizure practices.[49]

A more egregious intrusion into the lives of Americans can hardly be imagined. Nothing is more injurious to democracy and contradicts our Constitution more than government seizure of people's life savings. Such procedures intimidate citizens and reduce them to subjects rather than the citizens of a free democracy.

No greater threat to democracy can exist than the suppression of political views not to the liking of the government. Yet this is exactly what the IRS has done by deliberately targeting so-called *Tea Party* groups for tax exempt status.

The phrase *Tea Party* refers to the protest of Boston colonists who in 1773 boarded a ship bound for England and pitched crates of its tax tea cargo into Boston Harbor. In 2009 the modern tea party movement got underway shortly after Pres. Barack Obama took office and he and House Democrats passed the American Recovery and Reinvestment Act without a single Republican vote. Although ridiculed and insulted by the media, citizens who objected to the overreach of the federal government increased their popularity considerably.[50]

On May 10, 2013, the then director of the Exempt Organization Division of the IRS, Lois Lerner, publicly acknowledged and apologized for the practice of targeting Tea Party groups for special scrutiny. Consequently the treasury department's inspector general for tax administration, J. Russell George, confirmed that conservative groups had indeed been targeted by Ms. Lerner using inappropriate criteria when used to identify tax-exempt applications for review. George and his investigators discovered that the IRS Organization Division had sent a memo to its staff called "Be on the Lookout" to the effect that Tea Party linked groups were to be subject to detailed examination regarding their eligibility for tax-exempt status. This led the chairman of the House oversight and Government Reform committee, Darell Issa, to proclaim, "this was the targeting of the president's political enemies effectively."

Undoubtedly it will come as a shock to many Americans that the IRS has actually succeeded in forcing some American citizens to give up their US citizenship. The fact is that a record number of Americans are giving up their US citizenship in an effort to escape onerous requirements enforced by the IRS. Visa requirements are enforced no matter where in the world a citizen lives. In addition, a number of foreign banks around the world are refusing to even accept American customers in order to avoid US government bullying and mountains of regulations.

The Wall Street Journal reports that almost 2,400 people a year have given up their US citizenship or turned in their green cards. This means that the number who have renounced their citizenship has increased 33% over what it was a decade ago.

The biggest reason for the surge in numbers who renounce their citizenship is the tax laws, which demand higher and higher taxes accompanied by harassment from the IRS. In addition to IRS harassment, there is also The Foreign Account Tax Compliance Act, which passed Congress in 2010. This act demands that financial institutions all over the world report information about US citizens and green card holders to the US federal government. For example, Ruth A. Freeborn, a native of Oklahoma, married a Canadian and has lived in Canada for over 30 years. Now The Foreign Account Tax Compliance Act demanded that her foreign bank hand over all of her family's financial information to the Obama administration. Her Canadian husband opposed this. Nevertheless the only means that Ruth Freeborn had to avoid subjecting her family to intrusive prying by the IRS was to renounce her U.S. citizenship.[51]

IV. Political Nepotism and Collusion Create a Ritual Oligarchy in the US

Because Pope Calixtus III (1378-1458) did not have any children, as head of the Borgia family, he appointed his nephews to several important positions in the Church. Consequently his nephew Rodrigo became Pope Alexander VI and other nephews benefited equally. The appointment of these nephews led to the use of the Italian word for nephew, Nepote, and later to the English version nepotism.[52]

Political nepotism has become so common and so widespread in the United States that it has indeed defeated the intent of the founders of this country, who had hoped for a democracy "of the people for the people and by the people." Instead, a ritual oligarchy has developed in the United States which may be described as the American ruling class. As soon as the Republic got underway and within the lifetime of its founders, nepotism had already begun this defeat of democracy. John Quincy Adams became president in 1825 because he was the son of the second president of the United States, John Adams.

176 years later, the first son of George Herbert Walker Bush, the 41st president of the United States, became the 43rd president of the United States. George W. Bush served two terms from 2001 to 2009. The second son of George Herbert Bush, John Ellis "Jeb" Bush, was elected governor of Florida and served from 1999 to 2007. In 2016 he became a candidate for the Republican presidential nomination but did not succeed. It is nevertheless significant that yet a third member of the same family has the necessary corrections to make such a candidacy possible.

"All in the Family" also applies to Hillary Rodham Clinton, the wife of President William Jefferson Clinton. Using her political connections she not only became Senator from New York, a state in which she had never lived before, but she also became secretary of state and Democratic candidate for the presidency of the United States.

Another recent example of this political behavior was the appointment of Caroline Kennedy to be ambassador to Japan. Kennedy is the daughter of former President John F. Kennedy and was a supporter of President Barack Obama in his two efforts to gain election. At her confirmation hearings in the United States Senate, it became evident that she knew nothing about Japan. Yet, that ignorance did not prevent her from becoming confirmed as ambassador to that country.[53]

The political career of Lisa Murkowski is another example of blatant nepotism. She is the daughter of a former United States Senator and governor of Alaska, Frank Murkowski.

When her father Frank resigned his seat in the Senate to become governor of Alaska in 2000, he appointed his daughter to complete his unexpired term. Since then she has been repeatedly elected to the Senate and was only the second member of that body to be reelected by a write-in vote.[54]

The list of appointed and political officials whose sole merit is the relationship to some other politician is so long and so ubiquitous that it has become commonplace in this country.

In Arkansas the Secretary of State has appointed his son as well as his son's wife. All over the United States nepotism seems to be almost the only means by which a politician can gain office. Senators Dan Boren of Oklahoma, Al Gore of Tennessee, and Connie Mack of Florida all had fathers who were also senators.

Shelley Moore Capito of West Virginia, Jim Cooper of Tennessee, and Jim Matheson of Utah have been governors, as were their fathers. Stephanie Herseth of South Dakota was the granddaughter of a governor and was herself a congresswoman. William Schuster of Pennsylvania, Walter Jones of North Carolina, John Duncan of Tennessee, John Dingell of Michigan, Charles T. Walsh of New York, Alan Mollohan of West Virginia, Daniel Lipinski of Illinois, and Charles Bass of New Hampshire were all members of Congress and all had fathers who had been members of Congress. In Utah we find that representative Mark Udall is the son of former Congressman and presidential candidate Morris Udall. His cousin is representative Tom Udall, whose father was a cabinet secretary and cousin of Sen. Gordon Smith of Oregon, and representative James M. Jeffords of Vermont is the son of the Chief Justice of the Supreme Court in that state.

Representative Rodney P. Frelinghuysen has had five ancestors or relatives represent New Jersey before him. Sen. Chris Dodd is the son of the former Sen. Thomas Dodd and Sen. Robert Bennett is the son of a senator from Utah. Sen. Mark Pryor of Arkansas is also the son of a senator and Sen. Olympia Snowe of Maine is the wife of John R. McKernan Jr., who was governor of Maine. Representative Russ Carnahan of Missouri is the daughter of a Missouri governor and Lincoln D. Chafee of Rhode Island is the son of Sen. John Chafee of Rhode Island. Representatives Mary Bono of California and Lois Capps, also from California, and Joe Ann Emerson of Missouri are all widows of representatives in Congress. Former Sen. Jon Kyl of Arizona is the son of former representative John H. Kyl, and Representative Tom Allen of Maine has been a member of the Portland City Council, as were his father and grandfather. Representative Charlie Gonzalez is the son of the late Congressman Henry Gonzalez and Sen. Evan Bayh is the son of the late Sen. Birch Bayh. Missouri Gov. Matt Blunt is the son of former US House majority whip Roy Blunt.[55]

Representative John Sarbanes is the son of former Sen. Paul Sarbanes and Sen. Gordon Smith of Oregon has a brother Milan Smith, who was appointed by Pres. Bush to the Ninth Circuit Court of Appeals.

These examples are only a few of the numerous relatives who have become a part of the American oligarchy in a manner similar to that common in monarchies such as Saudi Arabia and the British monarchy of the 18th century from which the American colonists achieved independence precisely in order to escape the nepotism inherent in the monarchical system.

Nepotism is now also being used to get around term limits. For example, Ohio state senator Timothy Grendell has replaced his wife, who sat in the seat for eight years. In Michigan three women were elected to the state legislature after their husbands left because of term limits. In Oregon House Speaker Karen Minnis took the seat of her husband in 1998, and William Weld, the former Massachusetts governor, is the great grandson in law of Theodore Roosevelt. There is also a great deal of political necromancy. For example, Sen. Jean Carnahan is a widow whose husband died while on the stump for the seat she now holds.

Traditionally, the media made it their task to supervise elected and appointed officials and tell the voters about corruption, favoritism, and other abuses of power on the part of the people's representatives. This function of holding accountable those in power has been greatly eroded in recent years as professional journalists and professional politicians have become one happy family.

Numerous such examples include Chris Cuomo, son of former New York governor Mario Cuomo and brother of Andrew Cuomo, current governor of New York. Chris Cuomo is co-anchor of ABC's 20/20 and hosts CNN's morning news show. Then there is Jay Carney, who was appointed as Obama's news secretary. He is married to Claire Shipman of ABC *Good Morning America*. Likewise, Ruth Marcus, columnist for the Washington Post, is married to Federal Trade Commission Chairman Jon Leibowitz. The daughter of Pres. George W. Bush, Jenna Bush Hager, is a reporter for the *NBC Today* show. Ron Brownstein a Los Angeles Times reporter, claimed that he would treat Sen. John McCain objectively although Brownstein's wife, CNN producer Eileen McMenamin, is the senator's communications director. The daughter of Tom Oliphant of the Boston Globe worked on the Kerry campaign and Fox News named Greg Kelly, son of New York Police Department Commissioner Raymond Kelly, White House correspondent.[56]

Relatives of politicians are often rewarded financially. For example representative Bernard Sanders of Vermont, later to become a senator from that state, paid his wife and stepdaughter more than $150,000 for campaign related work since 2000, according to records filed with the Federal Election Commission. It is interesting that Sanders campaigned for the nomination for president of the United States on the Democratic ticket by claiming to represent the poor and the disadvantaged.[57]

The attack on democracy is particularly egregious when it is practiced by professional politicians who subvert the very constitution which they have sworn to defend. No better example of antidemocratic conduct can be found then the practice of deal making between Democratic and Republican County Chairmen determining who will sit as judge in American courts. Seven states of the union permit cross endorsements, also known as fusion voting. The states permitting this are Connecticut, Idaho, Mississippi, New York, Oregon, South Carolina, and Vermont. This is a process whereby two or more political parties, usually the Republicans and the Democrats, nominate the same candidate for the same office during the same general election.

These deals deprive voters of any opportunity to influence or vote for or against a candidate for the position of judge.

In Erie County, New York, for example, the Republican chairman, Nicholas A. Langworthy, participated with the Democratic chairman Jeremy J. Zellner, depriving voters of an opportunity to vote for judges in 2014. Langworthy and Zellner agreed to so-called cross endorsements of several judge candidates, so that voters had no choice, thereby making any vote meaningless. It was alleged by opponents of these methods that Zellner had asked for and had been given $4000 in contributions from the judicial candidates.[58]

In South Carolina there is not only fusion voting but also a "sore loser" election law. This law blocks a candidate from appearing on the ballot if he or she seeks and loses any party's nomination, even if a different party selects that candidate as its nominee. Evidently this scheme denies the voters of South Carolina the right to choose at the ballot box.[59]

V. Asset Forfeiture

A police state is a country in which the police can arbitrarily arrest anyone with or without a good reason and in which the police can enrich themselves by seizing the property of citizens who have committed no offense. Americans usually pride ourselves on our rights and our freedom because the vast majority of us do not know that in most states so-called civil forfeiture laws allow police to take and keep a citizen's property without a criminal conviction. Police officers can seize someone's property without proving the person was guilty of a crime; they just need probable cause to believe the assets are being used as part of criminal activity, typically drug trafficking. Police can then absorb the value of this property, be it cash, cars, or something else, through a law known as Equitable Sharing, which lets local and state police get up to 80% of the value of what they seize as money for their departments. Police not only can seize people's property without proving involvement in a crime, but they have a financial incentive to do so. In some states police can keep property only if they have proved a crime. The states prevent police abuse, which is common in those states which allow law enforcement to seize for profit. States which allow the police to make these unreasonable seizures force people to get their property back through court challenges, which take years and are very expensive.

Consider the case of college student Charles Clarke, who was at the airport when police took his life savings of $11,000. The police pretended to have smelled marijuana on Clarke's bags but could never prove that his money was linked to any crime or drug possession. In fact, Clarke provided documents that showed that the money came from past jobs and government benefits. This is only one example of how innocent citizens are being treated like criminals for the profit of so-called law enforcement.[60]

In sum, this chapter demonstrates that local, state, and federal governments in the United States are undermining democracy until "the land of the free and the home of the brave" is no more.

CHAPTER 3. RELIGIOUS VIOLENCE

Existence without the threat of violence is an essential prerequisite of democratic life. A democratic society seeks to provide adequate means for people to express their views, debate different positions, and either find ways to compromise or learn which view is predominant, then abide by society's decision. But this requires a great degree of responsibility and self-control, as well.

Antiabortion Violence

Among those who seek to suppress speech and actions not in accord with their opinion are those who call themselves antiabortionists. Among them are some who have committed all kinds of crimes directed at institutions and people associated with abortion. Vandalism, stalking, assault, kidnapping, and murder all been inflicted on people, while arson and bombing against property have also been used by some antiabortionists. The US Department of Justice has defined antiabortion violence as single issue terrorism. Among those who have committed such violence are Michael Griffin, James Kopp, Paul Jennings Hill, Scott Roeder, and Peter James Knight.[61]

Antiabortion violence is a political weapon against women's rights and it is associated with violence towards women generally. Antiabortion violence is also often a form of Christian terrorism. At least eight murders occurred in the United States since 1990 associated with antiabortion sentiments. In addition, there have been 41 bombings and 173 arsons at abortion clinics. In 2008, there were 1,793 abortion providers in the United States as well as 197 abortion providers in Canada. The eight people killed by antiabortionists include four doctors, two clinic employees, a security guard and a clinic escort.[62] On March 10, 1993, Dr.

David Gunn of Pensacola Florida was fatally shot during a protest. He had been the subject of "wanted"-style posters distributed by Operation Rescue the summer of 1992. Michael F. Griffin was found guilty of Gunn's murder and was sentenced to life in prison. The murder of Gunn was the first murder of an OB–GYN doctor whose killer sought to prevent the performing of abortions. Griffin, who was 31 years old at the time, waited outside of Gunn's clinic and shot him three times in the back. He then yelled, "Don't kill any more babies." Griffin waited for the police and told them, "We need an ambulance."

This killing led to the passage of the Freedom of Access to Clinic Entrances Act.[63]

On July 29, 1994, Dr. John Britton and James Barrett, a clinic escort, were both shot to death outside another facility, the Ladies' Center in Pensacola. Rev. Paul Jennings Hill was charged with the killings. Hill received a death sentence and was executed on September 3, 2003. Hill had a long history of using drugs and "raising hell." After he was baptized in a muddy swimming pool, he found Jesus. At first Hill talked about using that weapon of the spirit against abortion doctors. Later he talked about using a pump action shotgun, as he began to advocate the murder of abortion doctors.

Hill claimed that he would never commit murder himself. Yet on July 29, 1994, Hill went to the Ladies' Center in Pensacola, Florida, at 7 AM, where he had come to protest abortion for a year. Then when Dr. John Britton arrived for regular duty at the clinic wearing a bulletproof vest, Hill raised his gun and shot Britton and Britton's escort, James Barrett, and Mrs. Barrett. Both John Britton and James Barrett died in the car. Mrs. Barrett survived, badly wounded.

Hill had a wife and three children and had lived a comfortable life until he crossed the line from advocate of his cause to murderer.

The same clinic in Pensacola had been bombed in 1984 and was also bombed later in 2012.

On December 30, 1994, receptionists Shannon Loweney and Lee Ann Nichols were killed in two clinic attacks in Brookline, Massachusetts. John Salvi was arrested and confessed to the killings. He died in prison and guards found his body under his bed with a plastic garbage bag tied around his head. Salvi had also confessed to a nonlethal attack in Norfolk Virginia days before the Brookline killings.[64]

On January 29, 1998, Robert Sanderson, an off-duty police officer, was killed when the abortion clinic where he served as a security guard was bombed. The bomber was Eric Rudolph. He was convicted of this murder and received two life sentences. Likewise, on October 23, 1998, Dr. Bernard Slepian was shot to death by James Charles Kopp. Kopp used a high-powered rifle to kill Slepian in Amherst New York. Dr. Slepian was standing in the kitchen in his home when Kopp fired a single rifle shot from a nearby wooded area that entered the kitchen through a rear window.

Slepian was a well-known obstetrician-gynecologist who performed abortions at a women's clinic in Buffalo, New York.

After the murder of Slepian, Kopp fled to Mexico under an assumed name, and later fled to Ireland. There Kopp practiced traditionalist Catholicism. From there Kopp fled to France, where he was arrested on March 29, 2001, while living in the town of Dinan. The French extradited Kopp to the United States upon receiving assurances from Atty. Gen. Ashcroft that the death penalty would not be applied. The French will not extradite anyone who faces the death penalty. Consequently Kopp was found guilty of second-degree murder and was sentenced by a judge to the maximum of 25 years to life. There is a good possibility that the murder of Slepian was not Kopp's only crime. It is possible Kopp was also involved in the shooting of Ontario doctor Hugh Short.

Kopp received help from sympathetic antiabortion activists Loretta Marra and Dennis Malvasi. Both pled guilty to conspiracy and helping Kopp avoid capture.

During his trial, Kopp argued that he was innocent of murder because "I have separated murderers from their weapons of mass destruction. I wish I could do 10 life sentences or 10 death penalties to save them," he said. [65]

On May 31, 2009, Dr. George Tiller was shot and killed by Scott Roeder as Tiller served as an usher at a church in Wichita, Kansas. This was the second time Tiller was shot by antiabortion activist. The first time, in 1993, he was shot into both arms by Rochelle "Shelley" Shannon. Shannon was convicted of the shooting and will be incarcerated until 2018.

On January 21, 2010, Scott Roeder was found guilty of murdering Dr. Tiller and was given a 50 year sentence. Dr. Tiller was shot dead on May 31, 2009, during worship services at the Reformation Lutheran Church in Wichita, Kansas. Tiller was standing in the hall of the church speaking to a congregant when Scott Roeder approached him, put a gun to his head, and fired. Roeder then fled in his car, but was apprehended three hours after the shooting. He was charged on June 2, 2009 with first-degree murder and two counts of aggravated assault. Roeder was already known before the murder for vandalizing a women's clinic the week before and the day before killing Tiller. Once in prison Roeder confessed that he had shot and killed Tiller and said that he felt no remorse. [66]

According to Roeder's ex-wife Lindsay, Roeder had been suffering from mental illness and had been diagnosed with schizophrenia. Roeder had also been a member of the antigovernment Montana Freemen group. Roeder drove without a driver's license or vehicle registration or proof of insurance on the grounds of being a sovereign citizen. He also carried explosives and gunpowder in his car and failed to pay taxes. Roeder had been jailed on several previous occasions because he carried weapons of this car. These weapons were found by police who searched his car. However, a Court of Appeals ruled that the search of his car had been illegal. The searchers discovered an Army of God manual, which advocates the killing of providers of abortion and contains bomb making instructions.[67]

Numerous other attacks on abortionists and abortion clinics occurred over the years. Perhaps one of the most atrocious of these attacks was the murder of three people and the wounding of nine others, including five police officers, at a Planned Parenthood center in Colorado Springs on November 27, 2015. This mass murder was perpetrated by Robert Dean, a man of questionable mental capacity.[68]

In addition to murder and other forms of violence against people, the opponents of abortion are also responsible for numerous bombings, 173 forms of arson, 619 bomb threats, and 1,264 incidents of vandalism. In addition, there have been 100 attacks with butyric acid, known as stink bombs. There have also been innumerable incidents of invasions and vandalism.[69]

One of the most arrant examples of such vandalism occurred in 1984 at a Birmingham, Alabama clinic. Two men forced their way into the clinic at 7:45 in the morning and, using sledgehammers, did $8,000 worth of damage to suction equipment. One of the perpetrators of this violence was the Benedictine monk Edward Markley. Although convicted of first-degree criminal mischief and second-degree burglary, Markley later entered the women's community health center in Huntsville, Alabama where he assaulted at least three clinic workers. One of them, Catherine Wood, received back injuries and a broken neck vertebra. Markley was convicted of first-degree criminal mischief and three counts of third-degree assault and harassment in the Huntsville attack.[70]

Islamist Violence: Attacks on Christianity and Judaism?

Attacks on Christian installations in the Middle East and elsewhere are well known, and to the extent that they are the Muslim population's response to what they perceive to be American wars of aggression, they cannot be considered religious attacks at all. In assessing crimes by adherents of one religion against another, one must consider the context of the wars in the Middle East, where the Americans are seen as allies of Israel.

Both Christian and Jewish institutions have been attacked quite often by Muslims living in the United States and Europe. Since violence is not consistent with the teachings of Islam, most Muslims find these attacks outrageous. However, it is often said that such attacks are motivated by the belief on the part of the perpetrators that their religion is the only one that ought to exist and that Christianity, Judaism, and all other religions are illegitimate and have been condemned by Allah. As decades of war drive more and more impoverished Muslims to despair, it should not be surprising that they can be motivated to commit atrocities.

The long list of attacks on Christian institutions in the United States started with a group called The Nation of Islam. In 1973 there were seven attacks and has continued unabated until the present day (2017). As the Muslim population increased, the number of attacks also increased. Thus, in 2012 there were twelve violent attacks on Christians in this country.

In 2002, Muslims in the United States made ten unprovoked attacks on the American population. In every year since then, there have been several attacks on Christians by Muslims in this country. On June 1, 2009, a Muslim shot a soldier to death inside a recruiting center explicitly in the name of Allah. On November 2, 2009, a woman died from injuries suffered when her father ran her down with a car for being too Western-minded. On November 5, 2009, a Muslim psychiatrist gunned down 13 soldiers while yelling praise to Allah. On April 12, 2009, a non-Muslim Islamic studies professor was stomped to death by Muslim grad students swearing revenge for persecuted Muslims. On April 14, 2010, a Muslim convert shot his family members to take them back to Allah and out of the world of sinners.

Some observers consider the anti-Israel movement BDS to be an Islamic expression of religious hatred devoted to the destruction of the Jewish community in America. A pro-Palestinian movement, BDS stands for "boycott, divestment and sanctions" against Israel and Israeli-owned business. Officially positioned as a means of protesting Israel's aggression against the Palestinians, this movement looks quite different on the campuses of American universities, where it is particularly active. Foreign-born Arabs and other Muslims have attacked Jewish students both physically and verbally. These attacks are also supported by some faculty and students who paint swastikas on the doors of dormitory rooms. The fact is that anti-Jewish hatred is now commonly expressed on American university campuses, even as administrators do nothing to protect Jewish students from assault.

A recent study from the Brandeis Center For Human Rights found more than half of 1,200 Jewish students surveyed on 55 campuses nationwide have been subjected to anti-Jewish attacks. Worryingly, the same tactic of boycotting Jewish business was used against the European Jews starting in 1933.

Hatred of Jews in American colleges and universities has grown in tandem with the increase in foreign Muslims enrolled as students or teaching there. Such attacks on Jewish students and faculty are also widespread in Canadian and English universities. An example is the experience of two students Carleton University in Canada. Although these two students are not Jewish, they were taken to be Jewish by a gang of Muslims who began by yelling at them in English and Arabic and cursing them as Jews. As the two were leaving the scene, one of the Muslims went into his car and brought out a machete, which he hurled at the head of one of the students, barely missing him.[71]

On January 7, 2016, Edward Archer, a convert to Islam, ambushed and shot a Philadelphia police officer sitting in his patrol car. Although shot three times in the arm and bleeding profusely, the officer, Jesse Hartnett , got out of his patrol car and shot the assailant in the buttocks. Archer was then apprehended by other officers. Archer said that he committed this brutal assault in the name of Islamic State. Archer used a 9 mm Glock 17 which had been stolen from the home of a police officer in 2013. Archer argued after his arrest that the police were enforcing laws that were contrary to the teachings of the Koran.[72]

Secular Attacks on American Christianity

Many American Christians feel attacked by secularists, agnostics and atheists, and even the United States government. This perception has been called persecution by some Christians.

A poll undertaken by *The Washington Post* in April 2016 reveals that 63% of the respondents surveyed said they agreed or strongly agree that Christians are facing growing levels of persecution, up from 50% in 2013. An equal number, 60%, said religious liberty is on the decline in America. This survey indicates high rates of anxiety about the state of religious freedom. The poll reflects Christian opinion after the Supreme Court decision to strike down state laws defining marriage as a union between one man and one woman.[73]

The Right to Personal Belief

An outstanding example of government intrusion into the right of an American citizen to freely exercise religious and moral beliefs was the jailing of County Clerk Kim Davis of Kentucky for refusing to issue a marriage license to two men. Davis stayed in jail for five days in September 2012 after refusing to issue marriage licenses despite the Supreme Court's decision legalizing same-sex marriage. Davis claimed same-sex marriage violated her Christian beliefs.[74]

Numerous other examples of discrimination of Christians are the subject of complaints. For example, a Christian ministry in Florida has been providing food to the hungry and Lake City. All of that however was challenged when a state government worker showed up and said that a state agriculture department official would not continue a contract between the state and the Florida ministry unless they removed a picture of Christ, the 10 Commandments and a banner that read "Jesus is Lord". They were also told to stop giving Bibles to the needy. The food distributed by the Christian ministry came from the United States Department of Agriculture.

The Billy Graham Evangelical Association claims that the Internal Revenue Service targeted them when they notified the Association that they were conducting a review of their activities for the year 2010. The Rev. Graham wrote a letter to *Politico* to the effect that "I believe that someone in the administration was targeting and attempting to intimidate us. This is morally wrong and unethical — indeed some would call it Un-American".[75]

On February 2, 2011, two Christians, Mark Mackey and Brett Coronado, were arrested in front of the California Department Of Motor Vehicles in Murrieta, for reading the Bible out loud. The arresting officer said that it was illegal to preach to a captive audience. The defendants were placed in jail. When the officer discovered that no penal code prohibits preaching to a captive audience he changed the citation to "impeding an open business". Thereafter, the district attorney changed the charges once more claiming "trespass" because impeding an open business could not be used because the business was not open. This constant change of the charges leads reasonable people to conclude that the true purpose of these arrests was to censor the two Bible readers.[76]

In 2008 a Christian Air Force veteran was relieved of his duties for refusing to affirm homosexual marriage. Senior Master Sgt. Philip Monk had served in the Air Force for 19 years. Shortly after returning from deployment to Iraq he returned to Lackland Air Force Base in San Antonio and discovered that he had a new commander who was a lesbian. This commander asked Monk to comment on a disciplinary matter involving an Air Force instructor who had expressed his disagreement with homosexual marriage. When Monk revealed that he did not believe in same-sex marriage the commander told him that because of his convictions he would be relieved of his duties. Monk was also faced with a court-martial for expressing his opinions. Evidently, the Christian point of view is not welcome in the Air Force[77]

At Florida Atlantic University a student, Ryan Rotela, was told by his professor to write Jesus Christ's name on a piece of paper and stomp on it. When Rotella refused, formal disciplinary action was started against him. When the word about what was happening became known, Christians became outraged leading to a formal apology by the vice president for student affairs, Dr. Charles Brown. The professor, Deandre Pool, was put on administrative leave after the university received a complaint from the governor of Florida, Rick Scott.[78]

Christian Post published a list of 10 anti-Christian acts as viewed by Christian believers. The most frequent complaint by Christians concerned a California law signed by Gov. Jerry Brown, forcing public school curriculum and textbooks to celebrate homosexuals, trans-genders and bisexuals. Christians also felt demeaned when the NBC television eliminated the words "under God" from the Pledge of Allegiance as it led up to the US Open golf tournament.

A Christian man in Minnesota was fired from his job because one of his female coworkers attended a Bible study that his wife led. In Florida, a Christian teacher was suspended after school administrators discovered his support of traditional marriage posted on the Internet.

In Kalispell, Montana, pro-lifers were attacked by a fire bomb during a prayer vigil in front of an abortion clinic. A police officer was called who remarked that pro-lifers should expect this sort of reaction to the activities. A Bible study was shut down by San Juan Capistrano, Cal. officials claiming that the Bible study group needed a permit because Bible study poses a risk to public safety and health.[79]

Innumerable other anti-Christian acts could be cited here. It is therefore necessary to explain how this anti-Christian attitude has become so widespread in the United States and why Christians have been largely unable to prevent the widespread antagonism against their traditions in a country which was at one time a chief supporter of the Christian religion.

Non-Religion

No doubt one reason for this attack on Christianity in the United States is that nonreligious are now the country's largest religious voting bloc. This is the first time that the nonreligious outnumber the religious in a presidential election year. The Pew Research Center survey in January 2016 found that religious "nones" now constitute 1/5 of all registered voters and more than a quarter of Democratic and Democratic leaning registered voters. That represents a 50% increase in the proportion of nonreligious voters compared with 2008 when they made up just 14% of the overall electorate. Affiliation does not necessarily mean translation into actual votes. For example, in the 2012 election the unaffiliated made up 18% of registered voters in pre-election polls but only 12% of the people who actually voted. It is also noteworthy that the Pew study found that religion is becoming a less potent force at the ballot box. In 2008 to 72% of focus said it was important for president to have strong religious beliefs. In 2016 that number has declined to 62%. Likewise, in 2008 75% of Americans said that churches and other houses of worship contributed a great deal to solving social problems. In 2016 that number had fallen to 58%.[80]

It has been evident for some time that the so-called mainline Protestant denominations in the United States continue their decades-long membership decline. That decline began in the 1970s since when the Presbyterian Church had the greatest membership drop of the 25 largest denominations. Other denominations reporting declines include the United Methodist Church, the Evangelical Lutheran Church in America and the Episcopal Church.[81]

The reasons for this decline can be attributed in part the failure of young people to participate in church activities. Beginning in the 1960s, individual autonomy and freedom from institutional restraints became most popular. This counterculture of the 1960s was related to the American civil rights movement and to the unpopular involvement of the United States in Vietnam. The counterculture began with the assassination of President John F. Kennedy in November 1963 and ended with the resignation of Pres. Richard M Nixon in August 1974. At the height of the counterculture movement 500,000 people descended on a farm near Woodstock, New York in August 1969. Advertised as three days of love and music, the festival descended in to a wild melee of drug use, and injuries to numerous participants.[82]

Sociologists contend that strong religions promote a level of commitment that binds members of the group together while weak religions have low levels of commitment so that people cannot resist influences that lower it even further.[83]

People who have no religious affiliation are not usually anti-religion but are rather indifferent to religion. They find it not necessary to participate in organized form of religious practice in order to support whatever faith they do have. Repeated surveys have shown that the "nones" as statisticians have called them, because they answer the question of affiliation with religion as "nones," are seldom atheists. Instead, "nones" generally agree that all religions of the world are equally good ways of helping the person find ultimate truth and that Christianity is not the only religion with a valid claim to the truth. Such people believe that God did not only have a hand in writing the Bible but he was also involved in writing the Buddhist, Muslim and other religious texts. This leads to a further assertion on behalf of the unaffiliated that all the major world religions teach a common moral cold similar to the Judeo-Christian tradition contained in the 10 Commandments. Liberals also reject the doctrine that God consigns someone to hell. In sum, many Americans see no point in being involved in religious activities. In addition Roman Catholics have had to deal with numerous sexual scandals involving priests and the subsequent cover-up of these assaults by the higher clergy.[84]

*

The Assault on Religion by the Religious

In 2015 The Pew Research Center reported that a survey of United States Catholics shows that half of all US adults who were raised Catholic have left the church at some point in their lives. The motivation for Catholics leaving their religion is in many cases the outcome of the same forces which have led so many Protestants to leave their denomination. In addition however the revelations of priestly misconduct have dealt a severe blow to American Catholicism.[85]

Although sexual abuse by priests led to considerable criticism of the clergy and the Roman Catholic Church, the greatest amount of anger related to these events concerned what appeared to be a cover up of sexual misconduct by priests on the part of several bishops. It needs therefore to be understood that what appears to be a cover up one's conduct required of bishops and leaving Roman Catholic clergy for centuries. For innumerable years it has with the contention of the Catholic Church that his conduct on the part of priests was to be considered absolutely confidential at that any consequences for such sexual misconduct were to be applied by the church itself is not the secular authorities. In the light of these beliefs, the bishops who did not report sexual misconduct secular authorities but dealing with these matters in accord with Canon law.[86]

From the traditional American point of view such efforts to keep sexual misconduct by priests secret appears to be a direct assault on democracy because democracy depends on the equal enforcement of the laws. However, Catholic Church doctrine involves the cold of Canon law. According to Canon 614 Canon law prohibits the disclosure of sexual abuse by priests to the civil authorities. It is this interpretation promulgated in 1917 which has led a number of American bishops to cover up sexual abuse by priests. An outstanding example of such a cover up concerns Father Dino Cinel, who lived at St. Rita's church in New Orleans for nearly a decade. It turned out that during those years Cinel stockpiled an enormous number of commercially produced pornographic films featuring young children as sexual objects. Cinel had also collected a number of magazines of children performing oral sex on each other. The mere possession of such material violates child pornography laws in Louisiana and in the nation.

Cinel also had 160 hours of homemade pornographic videos of his own sexual conduct with seven different teenage boys. Many of these videotapes were made in Father Cinel's rooms, where they were discovered by other priests. The church kept these discoveries secret for more than two years. When an investigative reporter from a local television station became aware of Cinel's activities, he was ousted as a parish priest. His tapes were turned over to the district attorney after the archdiocese held onto them for three months. The district attorney, Harry Connick, was a devout Catholic and a parishioner at St. Rita's. He was unwilling to prosecute Father Cinel "because he did not want to embarrass "Holy Mother the Church". After Connick was no longer district attorney, Cinel was in fact charged with possession of pornography but omitting any charges concerning his sexual assaults on children.

After Cinel was dismissed from St. Rita's, he was appointed a distinguished professor of history at the College of Staten Island which is part of the City University of New York. There he earned $90,000 a year and was also given lifetime tenure. Cinel then married a lady history professor and kept telling people that his erstwhile sexual conduct was behind him and that he could not understand why anyone was making a big deal out of something that happened in the past. Sometime later Cinel was indeed arrested and tried for his crimes. However, his jury found him not guilty. One of the consequences of Cinel's conduct was that many of his former victims sued the Church, which has paid millions in compensation for misconduct not only by Cinel but also for similar behavior by a numbers of other priests. [87]

*

Hardly any members of any American religious community know much of anything about the principal doctrines of their particular denomination. Almost all refer to religion only with reference to the local congregations. This means the theological issues do not gain the attention of ordinary congregational members. The fact is that the vast majority of Americans are simply not interested in religion. Most of those who hold these views also reject the idea that missionaries tried to convert people who already have a religion. They rarely discuss religion with families or anyone else.

The evidence is that religious communities are unable to generate high levels of commitment, a condition which has been going on the 1950s. Such practices as Sunday school confirmation and youth programs have all failed to bring about a commitment sufficiently strong to prevent the declines in religious affiliation over the past 50 years. The evidence for this lack of commitment is that Sabbath observance, so-called immodest dress, excessive use of alcohol, drug use and other practices not in accord with religious teachings have been and are being ignored. Neither the clergy nor religious teachings have been able to prevent this.[88]

Chapter 4. Economic Dependency

No greater threat to democracy exists than economic dependency. The unemployed, those will need to feed themselves and their families, those who are being exploited by working long hours for cheap wages and who are desperate to survive, will easily give up their constitutional rights for a piece of bread.

Work Ethic and Welfare

As Frank Tannenbaum put it: "We have become a nation of employees. We are dependent upon others for our means of livelihood, as most of our people have become completely dependent upon wages. If they lose their jobs they lose every resource except for the relief supplied by the various forms of Social Security. Such dependence of the mass of the people upon others for all of that income is something new in the world ... the substance of life is in another man's hands."[89]

This fact is illustrated by data published by the Bureau of Labor Statistics. The United States labor force included 159,281,000 workers in July 2016. Of these, 51,517,000 were employed and 7,770,000 were unemployed. Only 10% of all those included in the labor force were self-employed in 2016. This left 94,233,000 adults who were not in the labor force because they were no longer seeking employment.[90]

In 2015, these nearly 94 million Americans who were not in the labor force told the Bureau of Labor Statistics the reasons for this abdication from work. Nearly 24 million adults claimed to be disabled, while 13 million of those who said they were disabled were 65 years old or over. Another 307,000 of the disabled were "marginally attached to the workforce," which really means they, too, were not trying to find work. Another 45,000 were "discouraged" workers. However,

69,732,000 persons with no disability were out of the labor force in 2015. Of these, 2,871,000 persons were deemed marginally attached to the labor force and 603,000 were considered discouraged workers.[91]

These statistics are of necessity unreliable. We will never know how many of those who say they cannot work because of family responsibilities, or because they are disabled, or because they are going to school or for any other reason, are telling the truth. It may well be that all of the nearly 94 million not in the labor force truly cannot work, although this is unlikely.

In 1971, President Richard Nixon addressed the nation on Labor Day. In that radio address he emphasized the work ethic and said, "The competitive spirit goes by many names. Most simply and directly it is called the work ethic." Nixon went on to say that labor is good in itself and that those at work become better persons by virtue of the act of working. "That work ethic is ingrained in the American character," said Nixon. He then lamented that the work ethic has come under attack and that some Americans would rather take the welfare road than the road of hard work. "No job is menial in America if it leads to self-reliance, self-respect, and individual dignity." So said Richard Nixon in 1971 and so said the Puritans in the 17th century.[92]

Since the days of the Puritans, America has changed immensely, although some essential American values are as valid now as they were in 1620 when the Mayflower landed in Massachusetts. No doubt a democratic society owes those incapable of supporting themselves the means by which they can survive. Nevertheless, democracy is undermined if a large number of citizens are unwilling to carry their share of the burden of paying taxes and otherwise participating in the common enterprise by working.

On the Job Fear

But as we have already shown, America has become a nation of employees. Therefore, millions whose livelihood depends on their subordinate positions in large organizations (or even in smaller places where bosses rule), fear expressing their opinions on any subject. It is a true threat to American democracy that freedom of speech has been largely curtailed in this country, although it is enshrined in the First Amendment of the Constitution and is without doubt the most essential component needed to maintain a free society.

A good number of "silent" employees are afraid. Silence becomes a collective behavior when most members of an organization choose to keep silent. This phenomenon takes various forms, including meetings where no one is willing to speak up, or to make suggestions, and low levels of participation in discussions.[93]

While silence in broad societal terms is usually associated with such virtues as modesty, respect for others, prudence, and decorum, there are many who keep silent for other reasons. These are folks who seek to avoid embarrassment or confrontation with others. Yet, silence conveys approval — or at least acceptance, even if those who say nothing do not really approve of conditions on the job or in other situations.

Richard Nielsen has identified a number of reasons why people remain silent even in the face of unethical behavior. First of these is fear of retaliation against so-called "whistle blowers" by powerful people engaged in unethical behavior. The fact is that many of those who reveal unethical behavior become victims, with devastating consequences. Nielsen next lists embarrassment. Many people are afraid to speak about such topics as sex, money, politics, or ethics. Implicating friends is another reason why many people keep silent in view of unethical behavior while others say nothing because they feel that they do not have the political skills to deal with such issues.[94]

By political skills, they mean that employees who have relevant ideas, information and opinions that they do not express may be keeping quiet because they wish to avoid calling attention to themselves, especially if they sense their view is not widely (or even unanimously) held. Some people are afraid of any degree of confrontation; and a good number of people are afraid to speak up because they wish to protect themselves from external threats.[95]

Unions Offered Some Protection

Before unions were organized, a single employee was helpless in dealing with an employer. He was dependent ordinarily on his daily wage for the maintenance of himself and family. If the employer refused to pay him the wages that he thought fair, he was nevertheless unable to leave the employ and to resist arbitrary and unfair treatment. Unions were therefore essential to give laborers opportunity to deal on an equal basis with their employers.[96]

Employees are also exceedingly vulnerable because they are generally immobile. This means that many employees need to remain in their homes or their communities, not only because of the needs of their families and children, but also because modern technology requires more and more specialization. Evidently, job security has become more important than ever before, making employees even more easily oppressed by their employers. The law has not helped employees to maintain their jobs. On the contrary, employers may dismiss their employees at will ... for good cause or for no cause. This makes employees who are not union affiliated the docile followers of the employers' every wish. Employers are therefore empowered to give employees unfavorable work assignments, transfer the employee frequently, or prevent his promotion permanently. Employees can even be forced to express political opinions in accord with the views of employers. Fearing loss of employment as well as the blemish of having been dismissed, which makes future employment more difficult, employees will submit to almost anything. This really means that slavery has not truly been abolished in the United States. It has been said that being fired is equivalent to economic capital punishment.[97]

Indeed, employers have an interest in whatever an employee does or believes. It is therefore entirely possible that an employee may say or do something that is not compatible with his professional position. Therefore, employees need to be protected against the overreach of employers. This means that an employee should at least have the right to enjoy all those guarantees included in the first ten amendments to the Constitution usually called the Bill of Rights. Yet it is possible that an employer could threaten to dismiss an employee for invoking his Fifth Amendment rights or for speaking out on any political issue. In a case called *Garrity v. New Jersey*, the Court of Appeals in New Jersey ruled that police officers accused of fixing tickets were unconstitutionally forced to incriminate themselves or lose their jobs. This form of coercion was held to violate the 14th Amendment. This ruling applied, however, only because the employees were working for a government entity. Had they been employed privately, this protection would not have been available to them.[98]

Going Along to Get Along

The threat of losing one's job could also lead to forcing an employee to engage in illegal activities against his will. For example, in *Comerford v. International Harvester*, an employee alleged that he was fired as a result of his superior's inability "to alienate the affections" of his wife.[99]

A second example of coercion is the case of *Susnjar v. United States*. Here an employee was forced by an employee to smuggle aliens into the country in violation of the Immigration Act.[100]

There have been numerous cases of business executives fixing prices and participating in other illegal acts because they were coerced to do so in order to hold their jobs. Likewise, corporate lawyers and accountants may be required to falsify records in order to avoid prosecution of the employers for income tax evasion or other crimes. Employees are also often forced by threat of discharge not to give testimony unfavorable to employers or to give up their lawful claims against the employer, a fellow employee, or some third party, or not to buy goods from or otherwise deal with a particular business concern. There are numerous cases in which employees are told to violate the law or lose their jobs. It is difficult to assess the number of employees placed into such a dilemma because those who would coerce them would also not tolerate any complaint.

The only protection which employees achieved against arbitrary discharge has been membership in a union. This has been obtained by including "just cause" provisions in union-employer contracts. Employees are of course just as reluctant to become pawns in the hands of labor bosses as they are to be pushed around by employers.

Therefore there is a minor amount of protection available to employees. This is so because some states prohibit employers from preventing employees from engaging in political activities. The problem with these laws is that they provide no redress for the injured employee. Furthermore, the risk of losing one's job is so great that hardly anyone would complain about an employer who violates these statutes. Employees who are fired not only lose income, but are also concerned with the stigma and mental anguish which failure to support one's family entails.[101]

The National Labor Relations Board is one agency of government which is empowered to reinstate an employee and provide him with back pay if he was fired for being involved in labor union activities. Likewise, The Fair Employment Practices Commission can interfere on behalf of the employee who has been the victim of ethnic discrimination. In 1965, Congress passed The Automobile Dealer's Franchise Act. This act protects dealers against arbitrary decisions by automobile manufacturers.[102]

The Right to Unionize, and Rights Infringed by Unions

In the 19th century and in the early 20th century, before the passage of the National Labor Relations Act, the Supreme Court of the United States struck down legislation which made it a crime for an employer to discharge an employee for labor union activity. In the case of *Adair v. United States*, the court held that an employee had the right to quit his job at any time for any reason and that therefore the employer had the same right to discharge an employee for any reason.[103] Then in 1915, the court invalidated state legislation seeking to protect employees from being arbitrarily dismissed. In *Coppage v. Kansas*, the court ruled that an employer's right to hire and fire whom he wished is a constitutionally protected property right.[104] It wasn't until 1937 that the Supreme Court finally upheld the National Labor Relations Act in *NLRB v. Jones and Laughlin Steel Corporation*. The court approved the right of employees to unionize free of intimidation and coercion by employers.[105]

The right to unionize is no guarantee that the individual worker is protected in exercising his civil rights. This is best understood by describing briefly the activities in the International Longshoreman's Union after it became the tool of organized crime. The mob manipulated the docks and the ILA because the method of hiring made labor at the docks utterly dependent on the hiring boss "who ran the docks like the Gestapo ran Hitler's Germany."[106]

This brutal dictatorship took advantage of poor immigrants. The method of hiring depended entirely on bribing the hiring boss by giving him a percentage of a man's daily wages. The hiring boss picked those who paid him the most from their meager incomes. The hiring boss, also known as the stevedore, would send a kickback of cash to the head stevedore, who would in turn kick it up to the ILA boss. With that cash, the ILA forces bribed politicians and cops or anybody else who needed to get paid in order to keep the money in the pockets of the big shots who ran the ILA. Anybody who would give the ILA any trouble would never work at the docks again and might as well have stayed home. This meant that the union could issue an economic "death sentence" and thereby insure the power of the "mob." This system has been called the shape/payback system because the men seeking work would line up or shape up before the hiring boss, who then hired the worst men imaginable, including many who had just been released from prison where they had been sentenced for committing the most violent of crimes, including murder. This system was begun by Joseph Ryan, who became known as "Boss Joe." Ryan organized fundraisers at which his men were compelled to contribute. The beneficiaries of these fundraisers were politicians. Ryan's rule came to an end in 1955 after he was convicted and served a prison term for using union funds for himself.[107]

Ryan's departure allowed Anthony Anastasio, also known as Tough Tony, to take Ryan's place and continue the exploitation of the dockworkers. Anastasio was the brother of Albert Anastasio, a major member of the Mafia whom the media called Murder Inc. Anastasio continued the practice of choosing only those day laborers who paid him off from their meager wages. It was also Anastasio who was responsible for the fire that sunk the French ocean liner *Normandie* while tied to a dock in New York Harbor in 1942. Anastasio maintained his control of the docks until his death in 1963.[108]

Another assault on democracy promoted by labor unions is the use of the member's dues for the political preferences of paid officers of the union. According to The Center for Union Facts, union bosses routinely use members' money to support candidates for public office without asking the members whether they want their money spent on the candidates preferred by union officials. This is a plain violation of the union member's right to vote as he pleases. In 2016, union membership is only about 11% of the American labor force. This means that the 14,300,000 total union members in the United States no longer represent the majority of American employees. The annual dues paid by members to unions amount to $8,595,485,222, of which approximately $753 million are spent on political activities. These activities are determined entirely by the officers of the unions to the exclusion of the membership and/or their wishes.[109]

Union officials are constantly complaining that their membership makes too little money and that the minimum wage should be increased. Yet the same labor bosses collect large salaries derived from the contributions of their members. For example, in 2016, John Nicolai, president of United Food and Commercial Workers collected a $604,280 annual salary. Likewise, Terrence O'Sullivan, president of Laborers International Union of North America, collected a $501,648 annual salary. The president of The International Brotherhood Of Boilermakers, Newton Jones, was paid $657,897 in 2016, and similar salaries accrued to other union officials.[110]

These outlandish salaries demonstrate that democracy is absent from American labor unions, as the membership is forced to support a few labor bosses with huge incomes even as the members themselves earn the most meager of salaries.

Women's Work is Never Done....for Equal Pay

For centuries women have been consigned to do unpaid housework. Since they did not have their own wages or salary, this made women dependent on men. Even in the 21st century, women in many places around the world are literally second-class humans because they don't have the opportunity to gain lucrative employment. In most of the West, women now have access to education and professional training, and are gradually achieving economic independence. Nevertheless, housework is still largely viewed as women's work, even in the United States. Therefore, despite the huge advances which women have made in education and among the professions, the gender division of labor still persists. There are some who say that housework should be paid, although this is a most unlikely prospect.

To some extent, it is difficult to distinguish between housework and other activities that occur at home. A mother playing with her baby can hardly be viewed as working, although such an activity occurs at home and is an important part of child care. Of course, child rearing is a lot more than dealing with babies, so that it can reasonably be argued that driving adolescent children to endless activities after school or during vacations is indeed unpaid labor. Yet, it can hardly be answered as to who determines what is work and what is leisure. It could be argued that any household activity that could also be done by paid labor such as domestic servants, gardeners, chauffeurs, and nannies could be paid work, even if done by a housewife. Anyone who asks a woman who does any and all of these things every day would find that women will call this unpaid work, although there's hardly any means of gaining an income from such labor unless it is done outside of the home as employment.[111]

Women constitute nearly one half of the American labor force. According to the Bureau of the Census, American women earn only $.79 for every dollar paid to a median man in 2016. This discrepancy is in part the consequence of anti-female prejudices which have survived into the 21st century. However, there are aspects to women's lives which contribute to the gender gap. The evidence is that when young women start jobs they usually earn about the same that men earn. However, as women marry and reach childbearing age, many of them leave the workforce for extended periods of time to raise children. In addition, working women are far more likely to take a day off when children are ill or some other family situation requires it. Furthermore, domestic duties prevent women from putting in extra time on the job by working at home. All these opportunities are open to men, who therefore improve their income. Women typically devote two hours or more daily to housework, while men spend only one hour or a little more on similar tasks.

Mothers in the United States who work full-time, year round, make an average of $40,000 a year, compared to $57,000 paid to fathers. Women are more likely than men to take less demanding jobs so as to accommodate their family obligations. All this indicates that the wage gap between the genders is much more likely to be linked it the roles that women and men must play in American society, not mere prejudice. Women concentrate in low-paying jobs, according to the Bureau of Labor Statistics.[112]

The Bureau of Labor Statistics reported on July 19, 2016, that the median weekly earnings of American women was $744, or 81.8% of the $909 median for men. Among those of both genders who held full time management or professional jobs, the weekly earnings for men were $1405 and the weekly earnings for women were $1019. Among those employees with master's degrees or more, the highest 10% of men made $3517 or more per week compared to $2593 or more for women.[113]

Gender equality is an essential aspect of American democracy. Indeed, women have made great progress in achieving that end. In comparison to the entire history of the United States, women are indeed better off today than during any earlier decade. Nevertheless, democracy can only rest on a solid foundation once gender equality has been achieved. It is therefore a shameful atrocity that domestic violence, consisting in the main of assaults against women by men, continues to be common in this country.

Domestic Violence

According to the Bureau of Justice Statistics, American women and girls experienced approximately 552,000 non-fatal violent victimizations as of 2008. 99% of these assaults were committed by male offenders. In addition to these nonfatal violent visitations, over two thousand women are murdered in this country each year by husbands or significant other males. In addition, the Bureau of Justice Statistics records approximately 44,000 rapes each year.[114]

The fact is that domestic violence is the leading cause of injury to women in the United States. Several reasons for domestic violence have been discovered. As more and more women earn more money than men and also contain a greater level of education as well as job prestige, there are some who want to retain a dominant position by the use of violence.[115]

A second reason for domestic violence is the wish on the part of some people to exercise control over their partners. There are of course a good number of women who control men without resorting to physical violence. However, those men who assaulted women are often motivated by a wish to control the women in their lives.[116]

There are also men who assault family members because they can. The cost to perpetrators is relatively low, and the benefits, as they see them, are high. This would be mainly where law enforcement scoffs at female victims of male aggression. Finally, economic dependency, also known as patriarchy, makes it difficult for many women, particularly those with children, to escape violent men.[117]

Cruise Line Crimes

Anyone who was ever seen advertisements showing the ships used by the major cruise lines which frequent American harbors would be most favorably impressed by the promised enjoyment of cruises originating in American ports. Florida is no doubt the principal originator of cruises, as many ships depart from Miami, Fort Lauderdale, Port Canaveral, Jacksonville, and Tampa. In addition to Florida, California, New Jersey, New York, South Carolina, Texas, and Virginia also associate with the cruise line industry. According to the American Association of Port Authorities, the cruise industry earns nearly $38 billion in revenue each year. In one year, 20,335,000 passengers travel on these ships, which furnish 314,000 Americans with jobs. This means that 60% of all cruise ship passengers originate in the United States. New cruise ships are being ordered almost every year because of the popularity of these vacations, which originate in 30 American embarkation ports. One half of all these cruises sailed to the Caribbean islands, and others to the Bahamas, Hawaii, Mexico, Europe, and Alaska.

Because so many American ports are involved and because the owners of the ships are mainly Americans (as are the passengers), those not acquainted with the cruise industry would assume that working conditions as well as the safety of passengers are subject to American law. This is unfortunately not the case, so that it can be said with certainty that worse conditions for labor and those on the cruise ships cannot be found anywhere else in American jurisdictions. The same is true of the rights of passengers, of whom Americans constitute 76% of the global market share. Despite their dependence on American customers and American embarkation ports, the cruise lines do not pay federal taxes and are exempt from American labor laws. The cruise line owners escape these normal obligations by registering their corporations and vessels in foreign countries such as Panama, Liberia, and the Bahamas. As a result, those who work on the cruise lines as well as US citizen passengers usually find no recourse in the courts for mistreatment on these ships. It is claimed that because cruise ships sail in the waters of many countries as well as on the high seas, no one is really responsible to compensate those who have suffered injury or crime on one of these cruises.

Several examples will illustrate the impotence of passengers who have been mistreated or who have been the victims of accidents on these cruise ships. For example, a woman passenger, an American citizen, was assaulted and killed by her cabin mate. Charges against the victim's cabin mate were not enforced on the grounds that the Death On The High Seas Act applies. According to that law, only financial damages can be recovered in an amount no greater than the earnings of the dead victim. Wrongful death or pain and suffering are not considered.

One of the most common crimes committed against cruise ship passengers is sexual assault by crew members, particularly cabin, table, and bar stewards. Unfortunately, most of the cruise lines do not have policies prohibiting socializing between the crew and passengers. If American laws were applied to the crimes committed by crew members against passengers, then rapes and assaults would certainly have had different outcomes than is currently the case. Of course, even under the best circumstances, the collection of evidence is always very difficult aboard a cruise ship. This is largely the case because crew members who have committed a crime are usually sent to the home country where they will never be found and never prosecuted. Instead, these criminal crew members gain similar employment on a different cruise line and there repeat these offenses.[118]

Cruise lines that register their ships in foreign countries do not pay federal taxes and are not subject to federal labor laws.

The abuse of crew members by the cruise line owners are numerous and are enforced in a variety of ways. First, cruise lines unreasonably overwork crew members. Cabinet attendants, galley employees, and waiters and other crew members work a minimum of 10 to 12 hours a day and sometimes more, seven days a week, for 8 to 10 months a year. Crew members are also forced "to work off the clock" which means that they work for free during those hours. Cruise lines underpay crew members. Many crew members who work extreme hours are often paid only by passenger tips. This means that the cruise lines who pay no taxes nevertheless acquire that taxpaying United States guests pay the cabin attendants and waiters for the long hours they have to work. Cruise liners also use automatic gratuities, in some cases to steal the money. Cruise lines prohibit crew members from organizing or protesting by firing anyone who attempts to unionize or otherwise resist the exploitation. Moreover, crew members can be fired at will for any reason or no reason. Those who have been dismissed, particularly because of work related injuries, have no recourse of any kind, and are simply sent on a one-way flight back without money and without work. Cruise lines provide very few benefits to crew members, if any at all, so that very few crew members have any pension or any medical protection. Cruise lines also insert mandatory arbitration clauses in crew members' employment contracts so as to prevent them from being able to file suit in the United States before a judge and jury. Cruise lines also strip crew members from protection of all US laws, which is possible because many members of Congress believe that the court should be closed to foreign seamen despite the fact that the cruise lines use American ports of embarkation and that most of the customers are Americans.[119]

Cruise line employees are by no means the only exploited and impoverished citizens. The inhabitants of Appalachia, and particularly the coal miners living there with their families, are among the poorest Americans. These people are almost all the descendants of British and Scottish immigrants of the 18th century.

Mining —Hazardous for Many Reasons

Mining is an extremely difficult and dangerous occupation. The underground work is dirty and damp. The miners working there usually cannot stand up because the ceilings in the tunnels are too low. Therefore miners have to use picks and shovels and bend over for 10 hours a day. For two centuries, miners have loaded coal on small cars and pushed them to an area where at one time mules pulled the coal away from the face of the mines. Later, rubber tired vehicles called shuttle cars hauled the coal to the haulage system.

Mining towns were and are usually company towns. This means that the coal company owns the houses which they lease to the workers. This meant that if the miners ever quit work or went on strike the company could evict them. Companies also owned company stores where credit was available.

Miners were then paid with script, which could only be used in the company store.

Miners were traditionally paid by the ton, but only for large pieces, while small chunks were sold by the companies although miners received no pay for small chunks. And income of miners was seriously reduced by seasonal unemployment. Every day miners came home covered with coal dust, which caused miners to suffer from black lung disease. In addition to these certain threats to the health of all mining communities, miners face the additional nightmare of a mine disaster such as took place in 2010 in West Virginia. On June 6 of that year, 29 miners died when a huge underground explosion occurred in the Upper Big Branch mine in Raleigh County, West Virginia. Poison gas had accumulated at the blast site about 30 miles south of Charleston. This mine had a significant history of safety violations, including 57 infractions in just one month. Most serious was the failure of the Performance Coal Company to properly ventilate the highly combustible methane gas. After the explosion, rescuers bulldozed an access road above it so they could begin drilling three shafts over 1000 feet each to release methane and carbon monoxide.

The Performance Coal Company, which owned the mine, is a subsidiary of Massey Energy. That company had a poor record of safety violations, so that federal inspectors fined that company more than $382,000 for repeated serious violations involving its ventilation plan and equipment.[120]

On December 30, 1970, 38 miners were killed when mines exploded at the Hurricane Creek Mine in Hyden, Leslie County, Kentucky run by the Finley Coal Company.

Investigation of this disaster showed that 14 men were killed by the explosion at the number 16 mine, 19 men were killed by the explosion at mine number 15, and the others died from asphyxiation or carbon monoxide poisoning. Subsequent investigation of this disaster showed that unsafe practices in handling explosives in these mines were common. Evidence of smoking underground, such as burn patches, cigarette butts, and empty cigarette packages, was observed at numerous locations in the mines during ensuing investigations. It was also found that explosive charges were improperly secured with paper. These investigations were conducted by the United States Bureau of Mines.[121]

Over the years, innumerable additional mine disasters have occurred in this country. Indeed, these disasters are less frequent today than they were in previous years. Nevertheless, those who work under the circumstances risk their lives for little pay, and suffer poor health and a life of poverty and deprivation.

Because of these abuses, miners formed unions, so that the United Mine Workers of America became one of the most powerful unions in the country. In fact, one of its presidents, John L. Lewis, founded The Congress of Industrial Organizations.[122]

It is therefore no surprise that mortality is exceptionally high in the Appalachian coal mining region. In fact, Appalachia in general is linked to every kind of socioeconomic disadvantage. Associated with this disadvantage is a low educational achievement and very little economic diversification. Poor health is also associated with socioeconomic disadvantage, so that there is an elevated morbidity and mortality rate in these areas. Mortality is everywhere related to income, so that wealthy people live longer and poor people live shorter lives. Many of the effects of living in a coal mining area are delayed.[123]

It is significant that higher mortality rates occurred in both males and females in the Appalachian area, although women were not engaged in coal mining. The higher female mortality rate is therefore related to water and air pollution from mining activities.[124]

Appalachia has been a very byword for poverty for so long because the earliest settlers of the Shenandoah Valley of the 1730s were already dependent on outside investment at that time.

The citizens of Appalachia became impoverished after industrialization elsewhere in the United States led to far higher productivity outside Appalachia than within Appalachia. This meant that a far greater amount of time and work was required to produce the same unit of economic value than in the industrial areas of the country. This in turn led to unemployed workers receiving lower wages but also cheapening the value of the self-employed labor.[125]

Another reason for the impoverishment of Appalachia was the traditional practice of dividing landholdings among all male heirs. This remained useful as long as a sufficient amount of land was available. As the population increased, the amount of land inherited became smaller and smaller until landholdings no longer supported a family.[126]

Sweat and Tears

Many Americans believe that the sweatshop is a condition of the past belonging to days gone by. In any age, the newcomers tend to be most vulnerable; in the 1920s, these were mainly Jewish immigrant women, who were the victims of abominable conditions. However, despite American labor laws and unionization, sweatshops still exist in the American garment industry. Now, Latina women are the principal victims of the exploitation of those in need. For example, a recent advertisement in a trade magazine of the US garment industry announced that immigrants from El Salvador and American women from Puerto Rico can be hired for $.33 an hour. It is important to remember that natives of Puerto Rico are American citizens.[127]

Shortly after the Second World War, Puerto Rican women migrated and found garment industry jobs in New York City and other urban areas. These other urban areas were lower wage areas, so that Puerto Rican women confronted fewer jobs and deteriorating working conditions.[128]

The garment industry advertised in US newspapers and other media that: "Puerto Rican labor which is highly skilled in the textile field commands wage rates from 1/3 to ½ of others in the United States." The advertisement continued to the effect that Puerto Ricans suffered extensive unemployment and underemployment and that therefore they were orderly and tranquil and engaged in very few strikes. It was further announced that particularly women workers are noted for the dexterity and industry and, most important, labor laws had recently been liberalized to permit night work for women and textile industries.[129]

Although a segment of the garment industry moved to Puerto Rico, the New York City metropolitan region has accounted for 49% of employment for women and children's and women's garments. This is somewhat less that was true of the 1950s, when 78% of dresses and 73% of coats and suits were produced in New York City.[130]

Then, employment in the apparel industry decreased by 54,000 jobs between 1947 and 1958. In the next decade another 72,000 jobs were lost, and until 1975 so many jobs had been lost that fewer than 150,000 people worked in apparel, which was just one third of the 1969 labor force.

In the 21st century, employment in the apparel industry declined even more. In 2015, the Bureau of Labor Statistics recorded that only 141,520 people were employed as sewing machine operators, with a mean annual income of $24,680.[131] Although Manhattan has traditionally been the center of the New York garment industry, the Sunset Park area of Brooklyn has become the home of the Chinese garment industry in America. This development has come about because the owners of the sweatshops that employ mainly members of the American Chinese community can rent space in Brooklyn for a lot less than in Manhattan.[132]

These sweatshops have severe problems with ventilation. Because the shops are converted former warehouses and garages, they have very few or often no windows at all. In many of the shops, owners cover the few windows with rags or newspapers or lock the main entrance to conceal operations. Under these conditions, the air is filled with lint and dust, and workers sew under fluorescent lights in the daytime.[133] Traditionally sewing machine operators have been women. Now, however, an increasing number of undocumented male workers have taken over these positions in Sunset Park.[134]

It is easy to offer a week's work to people in need, and then kick the workers out empty-handed on the excuse they worked "too slow" or for some other complaint.

Among those who work in the sweatshops, there are some whose skills are minimal. Therefore 72% of the reported incomes of the less skilled workers have been reported to be below the poverty line for a family of four. This means that in the 1990s and even into the 21st century, many garment workers had an income of only $20,000 a year, so that many had to work long hours in violation of US labor laws just to sustain their families.

These poor workers are victimized in many ways by their employers. For example, employers sometimes close the shop and vanish without a trace while owing the workers several hundred thousand dollars in back wages. The states' labor departments discover that the owners are then hard to find, because many are themselves undocumented immigrants who had registered the shop with the name and Social Security number of someone else. That person is often a worker who did not know that the owner used his name so that no charges against the real owner could be instituted. This form of exploitation and labor law violations is widespread.[135]

American democracy has expanded over the life of the Republic. This is best understood by considering that in the early days of the United States only male property owners could vote. Later, all men were allowed to vote but women did not vote in any federal election until 1920, except for in Wyoming, where women voted already in 1869. The Afro-American population of the United States finally achieved voting rights in the 1960s during the voter registration drives of that decade.

Race, Crime and Poverty

Nevertheless, Americans of African descent are immensely overrepresented among the poor and suffer a far higher violent crime rate that of other Americans. This does not mean that poverty causes crime. The evidence is that white-collar crime is committed far more often by people with considerable incomes while violent crime is much more common among the poor and therefore among Americans of African descent. Criminologists assert that those who have been least rewarded by the American economy are far more prone to commit violent crime than those with high incomes or at least a middle-class position in the economic hierarchy.[136]

Associated with violent crime is the concept of relative deprivation. There are indeed many countries in which a large number of people are quite poor while a small minority are exceedingly wealthy. Yet in such countries such as Saudi Arabia or North Korea, there is very little violence on the part of the poor who have no aspirations and no expectations of ever gaining a higher income or achieving a better economic position. In the United States, however, it is universally agreed and taught both formally in schools and informally in the media that all Americans are created equal and that therefore everyone should be able to climb the ladder of success. For this reason, many Americans feel relatively deprived, not only because they have less of an income than other Americans, but because they compare themselves unfavorably to those who have more and sometimes much more. It is therefore the combination of poverty and relative deprivation which leads many Afro Americans to the conclusion that their lives are hopeless and that they will never be able to participate in "the American dream." Indeed, there are in the first decade of the 21st century a good number of Afro-Americans who have achieved middle-class standing and sometimes more. The election of a black man to the presidency is also an indication that the American people are gradually willing to promote the interests of the black population. Despite all this, however, there is a large economic gap between blacks and whites even in 2017 which has not changed in 50 years.

The evidence for this assertion begins with a look at the black unemployment rate, which has consistently been twice as high as the white unemployment rate. In fact, the Economic Policy Institute reports that this gap hasn't closed at all since 1963. In that year the unemployment rate was 5% for whites and 11% for blacks. Today it is 6.5% for whites and 12.5% for blacks. Furthermore, for the past 50 years, black unemployment has been well above recession levels.

This means that black America is nearly always facing an employment situation that would be labeled a particularly severe recession if it characterized the entire labor force. These conditions can also be seen by looking at the gap in the household income between blacks and whites which has not narrowed in the last 50 years. It is remarkable that during the recession of 1983–2010 the wealth disparity between whites and blacks grew even wider. According to the Urban Institute, from 1983 to 2010, average family wealth for whites has been about six times that of blacks.[137]

Looking now at the black family, we find that black children are four times more likely than whites to live in areas of concentrated poverty. Evidently, many African-Americans live in some of the least desirable housing in some of the lowest resourced communities in America. These poor neighborhoods have a way of perpetuating inequality as well as causing a higher exposure to health hazards and higher crime rates. Today, in 2017, schools are more segregated than they were in 1980, when segregated schools had dropped to 63%. Today over 80% of schools are once more segregated. The Pew Research

Institute reports that marriage rates have fallen for all Americans since the 1960s. Since then, the white marriage rate has fallen from 74% to 55%, while the black marriage rate fell from 61% to 31%. Since married people are better off than single people and since juvenile delinquency is a good deal less among children of married couples then of single parents, these conditions directly influence the black crime rate.[138]

That violent crime rate is indeed a threat to American democracy, as it is responsible for the excessive involvement of Americans of African descent with the criminal justice system. Some facts concerning violent crime among Afro-Americans are these: The Federal Bureau of Investigation reports that 93% of black homicide victims are killed by other blacks. It is true that 84% of white homicide victims are killed by whites. However, the white homicide rate is far lower than the black homicide rate because blacks commit violent crimes at 7 to 10 times the rate of whites. Thus, blacks commit 52% of homicides, although they are only 13% of the American population. Whites who compose at least 77% of the population committed 45% of homicides. Looking now at violent crimes other than homicide, it turns out that annually 39% of people arrested for rape, robbery, and aggravated assault are black. In the largest American cities, black crime is even more prevalent than in the country as a whole. For example, while blacks are 10% of the population in Los Angeles, California, they commit 42% of its robberies and 34% of all its felonies. In Chicago, as of September 2, 2016, there were 2,848 shooting victims in the first eight months of that year. In the entire year 2015 there were 2,988 shooting victims in Chicago. According to the Chicago Tribune, the overwhelming majority of these assaults which led to wounding and death were committed by black citizens.[139]

It is evident from this linkage of economic conditions and crime and violence that democracy demands the promotion of the American black community into far better educational, economic and family outcomes than is now the case. The fate of the Afro-American community is the product of all that has occurred in this country since the days of slavery and its consequences. The rescue of the Afro-American community can be achieved by means of education, family stability, economic success, and an understanding that this is really not a racial issue. We define race as a biological subdivision of the human species who have some physical characteristics in common. These physical characteristics have been interpreted as indications of inferiority or superiority, when in fact neither of these attributes is of a genetic origin. The condition of the American black community will without doubt improve, because indeed all men are created equal if given equal opportunities.

CHAPTER 5. THE AMERICAN CRIMINAL (IN)JUSTICE SYSTEM

Origins in the Constitution

The American criminal justice system is rooted in the United States Constitution, which is now over 200 years old. Therefore, a good number of changes have occurred in the manner in which the Constitution has been interpreted since then. Essentially, the Constitution protects the interests of the individual by promoting the right to privacy, the right not to incriminate oneself, the right to counsel and due process of law. Due process presumes the innocence of the accused and the right of the defendant to be proven guilty beyond a reasonable doubt.

The Fourth Amendment to the Constitution holds that the "right of the people to be secure in their persons, houses, papers and effects, against unreasonable searches and seizures, shall not be violated, and no warrant shall issue, but upon probable cause by oath or affirmation, and particularly describing the place to be searched at the persons or things to be seized". This is the privacy amendment.

The Fifth Amendment guarantees the right not to be a witness against oneself. The sixth amendment includes the statement that "in all criminal prosecutions the accused shall have the assistance of counsel for his defense". The sixth amendment also includes the right to a public and speedy trial and the right to confront the witnesses against oneself. The eighth amendment prohibits "cruel and unusual punishment" and also includes that "excessive bail shall not be required, nor excessive fines imposed." In addition the 14th amendment to the Constitution guarantees the equal protection of the laws and also holds that: "No state shall make or enforce any law which shall abridge the privileges or immunities of citizens of the United States, nor shall any State deprive any person of life, liberty, or property, without due process of law; nor deny to any person within its jurisdiction the equal protection of the laws."

It is significant that these amendments relate to any person including those who were not citizens. This means that the founding fathers truly meant that all men are created equal, an opinion which was most unusual in the 18th century and which is unfortunately still unusual around the world.

Misconstruing the Constitution

It is therefore particularly egregious that the Constitution has been so badly abused and reinterpreted so as to deprive many a citizen and many others of the very privileges which the Constitution and its originators sought to promote.

This violation of constitutional guarantees is best understood when we review the prosecution, conviction and imprisonment of innocent people including those who are sent to their death for crimes they did not commit.

Judge Alex Kozinski, one of America's most prominent jurists, has written an article in the Annual Review of Criminal Law Procedure in which he points out that 12 widely held beliefs about criminal prosecution in America are, in fact, false.

These beliefs include the opinion that eyewitnesses are highly reliable when in fact they are highly unreliable. Kozinski writes: "[M]istaken eyewitness testimony was a factor in one third of all wrongful conviction cases." The belief that fingerprint evidence is foolproof is also false. Kozinski says that prints left in the field are often smudged and incomplete and are subject to significant error. Kozinski then shows that what is true about fingerprint evidence is doubly true of foot and tire print identification and ballistics. Kozinski shows that much of so-called forensic expertise is nothing but guesswork. Even DNA evidence is not infallible says Kozinski. He shows that DNA evidence is often compromised during the collection, preservation and processing and that many DNA examiners are not competent and not honest. Next Kozinski shows that a study by psychologist Elizabeth Loftus demonstrates that human memories are not reliable and that we all have memories that are malleable and susceptible to being contaminated or supplemented in some form.

Almost everyone imagines that confessions are infallible because innocent people never confess. Kozinski found that innocent people confess surprisingly often due to interrogation tactics by the police, the Stockholm syndrome, emotional or financial exhaustion, family considerations and feeblemindedness. Kozinski also discovered that juries seldom follow instructions delivered by the judge and make decisions based on their private prejudices. Next Kozinski shows that prosecutors often fail to turn over evidence favorable to the defense although by law prosecutors are obliged to do so. He mentions the case of Brady vs. Maryland in which the Supreme Court ruled that prosecutors must turn over exculpatory evidence to the defense which prosecutors seldom do. Moreover, Kozinski writes that the defendant is often at a disadvantage because prosecutors have a chance to argue the case before the defense during a trial. The evidence is that whoever makes the first assertion about something has a large advantage over anyone who denies it later. Kozinski says that police have the opportunity to alter or remove evidence, influence witnesses, extract confessions and more or less lead an investigation in such a way that they can stack the deck against somebody they want convicted. Finally, Kozinski shows that guilty pleas are by no means proof of guilt because many a defendant thinks that everything is stacked against him and that he therefore enters a guilty plea to a lesser charge in order to still salvage a part of his life.[140]

The principal reason for all these problems is the extraordinary power of prosecutors who regularly violate the law in order to gain convictions at any cost. Numerous examples of prosecutorial misconduct which have led to the imprisonment and even the death penalty for innocent people can easily be recorded.

Misconduct and Miscarriage of Justice

On December 27, 2016, a Texas Court of Appeals exonerated Brian Franklin who had spent 21 years in prison on the false allegation that he had raped a 13-year-old girl in 1994. After 21 years, she admitted that she had lied about Franklin's so-called rape and that prosecutors knew this at the time of Franklin's conviction.[141]

On October 6, 2015, John Hincapie was released from prison 25 years after he was convicted when a confession was beaten out of him. In September 1990 six young men robbed some tourists from Utah on a New York subway platform. In the course of the robbery Brian Watkins was fatally stabbed as he tried to protect his mother. At the time of the killing Hincapie was not on the subway platform where the killing took place. He had gone upstairs in that subway station and on his return discovered that his friends had murdered Brian Watkins. Nevertheless, the police arrested him and beat him until he confessed to a crime with which he had nothing to do. Prosecutors then railroaded Hincapie to prison with the aid of a judge willing to ruin the life of an innocent man. Some prosecutors don't care whether the innocent are imprisoned or even sent to their death. They only care about accumulating convictions in order to help their career.[142]

Randall Dale Adams was convicted of capital murder and sentenced to death in 1977 in the Dallas County court in Texas. In 1980 his death sentence was overturned and the sentence commuted to life imprisonment. Then in 1988 a key witness recanted his trial testimony and attested to Adams' innocence. In 1989 Adams' conviction was overturned and he was released from prison. The Texas court of appeals overturned Adams conviction, holding that prosecutor Douglas D Mulder withheld a statement a witness gave to the police that cast doubt on her credibility and allowed her to give perjured testimony. Further, the court found that after Adams' attorney discovered the statement, Mulder falsely told the court that he did not know that witness' whereabouts.[143]

Errol Morris, a film producer and director, released a film called the "The Thin Blue Line" in 1988. The movie showed that Adams was walking along a Dallas Street after his car had run out of gas. At that point David Ray Harris came by in a stolen car and offered him a ride. The two spent the day drinking, smoking marijuana and going to a drive-in movie. Shortly after midnight, a Dallas police officer, Robert Ward, stopped a car for a traffic violation and was shot and killed. The investigation led to David Harris, who then accused Randall Adams of the murder. A number of so-called eyewitnesses corroborated Harris's testimony and Adams was convicted. Sentenced to die by lethal injection Adams appealed the verdict, but the Texas Court of Criminal Appeals refused to overturn it. His execution was scheduled for May 8, 1979. Three days before the execution the United States Supreme Court ordered to stay on the grounds that death penalty opponents were excluded at jury selection.

Then Governor Bill Clements commuted Adams' sentenced to life in prison leading the Texas appeals court to argue that now there is no error in the case. Meanwhile, Adams' accuser, David Harris had accumulated a long criminal record and was on death row for an unrelated murder. Harris at one time had bragged about shooting a police officer and then recanted and blamed Adams. It appeared to Errol Morris, the movie director, that Harris was probably guilty of the murder of the police officer and that Adams was wrongfully convicted. The result was the movie "The Thin Blue Line" which led a judge to grant Adams another hearing. Then in 1989 the Texas appeals court ruled that Adams was entitled to a new trial because of perjured testimony. Three weeks later he was released on his own recognizance, and two days after that the Dallas district attorney dropped all charges. Adams was never compensated for the atrocities he had suffered.[144]

Ken Bloodsworth was convicted of first-degree murder, first-degree rape and first-degree sexual offense; sentenced to death in Baltimore County, Maryland in 1985. In 1986 his conviction was overturned because the prosecution failed to reveal exculpatory evidence to the defense. This is called a Brady violation. In 1987 Bloodsworth was tried a second time and convicted again. Six years later in 1993 Bloodworth was exonerated by the use of a DNA test. He was released from prison and pardoned. His conviction had been overturned because prosecutors Robert Lazzaro and Ann Brobst withheld evidence pertaining to another possible suspect. [145]

In 1989 the Texas Court of Criminal Appeals overturned the conviction for capital murder of Clarence Brandley after a witness told authorities that another man had confessed to the crime. Brandley was convicted of capital murder in 1981 and released in 1990. The court had found that the prosecutor James Keeshan and the police failed to investigate leads pertaining to other suspects, suppressed evidence placing other suspects at the crime scene at the time of the crime, failed to call a witness who did not support the state's case, allowed the perjured testimony of witnesses to go uncorrected and failed to notify Brandley that another man later confessed to the crime.[146]

Kerry Max Cook was convicted of capital murder in Smith County Texas in 1978. In 1991, thirteen years later, his conviction was overturned by the Texas Court of Criminal Appeals due to erroneous admission of psychiatric testimony. The court also discovered that the prosecutors including A.D. Clark, Michael Thompson and David Dobbs withheld and/or lied about evidence on a variety of matters concerning Cook's guilt. They also lied about the credibility of state witnesses and attempted to interview Cook without the knowledge or consent of his lawyer. The court also noted that a state expert witness admitted that Clark pressured him to present false and misleading testimony. In 1991 Cook pled guilty to a lesser charge.[147]

In 1985 Rolando Cruz and Alejandro Hernandez were convicted in DuPage County, Illinois of kidnapping, rape and murder even though another man had confessed to these crimes.

In 1988 their convictions were overturned, but in 1990 Cruz was re-convicted and in 1991 Hernandez was reconvicted. In 1994 Cruz' conviction was overturned again and in 1995 Hernandez' conviction was overturned because DNA exonerated him. Cruz was finally acquitted at a third trial and the charges against Hernandez were dismissed. These convictions were overturned because prosecutor Thomas Knight had improperly used co-defendants statements at trial. In addition, prosecutor Robert Kilander improperly impeached a witness. In 1996 prosecutor's Knight, Kilander and King along with four Sheriff's detectives were criminally charged with conspiring to convict Cruz and Hernandez by fabricating evidence and withholding exculpatory evidence. All were acquitted in 1999.[148]

Paris Carriger was convicted of robbery and murder in Maricopa County in Arizona in 1978. In 1987 and again in 1991 the state's key witness confessed to the crime for which Carriger had been imprisoned. In 1997 the United States Court of Appeals for the Ninth Circuit granted Carriger and new trial because the prosecutor, Richard Strohm, failed to disclose information that could have undermined the key witness's credibility. Carriger was therefore imprisoned for 19 years although someone else committed the crime for which he was convicted.[149]

Henry Arthur Drake was convicted of murder and armed robbery and sentenced to death in Madison County, Georgia in 1976. In 1981 the state's key witness, the codefendant, admitted that he lied at Drake's trial and that he, not Drake, was responsible for the murder. Four years later the conviction was overturned. In 1985 United States Court of Appeals for the 11th District reversed Drake's death sentence because of prosecutor Brian Hoff's improper remarks during the sentencing phase of the trial.[150]

Michael Ray Graham and Albert Ronnie Burrell were convicted of first-degree murder and sentenced to death in separate trials in Union parish Louisiana in 1987. In 2000 the charges were dismissed and after 13 years in prison the two men were released. In granting a new trial for Graham in March 2000, a judge ruled that prosecutor Dan Grady had failed to disclose several pieces of exculpatory evidence. The judge also noted that Grady later provided an affidavit in which she admitted the case against Graham and Burrell was so weak it should not have been brought to the grand jury.[151]

Ricky Hammond was convicted in 1990 in Hartford, Connecticut of kidnapping and sexual assault. In 1992 his conviction was overturned and a new trial granted. At the new trial Hammond was acquitted. Despite pretrial biological tests that exonerated Hammond prosecutor John Malone claimed the evidence had been contaminated, a claim the appellate court deemed highly improbable. The court also ruled that some of Malone's comments during the closing argument were improper.[152]

Ronnie Marshall and Robert Spurlock were convicted of first-degree murder in Sumner County, Tennessee in 1990. In 1992 Marshall's conviction was overturned. In 1993 Spurlock's conviction was overturned. In 1995 Spurlock was re-tried and convicted again and Marshall bargained for a reduced sentence. In 1995 and 1996 the real killer confessed. Therefore in 1996 Spurlock and Marshall were released. The Tennessee Court of Criminal Appeals ruled that the prosecutors, Lawrence Ray Whitley and Jerry Kitchen failed to provide witness statements that pointed to other suspects, that they failed to correct the false testimony given by prosecution witnesses and used false evidence.

This case like so many others indicates that prosecutors will use the most illegal and egregious methods to gain convictions of innocent people. Yet prosecutors are never charged with illegal activity.[153]

These 11 cases are only a tiny portion of cases in which innocent people are convicted every day by fraudulent prosecutors allowed to perpetrate these crimes at the expense of innocent Americans. It is therefore imperative that the power of prosecutors be greatly curtailed and that police not be permitted to interrogate anyone unless a video recording of the interrogation is made available to the defense attorneys of the accused.

Not only prosecutors but also so-called forensic scientists have repeatedly been discovered to deliver false testimony or forensic fraud. Such examiner misconduct has led to numerous convictions of innocent people. Prosecutors and the police employ these forensic scientists who are therefore tempted to testify that there is scientific evidence is in accord with the wishes of those who pay them.

Some recent examples of forensic fraud include the Washington State Patrol Crime Lab. Since 1999 that crime lab has been the target of numerous scandals. Dr. John Brown, who worked in the lab for years was terminated for DNA fraud, and the lab manager, Kevin Fortney, resigned his post while under investigation for fraud relating to numerous cases. Since he left new revelations have been uncovered every week. In fact, the former lab director who functioned before Fortney, Barry Logan, and his subordinate, Annie Marie Gordon had committed numerous frauds in that laboratory.

The Scottsdale, Arizona Police Department crime lab has been accused by the defense in many cases of deliberately falsifying blood alcohol evidence.

One of the most extreme cases of fraud involving a crime lab concerns the Hinton Drug Lab in Jamaica Plain, Massachusetts. There Annie Dookhan, has been indicted on charges related to her many acts of fraud. As a result of her deceit hundreds of cases have been overturned and the crime lab became so bankrupt of scientific integrity and accountability at all levels of management that it had to be shut down. Likewise, Debra Madden, employed as a scientist by the San Francisco Police Department crime lab caused numerous cases to be dismissed because she hid evidence for four long years.

The commanding officer of the Crime Scene Service Section of the Massachusetts State Police, Detective Lieut. Kenneth F. Martin was stripped of his command and reassigned when it was discovered that he was moonlighting as a defense expert in local cases. The Canton, Stark County crime lab in Ohio hired a fraudulent scientist, Michael Short and also hired an unqualified police officer as lab director. In the West Virginia Beckley Police Department, Gabriela Brown, an evidence technician, stole drugs from the evidence locker under her charge. Her education consists of an online master's degree in forensic science from Marshall University .She was sentenced to four years' probation. Likewise, forensic chemist Sonja Faraka was indicted for stealing drugs and otherwise tampering with evidence at the Massachusetts State Drug Lab in Amherst.

Numerous local trials were compromised when Herman Brown, a criminalist at the California state crime lab in Ripon, skimmed from the drugs submitted by law enforcement, and altered weights and then misreported the true weights in logbooks and reports. He was sent to jail for 16 months.

Cynthia Burbach, the lab director at the Colorado Department of Public Health Forensic Laboratory tampered with evidence and lied about forensic tests in court. Her testimony was designed to support prosecution bias.[154]

The discovery of DNA (deoxyribonucleic acid) by the chemist Erwin Chagall had a considerable impact on American criminal justice after Chagall came to the United States as a consequence of the anti-Jewish persecutions during the Nazi era in Europe. DNA distinguishes all human beings from one another as no two people exhibit the same DNA. Therefore it became possible to apply DNA tests to persons accused of crimes with the consequence of discovering innocent people accused of crimes. Likewise, it also became possible to identify guilty people by the use of DNA.

The use of DNA identification has led to the discovery that hundreds of people have been imprisoned and even sent to death row although innocent. One reason for the conviction of innocent people are false confessions. Those unfamiliar with criminal justice proceedings are rarely willing to believe that innocent people would confess to a crime which they did not commit. Yet the fact is that about 16% of confessions are false. These false confessions are usually the result of coercion consisting at best of questioning the accused by relays of detectives for hours at a time and preventing the accused from sleeping. Driven to exhaustion and unable to defend oneself many accused will confess to the crime charged so as to gain relief from the torture endured. There are also police who will beat and assault the innocently accused and then lie about this in court. In fact, nothing is more certain than police telling lies during trials designed to support the prosecution's case. In addition interrogators usually pressure a suspect to accept a particular account of the crime story that squares with the interrogators preordained theory of how the crime occurred. The interrogator then uses leading questions, deliberately suggesting specific facts about the crime to the suspect, which are then parroted back in form of a confession.[155]

All of these efforts to send innocent people to prison were enhanced by the 1991 case *Arizona vs. Fulminante* in which the Supreme Court ruled that the admission of an involuntary confession is a harmless error. That decision encourages detectives to coerce confessions because jurors will therefore convict defendants on the basis of these unreliable confessions.[156]

Although the Constitution of the United States seeks to protect criminal defendants by invoking the privilege against self-incrimination, the right to the effective assistance of counsel and the right to a jury trial and the requirement that prosecutors prove defendant's guilt beyond a reasonable doubt and the ability to access appellate review have all failed again and again to protect the innocent. [157]

Those imprisoned innocent people spend an average of 13 years for other people's crimes and are incarcerated before being released, on the average, one year after it has been conclusively proved that the prisoner is innocent. These are nevertheless the lucky ones compared to those innumerable innocent people living behind bars with no real hope of ever proving their innocence. It is significant that the DNA exonerates are mostly convicted of raping a stranger. 68% were convicted of rape alone and an additional 21% convicted were convicted of rape-murders. This skewed statistic comes about because DNA evidence is most often available in rape cases. DNA is usually unavailable in property crimes which are just as likely to be adjudicated by means of coercion resulting in false confessions and by other illegal means designed to enhance the conviction record of prosecutors.[158]

Juvenile courts are even more prone than adult courts to find the innocent guilty. The reason for this is that the juvenile courts claim that they are not seeking to discover guilt or innocence but are rather interested in protecting children and are therefore seeking only the best interests of the child by examining his total life situation. The truth is, the juvenile judges send children to reform schools or other institutions. The outcome of such proceedings is that many a young child remains institutionalized until the age of 18 or later without any recourse to a Court of Appeals. In *Gault v. Arizona* the Supreme Court dealt with this problem and spelled out the rights of children under the Constitution. Nevertheless, few children who come before a juvenile court can afford a private lawyer and they are therefore defended by so-called guardians or court-appointed lawyers who do very little to prevent the injustices commonly visited upon children.[159]

Fraudulent testimony in a court of law is a common occurrence. Such testimony is usually provided by private investigators, technicians, and experts. Many a jury believes what these so-called scientists say because of the authority of scientists who are believed to be totally objective and interested in any motivation other than establishing the facts. The truth is otherwise as numerous experts have falsely testified in court in order to please those who pay them. An excellent example of this kind of fraudulent testimony is that of Salem Zain who testified as a forensic expert in more than 100 trials between 1972 and 2002. Zain had served as a West Virginia state trooper before starting work in the state police crime lab. Zain was eager to please prosecutors with testimony tailored to their demands. Zain needed only a trace of blood or semen or hair follicle to claim that they belong to the accused. Although serious questions were raised concerning Zain's honesty, prosecutors turned a blind eye. Fred Zain was such an excellent tool used to gain convictions that prosecutors were unwilling to admit Zain was a liar.[160]

Another example of scientific fraud was the manner in which Dr. Pamela Fish repeatedly gave wrong testimony in Chicago courts in order to please the district attorney. For example, in her lab she recorded that the semen of a man accused of rape revealed that he had blood type A. At the time of the trial, however, she changed this note to read blood type B because the defendant had blood type B. As a result of her testimony, John Willis was sentenced in 1991 to 100 years in prison. When another man confessed of having committed that rape the authorities discovered that Fish had given false testimony in at least nine other cases. Nevertheless, Fish continued for several years in her job as forensic scientist. She was never dismissed from her appointment although the state did not renew her contract in 2004 after innocent victims were given large financial settlements.

Another example concerns Texas pathologist Ralph Erdmann. Erdman was such a fraud that he claimed in an autopsy that he had measured the spleen of the deceased when it was later discovered that the deceased did not have a spleen. When a child drowned Erdman claimed that the child had died from a blow to the stomach. Therefore the father was indicted. When other pathologists conducted yet another autopsy they concluded that there was absolute evidence that the child had drowned as the father had contended all along. Finally, an investigation of Erdman's work revealed that he was guilty of producing numerous incorrect reports. He was convicted and sentenced to community work.[161]

For centuries law has relied upon simpleminded trust in its means and procedures. Even after the so-called Miranda decision sought to protect the right of suspects not to incriminate themselves when taken into custody nothing changed. Arresting officers viewed Miranda as empty verbiage and continued to coerce an arrested person. The evidence is that words mean little when the power of police and prosecutors descend upon innocent suspects.[162]

There can be little doubt that prosecutors, police and judges enjoy convicting, sentencing and jailing guilty as well as innocent people who come before them. The judges in particular play the role of the righteous while the police and prosecutors enjoy gaining access to the lives of other people's families.

Police Conduct and Misconduct

Police work is in itself a dilemma. There is hardly any citizen who does not want to be protected by the police or helped by the police in an emergency. Yet the same citizens usually resent the authority of the police not only because the American ethos includes the right of each individual to be free of government interference, but also because there is without doubt a good deal of police brutality provoked in part by unwarranted assaults on the police.

Police misconduct has been repeatedly documented. For example, the Rampart division of the Los Angeles Police Department falsified reports, stole drugs from suspects, framed people and abused unarmed suspects leading to about 200 lawsuits filed against the city and more than 100 tainted criminal convictions have been overturned.[163]

Even as police misconduct is widely publicized and resented, the public is concerned with under policing and police abuse at the same time. Everyone wants excellent law enforcement in their neighborhoods and increased efforts to control crime. At the same time the black community and many Hispanics believe that police corruption and use of excessive force occurs all the time in their city. Minorities testify everywhere that they have personally experienced some kind of police abuse. This means that 43% of Blacks and 26% of Hispanics but only 3% of whites report that they have been stopped by the police solely because of their race or ethnicity. Since almost all contacts between police and citizens are unsupervised and unrecorded it is very difficult to document abuse. Police say that they are dealing mostly with problem citizens and not the general population. They therefore develop an "us versus them" mentality towards everyone. The consequence is that the police subculture insulates the police fraternity and enforces a code of silence that shields cops from scrutiny. Sociologists have shown that police officers usually trust only fellow officers and distrust members of the public. They therefore deal aggressively with anyone who questions their authority. [164]

The biggest problem facing American police is distrust among Afro-American citizens. Research has shown that this could be in part alleviated by appointing more black officers to serve in black neighborhoods. Black officers are evidently more likely than white officers to engage in supportive activities in black neighborhoods, including offering information, providing assistance, making referrals to other agencies, behaving respectfully, and comforting residents.[165]

In the past American police were largely unaccountable for their actions. This was and is in part true because police usually patrol alone or with a partner who will protect them from criticism. Police are often confronted with situations which require immediate action and are then misunderstood on later review. Citizens are often suspicious of internal reviews of officers who have been targeted by complaints. In order to alleviate the situation many departments now mount video cameras on the dashboards of police cars. This records the interaction between police and citizens. A study in Kansas City revealed that 2% of officers were the targets of 50% of all complaints. This indicates that there are a few police who are responsible for much of the bad reputation many police have in the minority communities. To alleviate this a good number of police now have early warning systems which restrain police misconduct. These early warning systems promote prompt intervention with problem officers.[166]

In the past there have been a number of riots in the streets of major American cities caused by police behavior. This is a conclusion reached by the President's Commission on Civil Disorders.[167]

Hostility Goes Both Ways

That conclusion however needs to be considered in the light of black hostility toward the police generally. Such hostility is so common and so intense that the mere presence of a white policeman performing routine duties is often sufficient to ignite explosive violence. For example, on September 14, 2016, Marc Payne, and Afro-American drove his car into three police officers standing on the street in Phoenix Arizona. The attack was sudden and unprovoked. The suspect had attempted to kill police officers at an earlier occasion. [168]

In Baton Rouge, Louisiana three law enforcement officers were killed in an ambush shooting on July 17, 2016. In addition three more officers were wounded.

Officer Matthew Gerald, 41, had only just begun his career with the Baton Rouge Police Department when he was killed. He graduated from the police Academy in March, 2016 and had only just been released to work on his own on July 5. He leaves behind a wife and daughters. Deputy Brad Gerarfola, 45, had worked with the East Baton Rouge Parish Sheriff's office for 24 years. He was assigned to the civil processing foreclosures division. He leaves behind a wife and four children. Officer Montrell Jackson, 32, worked for the Baton Rouge Police Department for 10 years. He leaves behind a wife and a four-month-old child. [169]

According to the Federal Bureau of Investigation, 41 law enforcement officers were feloniously killed in the line of duty in 2015. This is a decrease of almost 20% compared with 51 officers killed in 2014. According to *The National Law Enforcement Officers* Memorial Fund 64 police officers were murdered in 2016.While the vast majority of officers killed were murdered with a firearm three victim officers were killed with vehicles used as weapons. In 2013, 27 policemen were deliberately murdered. The average age of the officers is 39. Two of the 27 victims were black and two were female. Six of these offices were killed while making arrests and five were ambushed.[170]

The number of citizens killed by the police cannot be accurately established. Police unions say that shooting by officers are rare and more rarely unjustified. The Afro-American community claims that racial motives lead police shootings as the police deliberately execute black and brown men. There are also citizens who not only despise the police but who hate the government and believe that they are defending the American people against governmental oppression and therefore murder police and, if possible, other government officials. The police are of course much more available and much more visible than anyone else in government and therefore become the most likely targets for such fanatics.

Even as Blacks assault and kill police,, the reverse is also true. Furthermore, more whites are killed by police each year than Blacks. In 2015, 1502 people have been shot and killed by an on duty police officers since January 1of that year. Of these 732 were white and 381 were black and 382 were of another or unknown race. Since there are 160 million more white people in America than there are black people, white people make up roughly 62% of the United States population but only about 49% of those were killed by police. African-Americans account for 24% of those fatally shot and killed by the police despite being just 13% of the United States population. In 2015, 50 unarmed white people and 50 unarmed black people were killed by police. Because the white population is five times larger than the black population it is evident that black Americans were five times as likely as unarmed white Americans to be shot and killed by a police officer. Civil rights activists claim that the reason for this discrepancy is to be attributed entirely to racism and to the intent of the police to murder Blacks indiscriminately. The police counter this argument by citing FBI statistics that show that Blacks commit six times more violence than whites. Moreover, the entire dispute concerning the killing of so many black men every year avoids rigorously a discussion of the huge black on black murder rate in this country. According to FBI numbers from 2014 and 2015 and part of 2016 about 90% of black homicide victims were killed by other black people. Other forms of violence are also disproportionately high in the black population. This means that 62% of robberies, 57% of murders and 45% of assaults in this country's 75 biggest counties can be attributed to Blacks even though the black population is only 13% of all Americans. Recently, Heather McDonald wrote a column in the Wall Street Journal headline "The Myths of Black Lives Matter". McDonald claimed that the majority of victims of police shootings were armed or otherwise threatening the officer with potentially lethal force. McDonald further argues that Blacks commit 75% of all shootings, 70% of all robberies and 66% of all violent crime in New York City where they consist of 23% of the population. She further claims that only 4% of black deaths were caused by police officers while 12% white and Hispanic homicides were caused by police officers. McDonald then argues that "white and Hispanic lives matter" will therefore be more appropriate. McDonald also challenges the phrase "unarmed" since at least five black victims have tried to grab the officers' guns or had been beating the cop with his own equipment. Some were shot from an accidental discharge triggered by their own assault on the officer. Further several so-called "unarmed" black men were struck by stray bullets aimed at someone else.

McDonald recites an occurrence in Virginia Beach, Virginia where officers approached a car parked at a convenience store that had a homicide suspect in the passenger seat. The suspect opened fire, sending a bullet through an officer's shirt. The police returned fire, killing their assailant as well as a woman in the driver's seat. That woman entered the database without qualifications as an unarmed black victim of police fire. In 2015, according to McDonald, three officers were killed with their own guns which the suspects had wrestled from them. Yet, the killers were said to be "unarmed."

Finally, McDonald holds that Blacks are more likely to kill police then be killed by police. This contention comes by inspecting FBI data which found that 40% of police killers are black.[171]

The dispute concerning black and police violence can continue forever unless Americans of all races and all occupations in both genders agree that all lives matter. Such an agreement would benefit everyone. If there is anything we all have in common it is that we all want to live, that no one wants to be murdered. Such an agreement should be easily attainable provided we respect one another and support the right of every human being to live a life free of fear of his fellow man.

Comparison of the United States Constitution and its application in the 21st century reveals that the many guarantees securing individual rights and protecting citizens from the power of government have been greatly eroded. This is true in part because many employees of the criminal justice system are willing to ignore the oath they took on attaining office. Further, this erosion of individual rights is facilitated by popular beliefs concerning confessions made by innocent people.

The assumption by jurors that the police tell the truth in court, the overwhelming power of prosecutors and the lack of means, despite DNA, allowing innocent people to get out of jail or avoid the death penalty.

Additionally, we have not been able to solve the black versus police attitudes so that both sides of the endless dispute lose. Despite all the problems of the criminal justice system as here portrayed we must nevertheless grant that, paraphrasing Winston Churchill's famous comment on democracy: "[the American criminal justice system] is the worst system in the world except for all the others".

Chapter 6. Assault on Free Speech in Higher Education in America

The most fundamental means of securing democracy is free speech. This is the reason why the First Amendment to the Constitution includes this important right.

Traditionally, American colleges and universities were devoted to the proposition that all opinions on all subjects could be peacefully discussed. This meant that the right to speak one's mind was encouraged on the campuses of American institutions of higher education with a view of making the future leaders of America supporters and defenders of democracy.

The very word education may be derived from the Latin word "educere," meaning to lead, as well as "educare," meaning to train. Therefore, American college graduates for years were trained to lead in all American institutions with a view of preserving such American values as free expression, free publication, and the opportunity to speak openly and without fear on any topic at any time. It is therefore most painful to view the deterioration of our universities and colleges into one sided propaganda machines prohibiting any and all opinions not to the liking of that segment of the college population who are labeled "liberal" by the media, when in fact the word liberal once meant the support for freedom. Evidently George Orwell accurately predicted the abuse of language in the interest of conformity.[172]

Shutting Down the Debate

For a number of years, beginning shortly before the turn of this century, numerous American colleges and universities have prevented commencement speakers and others from appearing on American colleges on the grounds that their opinions or their beliefs were not to be tolerated. Examples of this kind are so numerous that they cannot all be listed here. Suffice it to say there is an increased effort by students and faculty to disinvite speakers with whom they disagree. During the 2015–2016 school year, numerous speakers were either canceled or interrupted for their beliefs or associations. For example, Janet Mock, a TV host and transgender rights activist, withdrew from speaking at Brown University after the students protested, not because of the content of Mock's speech but because a Jewish student organization cosponsored her lecture. Likewise, at the California State University at Los Angeles, Ben Shapiro, an author of a number of conservative books, was invited to speak, only to find the university had revoked his invitation on the grounds of Shapiro's unpopular beliefs. Shapiro called those who prevented him from speaking "jackbooted thugs." At the University of Chicago, Anita Alvarez, the Cook County Illinois state attorney, was interrupted during her speech and did not continue because of loud screaming protesters. The protesters claimed that she was responsible for violence against black and brown people in Chicago. The truth is that the huge murder rate in Chicago is a reflection of the fact that members of the black population kill each other.[173]

Also at the University of Chicago, Bassem Eid, a Palestinian Arab, was interrupted during his speech and shut down because he made comments that were considered supportive of Judaism. At the University of Pennsylvania, John Brennan, director of the CIA, was shouted down by protesters for his involvement in drone strikes in the Middle East. At San Francisco State University, a group of anti-Jewish protesters forced the mayor of the city of Jerusalem, Nir Barkat, to end his speech early. John Derbyshire was to speak at Williams College when the president, Adam Falk, canceled the speech on the grounds that some considered Derbyshire's writings to be racist. Also at Williams College, Suzanne Venker, a journalist and social critic, had been invited to speak until the college revoked her invitation on the grounds that she wrote an op-ed for Fox news titled, "Why men won't marry you."[174]

The list of additional dis-invitations of potential college speakers as well as violent interruptions of speakers whose views were not in conformity with the opinions of students and professors is far longer than can be presented here. It includes such renowned universities as Harvard and Yale and Columbia, whose reputation as objective scholarly institutions have been severely compromised by the suppression of free speech and their violent attacks on anyone with whom they disagree.

This perversion of American values on the campuses of our colleges and universities has come about mainly because numerous professors have for years abused their power and influence on college students by using the college classroom as a platform for the dissemination of their political opinions. All this is to the detriment of young students, who are thereby prevented from learning subject matter and understanding the difference between propaganda and objective fact.

Perhaps one of the most dramatic declines of any American university pertains to Columbia University in the city of New York. There is little doubt that at one time Columbia University was regarded as a major scholarly institution and that for good reason.

Since the early years of the 21st century, Columbia has been beset by a succession of scandals. For example, in 2003, an assistant professor, Nicholas De Genova, told students at an antiwar teach-in on the Columbia campus that "US patriotism is inseparable from imperial warfare and white supremacy," and that the only true heroes are those who find ways that help defeat the United States military." In 2004, a group called the David Project produced a documentary titled "Columbia Unbecoming." This documentary featured several students and former students and Columbia's Department of Middle East and Asian Languages and Cultures recounting incidents of political sermonizing, personal harassment and general intolerance they experienced at the hands of Columbia faculty. According to the students, professors used their courses to vent their political venom against Jews, Israel, and Zionism. They treated Israeli Arab relations as a closed subject rather than as an academic question, in the process fostering a culture of academic intimidation. Then, in October 2006, the founder of an anti-illegal immigration group, the Minutemen project, was driven off the stage of the school's Roone auditorium and prevented from speaking by a mob of student demonstrators. The students first shouted down the speaker, Jim Gilchrist, then slandered him as a racist, and finally mobbed the stage, shutting down the event. Students articulated their anti-intellectual, ant-democratic attitude by shouting down anyone who thought immigrants to the United States should be admitted through a legal process and screamed "they have no right to be able to speak."

These are not isolated incidents. Instead these political agendas are at the very core of the liberal arts curriculum at Columbia University. Scholarly objectivity has long been disregarded at Columbia. Instead, "liberal" doctrines are taught religiously and one sided reading lists are distributed. One sided lectures are presented by professors who are nothing more than political activists rather than academics. Entire departments like anthropology and African-American studies are nothing more than Marxist indoctrination courses, so that propaganda is taking the place of education.

In a good number of courses taught at Columbia, grades depend on the students' political activities and the extent to which a student embraces approved political views.[175]

Columbia University also operates a teachers' college, which includes their Peace Education Center. The purpose of this Peace Education Center is to show students how to look upon teaching as a way of promoting political ideals related in the main to Marxist opinions. The Center is evidently not interested in turning out good teachers but rather political activists. One of the principal messages of courses taught in the Peace Education Center is the view that the United States is an oppressor and that the numerous dictatorships around the world are fully justified. Finally, Columbia University continues the age-old practice of anti-Jewish propaganda, derived directly from centuries of arguments favoring religious persecution of the Jewish people. Today these centuries old arguments are slightly altered by using the word Israel instead of the word Jew, although the intentions have the same effect as they have had for 1900 years.

The journalism courses at Columbia University were at one time considered the most objective and reasonable form of preparation for a career in that profession. Yet today, journalism at Columbia has become the tool of political advocacy on the part of so-called liberals.

At the University of Delaware, an indoctrination program was delivered to freshmen who were confronted by resident assistants in the dormitories. These resident assistants asked students to answer such questions as: "when did you discover your sexual identity?" and were further forced to pledge allegiance to university approved views on race, sexuality, and the environment. Evidently, the University of Delaware turned residence halls into a reeducation camps as found in communist dictatorships. Students were forced to "learn," which was defined as having specific attitudes and behavioral changes. The University forced an unarguable dogma on students. One of these documents was the belief that all whites are racists regardless of class, gender, culture, or sexuality. Students were asked whether they approved of such things as affirmative action or homosexual marriage. No discussion of differences of opinion was allowed. Students were told they are racists and that students should focus on their oppressor or victim status.

Officially this entire program was canceled after the president of the University received numerous complaints concerning this indoctrination. Nevertheless, so-called liberal ideology continued to be preached at the University of Delaware, to the detriment of scholarly objectivity normally expected at any institution of higher learning.[176]

At the University of Pittsburgh, freshman introductory writing courses have become a form of imposed ideology, consisting of Marxism, hardline feminism, post-modernism, colonial studies, identity politics, and other isms. Students read such authors as Edward Said, a known anti-Jewish religious bigot, and Stanley Fish, a preacher for post-modernism, which rejects so-called "high" culture and instead celebrates popular culture and group experience as more important than individual expression. This reading list and the lecturers that accompany it can well be designated as belonging to the far left, who interpret everything to the effect that one must hate America.[177]

On November 12, 2002, a Republican student, Steve Hinkle, attempted to post a flier in a California Polytechnic State University Multicultural Center announcing a speech by black conservative C. Mason Weaver, author of: *It's Okay To Leave the Plantation: The New Underground Railroad*. In this book, Weaver argues that dependence on government programs puts many African Americans in a situation similar to slavery.

When Hinkle attempted to post the flier on the public bulletin board located in the student lounge area, he was approached by several African-American students who claimed to be holding a Bible study meeting nearby. Though the flyer listed only Weaver's name, the title of his book, and the time and place of the lecture, the students told Hinkle the announcement was offensive. They told Hinkle not to post the flier and said they would call the police if he didn't leave.

After briefly trying to discuss the students' comments with them, Hinkle left the lounge without posting the flier. Nevertheless, one of the students called the campus police to complain. The police arrived immediately and reported that they had been dispatched to the Multicultural Center to investigate a suspicious white male passing out literature of an offensive racial nature.

Thereupon Hinkle was summoned to meet with school officials. They told him that the lecture announcement was offensive to the African American students in the lounge. One administrator told him that being white and having blonde hair and blue eyes was offensive. Then on January 29, 2003, Hinkle was formally charged with "disruption" of a campus event in violation of the California Code of Regulations. As a result of the charges, Hinkle was subjected to a seven hour judicial hearing on February 19. Several weeks later, Hinkle received a letter from vice president David Conn which told him that his flier had disrupted a Bible study meeting and ordered him to write a formal letter of apology to the complaining students, to be approved by the Office of Judicial Affairs. Hinkle was warned that if he did not accept this punishment he would face much stiffer penalties, up to expulsion. Officials of the University made it clear that the problem was not any physical interruption of the Bible meeting, but the offensive nature of the lecture announcement. This meant that Hinkle was punished for the content of his expression, although this is constitutionally protected by the First Amendment. Hinkle refused to apologize on the grounds of his First Amendment rights. When Hinkle asked the Foundation for Individual Rights in Education to help him, the foundation wrote a letter to Cal Poly president Warren Baker reminding him of Hinkle's First Amendment rights. Despite this letter, Baker left Hinkle's conviction in his permanent school record, so that the threat of future punishment hung over his head.

Therefore, the Foundation for Individual Rights in Education referred this issue to Carol Sobel, a lawyer who filed a lawsuit on Hinkle's behalf in federal district court in Los Angeles. The court ordered the University to expunge the allegations and conviction from Hinkle's school records.[178]

Witch Trials

Professors as well as students have become the victims of antidemocratic procedures and opinions at American universities. The literal persecution of Professor Hans-Hermann Hoppe at the University of Nevada is only one example of the manner in which academic freedom has been subverted at so many of America's institutions of higher learning.

Prof. Hoppe is an Austrian born economist with an international reputation as a scholar. Nevertheless he became the victim of a complaint which had absolutely no merit other than to give the complainant a forum.

In March 2004, during a 75-minute lecture in a class on Money and Banking, Dr. Hoppe explained that homosexual couples are more present-oriented than heterosexual couples because homosexuals have no children — unless they adopt them. The professor therefore concluded that homosexuals are less likely to save money than heterosexuals, who intend to leave their savings to their children.

This perfectly reasonable and rational discussion led a homosexual student to complain to the university's affirmative action official. The complaint argued that the homosexual student was made to feel bad by that lecture. The official, himself a homosexual, called the professor at home and told him that he would shut down his class if he continued to make such remarks.

Subsequently the official met the professor in his office and lectured the professor on how he was to teach his class. Later, the student filed a formal complaint arguing that his feelings had not been taken seriously and that he felt hurt, and that he was learning in a hostile environment. Thereafter the university official acted as a prosecutor. He ordered the professor to appear before an administrative committee to investigate whether the professor's lectures were correct and provable. This was of course a direct interference in the right to speak freely. It constituted a serious violation of the First Amendment.

When the professor asked that the meeting be taped, this was denied. His request to hear witnesses was also denied. Then the officials interviewed a student whose testimony contradicted what they wanted to hear. They therefore suppressed the opinions of that student. In fact, whatever the professor or anyone else said in favor of his rights was brushed aside and regarded as irrelevant.

The college officials then reviewed the professor's writings and used them to find the professor guilty as charged. The officials recommended to the Dean that the professor be sent a letter of reprimand and that he forfeit a week's pay. In addition, Dr. Hoppe was ordered to appear for yet a second trial at which a committee composed of the dean of natural sciences, the associate dean of the hotel college, a biology professor, and the president of the student government participated. This committee also brought with them a lawyer, forcing Prof. Hoppe to pay for the lawyer as well. Dr. Hoppe's lawyer sought to have the meeting taped or have a court reporter present, but both requests were denied. At the meeting the student once more talked about his hurt feelings. At that meeting also, several student letters written on behalf of the professor were not admitted as evidence.

Thereafter the official in charge of affirmative-action ranted a tirade against Dr. Hoppe which lasted for over one half hour, so that even the University lawyer told him to "shut up."

In January 2005 the university's code officer called the professor's lawyer and told him that the committee had found that the professor had created a hostile environment and that therefore the committee would recommend to the Provost a letter of reprimand and forfeiture of his next merit increase.

Dr. Hoppe refused to subject himself to these demands and asked the American Civil Liberties Union to defend him. The ACLU requested an immediate end to that charade or the University would be taken to court. When local news stories appeared and angry calls began to pour into the University, the Provost sent the professor a letter of "non-disciplinary instruction." Thereafter, a flood of protests assailed the university, which had a public relations disaster on its hands. This led the Chancellor of the entire Nevada system to order the president of the Las Vegas campus to withdraw all charges against Dr. Hoppe. Prof. Hoppe has since then retired from the University of Nevada and now lives in Istanbul, Turkey.[179]

Hans Hoppe is an internationally famous economist who had the alternative of finding employment in Istanbul. That is certainly not true of the vast majority of professors, who are of course intimidated by the events surrounding Hoppe. Since academic appointments are difficult to obtain in any event, it is obvious that free speech has become the victim of policies which allow a student who claims to feel insulted to ruin a professor's career. Therefore, threats to freedom of speech in the classroom are a direct assault on American democracy. The fact is that it is impossible for anyone to speak in public when any phrase or any sentence, and even a very rational explanation of human behavior, can be twisted into some sort of insult to somebody. This results in all kinds of harassment of professors on the part of students who are thereby taught that they have the power to make the lives of professors miserable.

Beyond Affirmative Action

This dictum is well illustrated by the assault on Teresa Buchanan, who was fired from her teaching position at Louisiana State University in June 2015 for an alleged, occasional use of profanity and discussing issues related to sexuality in the classroom. In December 2013, Buchanan was informed that a student had made allegations against her for inappropriate teaching conduct that fostered a hostile classroom. The phrase "hostile classroom environment" has become a club with which students are encouraged to assault professors and also seeks to abridge speech that is protected by law. As a result of these allegations, the LSU dean of human sciences and education, Damon Andrew, suspended Buchanan from teaching until a faculty committee and the Board of Supervisors separately tried her case. According to Buchanan, no one gave her further details about these allegations until her initial trial 18 months later with the faculty committee. This prevented her from attempting to clarify possible misinterpretations with the accusing student. Consequently, hearsay was taken out of context. Buchanan did not deny that she talked to some of her female students about the consequences of sexual relations with their boyfriends. She also admitted to occasionally using a few "four letter" words. The faculty committee, having heard all sides of this dispute, recommended that the dean allow her to keep her job, although she was asked not to use profanity in the classroom in the future. Despite the faculty recommendation, however, Buchanan was fired on June 19, 2015 by the dean and the LSU board of supervisors. No reasonable person could possibly consider Buchanan's remarks as sexual harassment. Nevertheless, Dean Alexander claimed that the accusations proved that she had infringed upon a student's rights under the federal Americans with Disabilities Act. This allegation had been totally rejected by the faculty committee that had met earlier. Teresa Buchanan was hired in 1995 and since then had received nothing but positive performance reviews. She had founded a nationally recognized and highly selective teacher training program called the PK 3 Teacher Education Program.

It soon became evident that the allegations had stemmed from a jealous and vengeful student who wasn't admitted to the PK 3 teacher education program.

Whatever the reason for Buchanan's termination, it was obvious that the university had violated her rights to freedom of speech in the classroom and due process throughout her trial. Consequently, the Louisiana Chapter of the American Association of University Professors has started a fund for Buchanan's legal defense counsel, as she cannot afford the counsel on her own.[180]

The actions of administrators at California Polytechnic State University, the University of Nevada, and Louisiana State University are clearly attacks on the First Amendment rights as anchored in the United States Constitution. The First Amendment protects a large number of distasteful, defamatory, profane and anti-American forms of hateful speech. Several cases have been decided by the American courts in favor of some of the most outrageous forms of speech. For example, the court protected a factually false statement regarding military service.[181] In another case the court protected a man wearing a jacket bearing the legend "fuck the draft".[182] Further, the courts held that even hateful speech is protected. Therefore an anti-gay, anti-American protest near a soldier's funeral was supported by the court, despite its evidently cruel intentions.[183]

This kind of legal protection has been justified on the grounds that the First Amendment prevents the government from prescribing orthodoxy in politics, nationalism, religion, or other matters of opinion. It is therefore evident that public colleges and universities are wrong in attempting to regulate hate speech while seeking to force students and faculty to limit their speech to only approved expression. The foregoing examples show that public higher education's effort to quash hate speech through regulation and inculcation is a direct assault on American democracy.

In the beginning of the 1980s and the early 1990s, most colleges and universities adopted speech codes seeking to regulate campus speech. These codes led to litigation in which such policies were rejected by judicial scrutiny.

In 1989, the University of Michigan adopted a "policy on discrimination and discriminatory harassment" that forbade and punished verbal or physical behavior stigmatizing or victimizing individuals on the basis of race, sex, religion, sexual orientation, or veteran status. Students violating this policy are subject to formal or informal proceedings that could result in sanctions ranging from a reprimand to suspension or expulsion. Thereafter a student filed suit on the grounds that he would be charged under this policy for leading a classroom discussion on controversial theories on biologically-based differences between sexes and races. This lawsuit led a federal district court to permanently enjoin parts of the policy that restricted speech. The court ruled that Michigan's policy was applied to protected speech. The court cited three examples of the University regulating protected speech.[184] The point here is that college administrators are hardly willing to observe the First Amendment when it comes to views that administrators find offensive.

This is well illustrated by the assault on Professor John McAdams, a member of the political science department at Marquette University in Milwaukee, Wisconsin. Marquette University is a Catholic Jesuit institution.

McAdams was targeted by the administration because he publicly criticized a teaching assistant for not allowing discussion of gay marriage in an ethics class. A student had objected to the teaching assistant's handling of the class discussion. The student meant to express arguments against gay marriage. However, the teaching assistant told the student that "some opinions are not appropriate, such as racist opinions, sexist opinions."

The student then argued that it was his right as an American citizen to make arguments against gay marriage. To which the teaching assistant, Cheryl Abbate, replied: "You don't have a right in this class to make such an argument." When Professor McAdams learned of the teaching assistant's suppression of free speech, he publicly objected to Abbate's decision not allowing the gay marriage discussion. McAdams' objections led the University administration to review the concern raised by a student and by a graduate student teaching assistant.

While the review continued, an administrator at the University, Brian Dorrington, announced that McAdams had been relieved of his teaching and other faculty duties. He was also banned from setting foot on campus, even as Marquette University had begun the process of firing McAdams. The president of the University, Michael R. Lovell, sent a campus-wide letter in which he claimed that the guiding values of the University had been violated by Mc Adams' opinions and that he therefore had violated Jesuit tradition and Catholic social teachings. In fact, the Catholic Church relies upon the Jewish Bible, also known as the Old Testament, in rejecting homosexual behavior. In Genesis 19 the Bible tells the story of Sodom and Gomorrah, implying peripherally that homosexuality must not be allowed. In addition, Ezekiel 1 6:50 holds that Sodom and Gomorrah were destroyed because of homosexual behavior. Then in Leviticus 18:22 and 20:13 homosexuality is described as an abomination, a view enhanced by Romans 1:26-28,32 which forcefully rejects homosexual behavior.[185] It is indeed surprising that the president of Marquette University would argue that objections to homosexuality violated Jesuit Catholic social teachings. Instead it is evident that the administration of Marquette University is not acquainted with the dogmas of its own church.

Lovell further argued that the University would not tolerate personal attacks or harassment. Subsequently John McAdams received an email from the dean, Richard Holz, informing him that until further notice he was relieved of all duties and activities that would involve interactions with Marquette students, faculty, and staff.[186]

In May 2016, John McAdams and the Wisconsin Institute for Law and Liberty filed suit in Milwaukee County Circuit Court against Marquette University. The lawsuit seeks McAdams' reinstatement as professor, and unspecified damages. The suit alleges the University illegally suspended McAdams in 2014 and officials made the decision to terminate his tenure and fire him from Marquette. His lawyer, Rick Esenberg, General Counsel of the Wisconsin Institute for Law and Liberty, earned his law degree from Marquette and is now using it to sue the university on McAdams' behalf.[187]

At Brown University, located in Providence, Rhode Island, the main campus newspaper, *The Brown Daily Herald*, has engaged in censorship in direct opposition to the First Amendment's guarantee of freedom of speech and of the press. Evidently a columnist using a pen name published an essay entitled "The White Privilege of Cows," followed by a second essay entitled "Columbian Exchange Day." Because some Native Americans and others refuse to honor Columbus Day on the grounds that Columbus persecuted Native Americans, some students at Brown participated in an anti-Columbus Day demonstration.

The anonymous columnist wrote in effect that Native Americans should celebrate Columbus Day because Old World culture and technology improved life in the New World, even if Christopher Columbus himself should not be honored.

Because the columnist, who called herself Maier, advocated that Columbus Day be recognized, the editors of *The Herald* retroactively excised these columns from the internet and censored the author. When students restrict campus freedom of speech, it is indeed alarming, particularly when this occurs at a university founded in colonial days which has prided itself on promoting diverse student voices. Yet a survey of student opinion revealed that students were generally far more opposed to the publication of these columns than the censorship ensuing thereafter.

Brown University is, of course, not the only institute of higher education where students seek to silence dissenting voices. In fact, at Wesleyan University in Connecticut, some students wanted the school newspaper, *The Argus*, to lose its funding because it ran an op-ed that critically questions the Black Lives Matter movement.[188]

Harvard University, at one time a bastion of free speech, has also become a proponent of censorship. There the faculty of arts and sciences has struck economics courses taught by Indian scholar Subramanian Swamy without giving him an opportunity to defend himself. Evidently fair procedure has been absent from Harvard for 25 years.

Professor Swamy reacted to a terrorist attack at Mumbai in 2010 by writing in an op-ed that Islamic terrorism should be opposed by means of six methods. He recommended the settlement of Indian soldiers in Kashmir, the removal of mosques located at Hindu holy sites, the annexation of part of Bangladesh in compensation for illegal immigration into India, and the renaming of India as Hindustan as well as the prevention of non-Hindus from voting.

Swamy's expression of these opinions led a number of Harvard students to circulate a petition calling for his removal. This prompted the faculty of Arts and Sciences to take a vote stripping Swamy's courses from the curriculum, which effectively fired Dr. Swamy. The faculty attempted to excuse this assault on freedom of speech by pretending that freedom of expression was fully supported by the faculty, except that Swamy's opinions "cross the line." Here we find the same faculty which claims to support freedom of expression removing a faculty member precisely because he expressed an unpopular and controversial idea.

Censorship at Harvard became an issue in 2002 when a first-year law student used the abbreviation "nig" in a course outline discussing Supreme Court opinions that invalidated racially restrictive covenants on real estate deeds. This led Professor Charles Nesson to suggest defending the student in a mock trial. Nesson was therefore forced to give up teaching for the rest of the semester.

When a Harvard business school student published a cartoon that called administrators "incompetent morons," he was forced to resign as newspaper editor. Also in 2002, the English department at Harvard canceled a lecture and poetry reading by a Northern Irish poet on grounds of his political opinions. In 2015, the Dean of Freshmen, Thomas Dingman, pressured members of the freshmen class of 2015 to sign an oath pledging themselves to inclusiveness and civility. Such phrases, of course, are hard to define and useful in suppressing freedom of speech. The most widely publicized issue regarding freedom of speech was the manner in which Harvard president Lawrence Summers was driven out of office in 2005 because he discussed the lack of women in prominent scientific positions. Evidently, academic freedom has been abandoned at Harvard. Objection to academic freedom at Harvard was once more emphasized when a third-year student, Grace Stephanie, sent a private email to other students asking to see more research on the link between race and intelligence. When Law Dean Martha Minnow discovered that Grace was not convinced that there was no such link, she publicly admonished the student for daring to consider the question of race and intelligence. Minnow falsely claimed that the student viewed black people as genetically inferior to white people. The student then publicly apologized for holding the wrong opinion. The Dean has expressed satisfaction that the student no longer felt free to speak on controversial and unpopular topics.[189]

In their anxiety to prevent hate speech, college administrators are overlooking that the ideal of a university is that it is "the marketplace of ideas." It had traditionally been the role of the university to support open dialogue, including all ideas and all opinions. This raises the issue of whether hate speech is protected. This reminds us of the 14th amendment, which requires the equal protection of the laws. That amendment has been interpreted to mean that even remote criticism or failure to agree with current public opinion must be enforced on the grounds of the equal protection clause. Yet it seems that hate speech is as repugnant to the one amendment as to the other, so that the current effort to suppress all dissent on the campuses of American universities cannot be supported by citing the 14th amendment passed in 1868 after the Civil War.[190]

There was a time when it was important and most desirable that deliberate hate speech seeking to harm and threaten racial, religious, and sexual minorities had to be eradicated from American campuses. That has now been achieved by speech codes enforced universally in almost all American campuses. Now, however, the effort to remedy past wrongs has gone so far that it violates the right to free speech beyond all reason. It makes American colleges and universities complicit in promoting the parroting of popular opinion in a manner usually found only in the most obnoxious dictatorships. It is therefore imperative that colleges and universities balance the need for the suppression of hate speech while still allowing differences of opinion concerning any and all subjects. Neither the First Amendment nor the 14th Amendment should prevail. Equality cannot trump free speech, although proponents of regulating hate speech invoke the 14th amendment in pursuit of quality in education. Yet the tension between the first and 14th amendment disappears when free-speech for all is practiced. Evidently free speech cannot exist if aggressive hecklers are allowed to prevent speeches they don't want to hear. This is called "the heckler's veto." This court has ruled that hostile audiences are prevented from interfering with the first amendment rights of an unpopular speaker.[191]

American education is not confined to colleges and universities. On the contrary, the vast majority of Americans attend secondary schools whose students are old enough to express opinions and conduct themselves in a manner not always pleasing to adults. Consequently, the Supreme Court has repeatedly ruled on cases dealing with events occurring in high schools.

In 1985, a teacher accused a student of smoking in the bathroom. When she denied the allegations, the principal searched her purse and found cigarettes and marijuana paraphernalia. The family court declared the student a delinquent. The Supreme Court ruled that her rights were not violated, since students have reduced expectations of privacy in school.[192] In 1988 the court ruled that administrators may edit the content of school newspapers, when the principle of Hazelwood East High School edited two articles in the school paper, The Spectrum, that he deemed inappropriate. The student authors argued that this violated the First Amendment right to freedom of speech. The Supreme Court disagreed, stating that administrators can edit materials that reflect school values.[193] In 1975 the court ruled that students are entitled to certain process rights. Nine students at an Ohio public school received 10 days' suspensions for disruptive behavior without due process protections. The court ruled for the students, saying that once the state provides an education for all of its citizens, it cannot deprive them of it without employing due process protections.[194] In 1962 the Supreme Court held that school initiated prayer in the public school system violates the First Amendment. In the New York school system, each day began with a nondenominational prayer acknowledging dependence upon God. This was challenged in court as an unconstitutional state establishment of religion in violation of the First Amendment.[195] In 1987 the Supreme Court ruled that students do not have a First Amendment right to make obscene speeches in school. Matthew Fraser, a student at Bethel high school was suspended for three days for delivering an obscene and provocative speech to the student body.[196]

In earlier years the court had made several other decisions pertaining to secondary schools and primary schools. No doubt the most important and best known of these was *Brown v. Board of Education*, to the effect that separate schools are not equal.[197] This decision sought to eliminate racially segregated education in the United States.

Chapter 7. Greed, Fraud, and Crime

It can easily be shown that greed is the principal motivator of white-collar criminals. The phrase white-collar crime was coined by Edwin Sutherland at his inaugural address as president of the American Sociological Association in 1939.[198]

The white-collar crime most commonly associated with elected and appointed politicians is theft of money belonging to the taxpayer. Usually, this kind of theft is known by such labels as political corruption or malfeasance in office. Whatever its name, using political power for private gain corrodes democracy because it negates voting and the voicing of opinions by the taxpayer.[199]

Corruption and Democracy

Corruption also assaults democracy because it creates inefficient and ineffective government. Furthermore, it would appear to the taxpayer that government is arbitrary and that citizens are treated differently. Democracy is therefore weakened, as citizens no longer trust those in charge. Moreover, democracy depends on public procedures that have the force of law, particularly equal standing before the law and equal protection and evenhanded procedures.[200]

Corruption of political appointees and elected officials is as old as the republic. Recent examples would include charges of bribery and bid-rigging on the part of nine defendants associated with a New York construction company, L.P. Ciminelli. The charges were brought by the US attorney in Buffalo, New York. The defendants are accused of bribing a former Albany lobbyist in an effort to gain an unfair advantage over other contractors seeking work from the state. The defendants are accused of defrauding the state and the taxpayers. The accusation is to the effect that the Ciminelli company paid a former Albany lobbyist named Howe a bribe to win contracts from the state. Included in the complaint is the name of Alain Kaloveros, the president of SUNY Polytechnic Institute.[201]

According to the complaint brought by United States attorney Preet Bharara, Joseph Percoco, the former executive deputy secretary of the governor of New York, Andrew Cuomo, took more than $315,000 in bribes from the COR Developmental and Competitive Power, an energy company. A former Cuomo associate, Todd Howe, pleaded guilty to setting up bank accounts and shell companies to funnel bribes to Percoco's wife. Howe further pleaded guilty to charges of conspiracy to commit extortion, wire fraud, and tax fraud.[202]

On March 31, 2015, Representative Aron Schock of Illinois resigned from Congress. Schock needed to spend the money of the taxpayer like the proverbial "drunken sailor." He spent $40,000 on his Capitol Hill office. He had hired an interior designer, Annie Brahler, to do the work after he read about her in a magazine. It appears that Schock had a lifetime need to get ahead of everybody else. He had been the youngest school board member, the youngest Illinois state legislator, and one of the youngest members of Congress. Evidently he began his business career when he was only 12 years old and started his own IRA at age 14. At the age of 19 he was elected to the school board and after a short interval became school board president. He graduated from Bradley University after only two years while in the meantime earning $230,000 profit from real estate deals.

Once elected to Congress, he used private charter planes at the expense of the taxpayer, bought concert tickets, and traveled overseas and around the country, all at the taxpayers' expense. All of this led a congressional ethics committee to look at Schock's spending, which led him to resign in the middle of his term.[203]

Kent Sorenson, a member of the Iowa legislature, pleaded guilty to federal charges of accepting thousands of dollars as bribes before switching loyalty from Representative Michelle Bachmann to U.S. Representative Ron Paul in the contest for the 2012 Republican presidential nomination. Sorenson had been Bachmann's state campaign chairman in 2011. Yet six days before the Iowa caucuses, Sorenson suddenly announced his support for Paul. Sorenson admitted in his plea agreement of receiving monthly payments of about $8000 from October to December 2011 while he was still Bachmann's state chairman. He also pleaded guilty of causing a campaign to falsely report expenditures. Sorenson resigned from the Iowa Senate less than three years after his election. Several campaign aides of Sen. Ron Paul were also found guilty of participating in bribery and conspiracy.[204]

On August 12, 2013, Jesse Jackson Jr., the son of the civil rights leader Jesse Jackson, was jailed for 30 months and his wife to 12 months for spending $750,000 from his campaign funds on personal items. Jackson spent $15,000 in kitchen appliances and $43,000 on a Rolex. His wife Sandi was sentenced for omitting $580,000 in income from the couple's tax returns. The couple served their sentences at separate times in order to be with their two children. Jackson was also sentenced to three years of supervised release, as he is not eligible for parole. He must also pay back the campaign money to the government.[205]

In September 2015, Michael Grimm began serving an eight month sentence for filing false tax returns. Grimm resigned from the House of Representatives, where he represented the citizens of Staten Island. Grimm is a former Marine and former FBI agent. This makes it particularly egregious and peculiar that Grimm violated the tax laws. It appears that there are some Americans whose greed is such that they would take any risk for money.

Thomas DeLay, the House Majority Leader, was investigated in October 2005. He was found to have illegally channeled funds from "Americans for a Republican Majority" to Republican state legislators' campaigns. In 2010 he was convicted on two counts of money laundering and conspiracy.

Greed also motivates the judiciary. An outstanding example of this dictum is the removal of federal judge G. Thomas Porteous Jr. from the federal bench. In December 2010, Porteous was found guilty on four articles of impeachment and removed from the bench by the Senate. This was the first time in more than two decades and just the eighth time in the history of the United States that a federal judge was removed. This removal stemmed from charges that Porteous received cash and favors from lawyers who had dealings in his court under a false name deliberately designed to mislead the Senate during his confirmation proceedings. All 96 senators present found Porteous guilty on the first article, which concerned his time as a state court judge, and his subsequent failure to recuse himself from matters involving a former law partner, with whom he was accused of trading favors for cash. Porteous was also accused of accepting meals, trips and car repairs from a bail bondsman.[206]

In September 2008, Kyle D. Foggo, a high-ranking official at the Central Intelligence Agency, pleaded guilty to a felony corruption count, admitting that he had directed C.I.A. contracts to companies operated by a longtime friend.

Foggo admitted to theft of his honest services because he had concealed his relationship to Brent R. Wilkes, a San Diego military contractor. Foggo had been promised a high-paying job at Brent Wilkes' companies in return for steering military contacts to Wilkes. Wilkes himself had been sentenced to 12 years in prison for bribing Representative Randy Cunningham, who had pleaded guilty to corruption and is serving an eight-year prison sentence.[207]

Randy "Duke" Cunningham, an eight term congressman from San Diego, was sentenced to eight years imprisonment in 2006 for steering government contracts to firms that had given him a luxury house, a Rolls-Royce, Persian carpets, and other gifts. Cunningham was a Navy ace during the Vietnam War, having downed five enemy aircraft. Cunningham had taken $2,400,000 in bribes from military contractors in return for giving them government contracts. His sentence was the longest ever handed down for a member or former member of Congress. Cunningham had kept a "bribing menu" with the prices of influence. One column offered $16 million in contracts for the title to a boat, which the contractor had bought for $440,000. The card further detailed how much more contract work could be bought for every additional $50,000 paid to Cunningham. Cunningham also bargained for gifts like a sport utility vehicle, a Tiffany statue, and candelabras. Cunningham was ordered to pay $1,804,031.50 in back taxes and another $1,851,508 based on cash he received for his crimes.[208]

Because men are far more often appointed or elected to political office than women, men are also more often convicted of political corruption.

However, a casual perusal of politicians convicted and sentenced for extortion, bribery, money laundering, theft of campaign funds and various other schemes includes a good number of women, who evidently are as interested in gaining financial advantages by illegal means as men. If we confine ourselves to a list of politicians convicted between 2010 and 2016, we find a considerable list of such convictions, including a number of women.

In 2014, Arkansas state treasurer Martha Shoffner was convicted of the charges of extortion and bribery and sentenced to 30 months in prison. Shoffner accepted six payments in bribes from an investment or broker in return for steering the state's business to him.[209]

In California, state assemblywoman Mary Hayashi was charged with felony grand theft after being caught on video surveillance shoplifting $2,445 worth of merchandise from San Francisco's Neiman Marcus store.[210]

In May 2013, Diane Hathaway, a Michigan Supreme Court Justice, was sentenced to one year and one day in federal prison after pleading guilty to bank fraud. Hathaway was sentenced for hiding $1 million in assets so she could qualify for a short sale offer for a Grosse Pointe Park home. Evidently Hathaway pleaded hardship while still possessing more than $1 million in assets. She and her husband put their Florida home in her relative's name while dealing with the bank and then got the property back later.[211]

There are innumerable additional forms of political corruption on the part of women and men in all states of the union every year. In fact there are numerous instances in which politicians, both elected and appointed, seek to enrich themselves at the expense of the taxpayer.

The kind of corruption exemplified by Randy Cunningham and others exists not only in capitalism but also in all social systems, including feudalism, socialism, communism, and fascism. Corruption is evidently found in all age groups, both sexes, and all times, in the ancient world, in the middle ages, and the present.[212]

Corruption is of course far more common when those in power are not held accountable to other authorities or to the public by means of the media. Furthermore, the public does not necessarily support the court of ethics demanded of politicians, whether elected or appointed. Undoubtedly, corruption affects economic development, political institutions and social attitudes. In fact, few people know what corruption really is or appreciate its consequences. In every society there are politicians who try to get rich by corrupt means.[213]

Effects of Corruption

Corruption decreases respect and allegiance for the government. Evidently, those who give and accept bribes have no regard for their country or its people. They use political office to gain wealth. This is particularly the case when the government is weak and enforcement mechanisms are absent and there is no sense of national community. This in turn lowers respect for constitutional authority, as people who observe those in power gaining wealth by illegal means are induced to think that they should also gather money for themselves by any means possible. In a free society, an honest media can become a means of controlling excessive greed by those in power. It has been repeatedly observed that if those at the top are engaged in corrupt practices, such behavior becomes ubiquitous as it percolates down.[214]

The consequences of political corruption include hurting the poor in several ways. When public confidence in government is reduced, then public willingness to trust government agencies with spending large amounts of money for the poor who depend on government help is compromised.[215]

Another consequence of corruption is the involvement of legal assistance for those who have been caught. In every community there are lawyers who specialize in defending corrupt politicians. Such lawyers earn a great deal of money from defending white-collar offenders. Another consequence of corruption is that the cost of government to the taxpayer is increased by the money stolen by those who have access to public funds.[216]

How Not to Close the Income Gap — Voter fraud

Social scientists have identified relative deprivation as the principal explanation for so much theft and illegal efforts to gain money at any price. Relative deprivation refers to individuals who believe that members of their reference group are better rewarded than themselves and that such reference group individuals have more money and more social prestige than they have. This perceived discrepancy can lead to theft and corruption in an effort to close the gap between those who are believed to have more without being more meritorious. This dissatisfaction can therefore lead to crime. This then explains why some people with money and even highly prestigious occupations resort to all kinds of efforts to gain more income at the expense of others.[217]

Title 18 of the US Code # 611 specifies that: "it shall be unlawful for any alien to vote in any election held solely or in part for the purpose of electing a candidate for the office of President, Vice President, presidential elector, member of the Senate, member of the House of Representatives," etc. In April 2012, *The National Review* reported that illegal immigrant voters, along with immigrants who are prohibited from voting, have been detected voting in Florida. This joins confirmed reports of sizable numbers of noncitizens voting in Georgia and Colorado. Every illegal alien or noncitizen immigrant who registers to vote is committing a felony. Every illegal alien or noncitizen immigrant who votes and thereby steals a vote from an American citizen is committing another felony. This is well known to the supporters of illegal immigration amnesty. There are those who claim that a number of senators and representatives have been elected by illegal votes. However, the US government has made no effort to prove this.[218]

There is considerable evidence that aliens have been able to cast votes in elections in Maryland for years. This evidence can be seen by comparing how voters in Frederick County filled out jury duty statements compared with their voting records. Evidently thousands of people in Frederick County who stated that they are not US citizens on jury duty forms nevertheless cast votes in elections. These people wanted to escape jury duty but did want to vote. Someone who doesn't tell the truth when summoned for jury duty is committing a crime. Likewise, it is a felony for a foreigner to vote in the presidential election. It has also been discovered that about 40,000 people are registered to vote in both Virginia and Maryland so that they can vote more than once, which is also a crime. Someone who is not a citizen, even if he is legally in the United States, is not allowed to vote in federal elections and in many states cannot vote in local elections either. It turns out that one in seven Maryland residents are not US citizens.[219] In September of 2015, Olivia Lee Reynolds was convicted of fraud in Dalton, Alabama. In August 2016 the

Alabama Court of Criminal Appeals upheld that conviction. Reynolds was found guilty of 24 counts of absentee ballot fraud. Three additional persons were also convicted in this scheme. Reynolds filled out ballots for 24 people without their knowledge and submitted them.[220]

Andrew Spieles has been the target of an FBI fraud investigation involving voter registration applications filed in the names of dead people. Spieles worked for "Harrisonburg VOTES," a voter registration drive organization. Spieles has admitted this fraud, which involved 19 applications. As a consequence the FBI agents are examining all applications turned in by "Harrisonburg VOTES."[221]

Ruth Robinson, the former mayor of Martin, Kentucky, was sentenced to 90 months imprisonment on a variety of charges that included vote buying, identity theft, and fraud. Ruth Robinson and co-conspirators James "Red" Robinson and James Stephen Robinson threatened and intimidated residents of Martin in the run-up to the 2012 election, in which Robinson was seeking reelection. The Robinsons targeted residents living in public housing or in properties Robinson owned. The residents were threatened with eviction if they did not sign absentee ballots the Robinsons had already filled out. Robinson also targeted disabled residents, and offered to buy the votes of others. James "Red" Robinson was sentenced to 40 months in prison and his son James Stephen Robinson received a total of 31 months imprisonment.[222] Guadalupe Rivera and Grace Graciela Sanchez illegally "assisted" absentee voters in Rivera's 2013 reelection bid for city Commissioner. Rivera won the election by 16 votes, but the result was invalidated after a judge determined that 30 absentee ballots had been submitted illegally. Rivera pleaded guilty to one count of providing illegal assistance to a voter and was sentenced to one year of probation and a $500 fine. Sanchez also pleaded guilty to four misdemeanor counts of violating Texas' election code.[223]

Erin Vanessa Leeper registered and voted in the 2015 school board election. As a convicted felon, however, she was ineligible to do so, and pleaded guilty to perjury in May 2015. She was ordered to pay a $750 fine, $240 in court costs, and was sentenced to a suspended five-year prison term and two years of probation.[224]

Robert Munroe pleaded no contest to 13 counts of voter fraud, making him the worst duplicate voter in state history, according to Milwaukee County assistant district attorney Bruce Landgraf. The judge in the case rejected Munroe's claim that he was insane at the time, including that Munroe's mental state did not prevent him from appreciating the wrongfulness of his votes or from conforming his actions to election laws. Munroe will serve up to one year in jail, in addition to a suspended three-year prison sentence, five years' probation, 300 hours of community service, and a $5000 fine.

Munroe cast two ballots in the April 2011 Supreme Court election, two in the April 2011 recall election, five in the Walker–Barrett recall, one illegal ballot in an August 2012 primary, and two ballots in the November 2012 presidential election. In the presidential election, Munroe cast an in-person absentee ballot on November 1 and drove a rental car to Lebanon, Indiana. There he showed his Indiana driver's license to vote in person on Election Day, November 6.[225]

Voter fraud is widespread in the United States. For example, 12,000 noncitizens registered to vote in Colorado and about 5,000 of those voted in 2010. In North Carolina and Florida large numbers of noncitizens are registered. In Tennessee there were 645,075 votes cast in the 2012 primary. 266 persons did not show a photo ID at the polls. They were allowed to vote provisionally with the understanding that the ballots would be counted when they returned with a photo ID. Not all of these voters returned, so that those who did not come back were not counted. This demonstrates an effort on the part of Tennessee to eliminate noncitizens from the voting booth. In 2005, the United States Government Accounting Office found that up to 3% of the 30,000 individuals called to jury duty from voter registration rolls over a two-year period in just one United States District Court were not US citizens. 3% may seem a small number. However, these voters were more than enough to provide the winning presidential vote margin in Florida in 2000. The Census Bureau estimates that there are over 1 million illegal aliens in Florida, and the US Department of Justice has prosecuted more noncitizens' voting cases in Florida than in any other state.[226]

Illegal voting is nothing new in the United States. Throughout the 20th century, political machines stole elections in New York City and in Chicago. Irish immigrants were lined up and counted as citizens and voted almost upon arrival from Europe. Today, in 2016, there are roughly 11 million noncitizens living in the United States who could register to vote and often do so, because the law against foreigners voting is not enforced. The reason for this lack of enforcement is that politicians are willing to gain election by means of foreigners voting and therefore claim that these violations of the law don't exist.[227]

The fact that aliens do vote in American federal elections was visible when, in a mayor's race in Compton, California, aliens testified under oath in court that they voted in that election. As a result, a candidate who was elected to the city council was permanently disqualified from holding public office in California for soliciting noncitizens to register and vote. This election was contested by the incumbent, who had lost by less than 300 votes.[228]

Non-citizen voting is likely growing at the same rate as the alien population in the United States. Because of deficiencies in state laws and the failure of federal agencies to comply with federal law, there are almost no procedures in place that allow election officials to detect, deter, and prevent noncitizens from registering and voting. Instead, officials are largely dependent on an honor system that expects aliens to follow the law. The honor system is, of course, a failure, because most district attorneys will not prosecute what they consider a victimless crime.[229]

In Chicago a grand jury reported that many aliens register to vote so that they can obtain documents identifying them as US citizens. They then fraudulently use their voter's cards to obtain a myriad of benefits, from Social Security to jobs within the Defense Department. The US attorney in Chicago estimated that there were at least 80,000 illegal aliens registered to vote in that city, and dozens were indicted and convicted for registering and voting.[230]

In 2006, Paul Betancourt, voter registrar for Harris County, Texas, testified before the United States Committee on House Administration, that the extent of illegal voting by foreign citizens in Harris County was impossible to eliminate and will continue to occur. 22% of county residents, he explained, were born outside of the United States and more than 500,000 were noncitizens. Betancourt noticed the registration of a Brazilian citizen after she acknowledged on a jury summons that she was not a US citizen. Later she reappeared and again claimed to be a US citizen and was again given a voter card. The record shows that she was able to vote at least four times in general and primary elections.[231]

Organized Crime vs. Democracy and a Safe Society

Organized crime has plagued American democracy since the years from the 1820s to the 1850s, when large numbers of immigrants moved into the American cities of the East and West, so that the population of large cities quadrupled in 30 years. In fact, immigrants and their children comprised more than two thirds of the population of the largest cities in the northeast and more than three quarters of the population of New York, Boston, and Chicago. The immigrants were employed in the most dangerous, monotonous, and poorly paid industries. Women and children were also used as laborers. The immigrants lived in slum housing reserved for their own ethnic group. These immigrants became the victims of the most egregious bigotries concerning their religion, their lack of education, their foreign accents, and the entire culture. In view of all this, the immigrant had only one weapon with which to defend himself and that was his vote.[232] The votes of these new arrivals, who were not citizens, became the basis for the so-called political machines, whose boss was usually American-born. The relationship between these bosses and the immigrants was such that the bosses furnished the immigrants with work and a paycheck and the immigrants in turn voted as they were told. These political machines were usually able to provide immigrants with thousands of jobs. Such jobs as construction workers, street cleaners, police, firemen, and service workers of all kinds were provided by the political bosses.[233]

The politicians who profited most from these arrangements often operated gambling houses and saloons. These saloons were the nucleus of politics, as saloon keepers became the political powers in many American cities. The saloons provided social services. The saloons had newspapers in several languages, as well as free pencils and paper and mail service for immigrants who wanted to write letters home. Most important, the saloons had information on employment. In addition, saloons hosted entertainment such as dancing, music, billiard tables, union meetings, and wedding celebrations. All of this attracted the immigrants who, although usually not citizens, kept the bosses in power for years.[234]

That power was assured because the voters were often paid to vote, and voted under the supervision of party workers who could readily see which ballot a voter cast. In addition to this nefarious method, the bosses also employed gangs who voted several times in various precincts and who also attacked rival campaign workers and intimidated voters.[235]

These methods of defeating democracy continued until prohibition ended the relationship between the politicians and organized crime leaders. Before prohibition, the boss protected gangs and vice operators from law enforcement. This all changed when prohibition created a level of criminal violence unknown before. Now physical protection from rival criminal organizations became more important than protection from law enforcement, as prohibition converted gangs into crime empires.[236]

These crime empires and their criminal practitioners became immensely wealthy while prohibition of the use of alcohol was still in force. During those years, various criminal gangs fought in the streets of the United States over the profits to be made in the alcohol business.[237]

After prohibition was repealed in 1933, organized crime continued. Now organized crime concentrated on the numbers racket, prostitution, loansharking, drug smuggling, and union racketeering. All these activities were organized by professional criminals who used their enormous profits to corrupt politicians and officeholders of all kinds, so that elected officials became the tools for organized crime instead of serving the public, thereby undermining democracy. Although the majority of organized criminals were of Sicilian descent until approximately the 1970s, members of other ethnic groups have dominated organized crime in later years. Citizens of the former Soviet have more recently dominated organized crime in the United States, as have many of Mexican descent. These criminal gangs have competed successfully with the Sicilian and Italian Mafiosi and in part driven them out of business. Competition from South American gangs as well as successful government interference have weakened the Mafia even as South American gangs have gained the ascendancy in organized crime. Perhaps Colombia is the best example of a country engulfed in crime and violence. In Colombia, the homicide rate is 68 per hundred thousand. In the United States the homicide rate is five per hundred thousand.[238]

It may seem that events in Colombia should not concern Americans. But because Colombian-produced drugs enter the United States in large numbers by way of Mexico, about 30,000 Colombian natives have come to New York City and have brought with them drugs in huge quantities.[239]

All of these crimes could not well exist if it were not for support from politicians of all parties. As Merton wrote in 1967: "The supporters of the political machine include both the respectable business class elements, who are opposed to the criminal or racketeer, and the distinctly un-respectable elements of the underworld."[240]

Today, at the beginning of the 21st century, the old Sicilian-Italian criminal organizations have taken a severe blow from both federal law enforcement and competition from Mexican and other South American gangs. In addition, Asian drug dealers are competing for the huge market for drugs which the American public provides.[241]

While at one time Cuba provided drugs, gambling, bootlegging, and prostitution for Americans, that Cuban connection ended with the Cuban revolution of 1959. Since then, the drug trade in South America has come from Bolivia and Peru and from there was smuggled into the United States by way of Chile and Mexico. As the United States began to intercept a good deal of the Mexican drug trade, drug production developed in Colombia, which has a lengthy Caribbean coastline and therefore is in a favorable position to move illegal drugs to Florida by means of speed boats and airplanes.[242]

The market for drugs in the United States is so large and profitable that it yields over $500 billion a year. This means that the drug industry has several branches, all of which profit from it. Included in those who profit are the farmers who grow the weeds, the refiners, the trafficker, and the dealers and corrupt law enforcement. The drug business also produces a number of murders. For example, in 2010 there were 15,273 murders in Mexico related to the thousands of kilograms of drugs that cross the American-Mexican border every day. The drugs are delivered to dealers who sell them to users. None of this would be possible without the surreptitious involvement of politicians and law enforcers, all to the detriment of American democracy. Moreover, history teaches us that the final outcome of disorganization and widespread criminal behavior finally leads to dictatorship when a majority of the population prefers to relinquish freedom for security.[243]

The illegal drug trade is the second-largest profit-making industry in the world after the weapons trade. This is illustrated by the observation that the United States consumes 25 times more illegal drugs than Colombia, although Columbia produces 50% of the world's cocaine. 90% of the South American drug production passes into the United States through Mexico. This does not mean that Mexico produces all these drugs, since 104 countries are involved in the drug trade, although usually with far less results than are achieved by Colombia, Peru and other Latin American countries.[244]

The drug trade is responsible for a considerable amount of crime. Importing drugs into the United States is in itself a crime which is difficult to prevent, because each year over 60 million people enter the United States by air, 70 million by land in 116 million vehicles, and 6 million by sea on 90,000 ships carrying 400 million tons of cargo. This enormous traffic allows drug dealers to move their products into the United States with near impunity.[245]

It has been 46 years since President Nixon declared a war on drugs in 1971. Yet, drug dealing and all the evils associated with it are more widespread than ever in 2017. This increase in drug trafficking began in the 1970s, when a new form of organized crime was created by the global world economy, resulting in open borders, as crime groups changed from domestic organized crime like the Cosa Nostra (Mafia) to criminal organizations that are international and worldwide and not nearly as hierarchical as the Mafia. These transnational organized crime cartels are usually violent. This allows them to intimidate citizens and law enforcement personnel. Because these traffickers are international, they can exploit differences between countries, which allow them to escape apprehension and conviction. They attain influence in government and politics by bribing and corrupting officials, thereby undermining democracy. Major drug dealers make vast amounts of money, which they then use to enter into legal businesses and thereby gain the support of vast numbers of unsuspecting customers. To ensure that the crime bosses are never held accountable, these cartels develop a structure that insulates each layer of authority from those below them.[246]

Therefore "the war on drugs" has failed, which is best understood by looking at arrests made for dealing or possessing illegal drugs. For example, on February 3, 2015, eight people were charged in Arkansas for large-scale drug trafficking of methamphetamine and crack cocaine. The investigation led to the seizure of two firearms and several rounds of ammunition, four vehicles, and $10,000 in cash. Among those arrested were a number of persons previously arrested for the same offenses. Evidently, an occasional arrest cannot stop importation and distribution of drugs in this country.[247]

The best source for understanding the extent of drug crimes in this country is a look at the Bureau of Justice Statistics publications issued by the Department of Justice. This reveals that in one year in the United States there were more than 1½ million drug arrests. 40 years earlier, in 1973, the total number of drug arrests was only 329,000. In 1973 the population of the United States was 212 million or 29% less than the 317 million in 2013. Yet, drug arrests have increased fivefold since then. Likewise, drug arrests in 1990 were 742,000 in number. That was exceeded by 46% since 2006. The median age of those arrested is 26 and 11% of those arrested were juveniles. 18% involved those 50 years old or older. The cost of arresting drug users is very high.[248]

It has been estimated that it takes approximately one million hours of police time to make about 440,000 arrests for drug possession. It has further been noted that 47% of violent crimes and 19% of property crimes are drug related. Compared to arrests for all crimes it turns out that 47% of all violent crimes are cleared by arrest, matching exactly the arrest rates for drug-related crimes. This leads one to believe that violence not associated with drugs is hardly prosecuted, since the alternative explanation, that drug use is associated with all violence, is spurious.[249]

This discussion of greed, fraud, and crime demonstrates that our third president, Thomas Jefferson, recognized 250 years ago that every generation must defend freedom, liberty, and democracy over and over again. There always are those, born in the United States, and the beneficiaries of more liberty and freedom than any other country offers its citizens, who are nevertheless willing to betray and undermine it. This demonstrates that millions of Americans don't know what a great privilege it is to wake up every morning in the United States. That therefore once again reminds us of Winston Churchill's insightful remark: "Democracy is the worst form of government except for all the others."

Chapter 8. The Assault on Gender Equality

The history of mankind since its very beginnings on this globe has assigned to women a secondary role subject to men. This doctrine can be illustrated by reviewing the position of women in the family in the history of every culture on earth. Christianity is no exception to that rule, as best exhibited in the teachings of the New Testament concerning women. There are so many translations of the Bible from the Hebrew and the Greek that the wording among them is not always the same. Nevertheless, all these translations agree with Young's Literal Translation that St. Paul wrote in I Corinthians 14:34 : "Your women in the assemblies let them be silent, for it has not been permitted to them to speak, but to be subject, as also the law says." Paul was Jewish and therefore refers to the Jewish law with which he must have been well acquainted. For example, in Leviticus 15:19-30, menstruation is described as unclean and he warns men not to touch a woman during her period. In Leviticus 12:1-8 we read that after childbirth a mother needed purification for 40 days after the birth of her son but for 80 days after the birth of her daughter. Similar views concerning menstruation are found in Greco-Roman culture. For example, Pliny the Elder writes in *Natural History:* "Contact with the month flux of women turns new wine sour, makes crops wither, dries seeds and gardens, causes the fruit of trees to fall off, dims the bright surface of mirrors, dulls the edge of steel and the gleam of ivory, kills bees, rusts iron and bronze, and causes a horrible smell to fill the air."[250]

These beliefs, perpetuated for centuries and utterly divorced from reality, were brought to America with the Puritans in the 17th century and continued as unassailable fact among the millions of immigrants who came after them. As late as the Victorian Age, which really continued even after Queen Victoria's death in 1901, women were viewed as asexual victims of men's insatiable sexuality.

Normal women were also viewed as morally pure and passive. Therefore, education for men and women differed to accommodate these presumed inherited conditions.[251]

Education and Better Jobs

Consequently, women received far less education than men. This self-fulfilling prophecy then confirmed the prejudices against women as childlike and imbecilic. Even as late as the 1950s and into the early 1960s, these beliefs were commonly held, until Betty Friedan published her epoch-making book, *The Feminine Mystique*, in 1963.[252] She called the plight of women the problem that has no name. Widely disseminated, the book was truly revolutionary and instigated changes for women which had many consequences for the everyday lives of men and children as well.

It is an axiom of sociology that changes in any part of a society will inevitably lead to changes in all other parts of that society. Therefore it is not surprising that the liberation of women, beginning in the 1960s, has led to a more egalitarian and democratic family in America. Yet, there are now in the first decade of the 21st century those who seek to undermine these achievements in an effort to return the family and its women to the earlier status quo.

Although American women have not yet achieved economic equality with men, their progress in that respect has altered the American family considerably. Women are gaining ground in professional careers, which indicates that they are gaining positions where they can contribute their best skills while earning good incomes. Along with this they are gaining more respect, more of a voice in American business and society, and also more economic freedom.

For example, about 47% of all law degrees awarded during the five years ending in 2016 have been awarded to women. About one third of the 1,092,000 American lawyers are female, 20% of editors-in-chief of the fifty most prestigious law reviews are women, and so are 20% of law school deans. Five women have been presidents of the American Bar Association, and 22% of corporate lawyers are women.[253]

Similar advances have been made by women in the field of medicine. According to the Bureau of Labor Statistics, women constituted nearly 36% of the 934,000 American physicians in 2016, earning an average income of $145,000 a year.[254]

Even more spectacular has been the advent of women as executive officers of America's largest corporations. Mary T. Barra is the president of General Motors Company, which employs 212,000 people. Her compensation is $16.2 million annually. There are a number of other women who have achieved as much in the American economy, such as Virginia Romety, president of IBM, Mary Jackson Sammons, the president of Rite Aid, Jane Ellers, president of Children's Place, and Ursula Burns, the chair of the Xerox Corporation. [255]

These women are of course unusual, as the vast majority of women — or men — will never be corporation presidents nor doctors or lawyers. Nevertheless, the achievements of women in general have made a huge difference in the manner in which women are perceived in the America of the 21st century. American women are no longer viewed as second-class human beings. It also means, however, that the American family is changing, in that women earn their own income, vote in large numbers, and have attained a degree of independence of men never known before.

What is true of the economy and of education is also true in politics. In 2016, there were 20 women in the United States Senate and 79 women in the House of Representatives. In 2017 the 115th Congress includes 83 female Representatives and 21 female Senators. Numerous women are represented among America's governors, ambassadors, and members of the president's cabinet. Therefore it is reasonable to assume that the demeaning of women in America is over.

One of the consequences of increased female participation in the workforce is that it is no longer particularly unusual for married women to earn more than their husbands, since many men work at low wages, at part-time work, or temporary jobs, and may have fewer benefits and repeated joblessness.[256]

Equal Rights Amendment

These new conditions tend to mean that many men no longer automatically find themselves recognized as the head of the family. This can cause them to feel frustrated and to resent the superior education and income of the women in their lives. Not only some men, but also some women, have not been happy or supportive of gender equality in this country. This failure to support gender equality can be seen when we consider the opposition to the Equal Rights Amendment to the United States Constitution, first proposed in Congress by the National Women's Party in 1923. This amendment passed Congress after many attempts, but only 35 state legislatures ever voted in favor of the amendment, a number three states shy of ratification. Section 1 of The Equal Rights Amendment states: "Equality of Rights under the law shall not be abridged by the United States or by any state on account of sex."

This amendment was viewed by feminists as the only means by which all legal gender-based discrimination in the United States would finally be eliminated. Yet, the lead in opposing this amendment came from a woman lawyer, Phyllis Schlafly, who published a book titled *A Choice Not an Echo*, which sold 3 million copies. In this book, Schlafly claimed that The Equal Rights Amendment would eliminate laws against sexual assault and alimony. Schlafly also argued that mothers in a divorce case would no longer receive child custody, and that the all-male military draft would become unconstitutional. Schlafly predicted that single-sex restrooms would be banished by future courts. The opponents of the ERA baked apple pies for state legislators while they debated this legislation and hung "don't draft me" signs on baby girls.

Phyllis Schlafly was a truly liberated woman. She was named one of the 100 most important women of the 20ᵗʰ century by *The Ladies' Home Journal*. Schlafly held a law degree from Washington University, from where she had graduated Phi Beta Kappa. She also received a Master's in political science from Harvard University and an honorary Doctor of Humane Letters from Washington University in 2008. She founded a national organization of citizens called Eagle Forum. This maintained offices in Washington D.C. and in Illinois. The Eagle Forum of volunteers lobby Congress and otherwise seek to influence the public in their cause. Schlafly wrote 20 books on family and feminism, including *The Flipside of Feminism* and *No Higher Power: Obama's War On Religious Freedom*. She also published a column in 100 newspapers and a monthly article for *The Daughters of the American Revolution* magazine. In her role as a lawyer, she was a member of the commission on the bicentennial of the U.S. Constitution appointed by President Reagan. She testified before more than 50 congressional and state legislative committees and served five terms on the Illinois Commission on the Status of Women. She also filed numerous briefs with the US Supreme Court and courts of appeal.

In 1992, Phyllis Schlafly was the Illinois Mother of the Year. She had been married to her husband for 44 years when she became a widow. She had six children and 14 grandchildren. All six of her children became lawyers, doctors, PhDs and businesswomen.

In sum, Phyllis Schlafly was the opposite of what she expected of all other women, whom she encouraged to stay home even as she opposed the entire feminist agenda.[257]

Ninety-three years have passed since the Equal Rights Amendment was first introduced. During those years, women have found means of gaining gender equality other than through the ERA.

Pay Equity and Workforce Participation

It is possible that if the Equal Rights Amendment had been passed, the courts might have considered unequal pay based on gender unconstitutional. This will never be known. Over the years there has been a distinct improvement of women's income as a percentage of men's income. In 2015, women earned an average of $719 a week or 83% of the income of men.[258]

The Bureau of Labor Statistics publishes a vast list of occupations by salary and sex. All of these occupations depict a lesser income for women than for men in all categories. Some examples are: among chief executives, men earn a weekly income of $2,251 and women $1,836. Male managers on a lower level earn $1,525 and women in the same position earn $1,213. Men in the mathematical sciences earn $1,452 a week and women earn only $1,257 in the mathematical sciences. Even among social workers, who are predominantly female, men earn $943 a week but women only $862 a week. Among college professors, men earn $1405 a week on the average and women $1144. According to the Bureau of Labor Statistics, the average earned by physicians, i.e. their median income, is $1,915 for men and $1,533 for women. That statistic seems rather low for the medical profession because the income of residents is included. According to The Med Career Guide, male physicians earned an average of $284,000 a year in 2015 and women earned $215,000 that year.[259] Although the financial gender gap still exists in 2016 in the United States, it is important to note that women's participation in the paid labor force rose steadily in the latter part of the 20th century and in the early 21st century. As we have already seen, this increase was principally fueled by the educational attainment of women all the way from primary school to college and professional and graduate schools. These changes in the position of women in the family have affected men as well. One indication of this change is that the amount of housework undertaken by women has declined while the amount of housework done by men is increased.[260]

Yet, there has been a slowdown in the rate at which women's labor force participation has increased, as well as in the rate of decline of the gender wage gap. The rate of change has declined, but nevertheless more women have obtained management positions than ever before. That decline came about because the proportion of management positions for women is a direct outgrowth of the percentage of women in non-management jobs. This means that some of the traditional opinions concerning men and women continue, although the idea of separate spheres for the sexes has been rejected by the majority of Americans. Progress in this respect has been somewhat slower than was true in earlier years. The principal reason for this slowdown is that there is not as much pressure towards resolving the gender gap as was true at the outset of the feminist movement.[261]

The Institute for Women's Policy Research has published a paper entitled *The Status of Women in the United States*. This publication deals with the percentage of women in a given state who registered to vote. Such registration is an indication of women's political participation in that state.

By comparing voter registration by women between various states of the union, it is possible to discover whether states and regions of the United States differ to the extent to which women have achieved equality. To answer this question, Sugarman and Strauss invented a Gender Equality Index. This index combines seven indicators of economic gender equality, four indicators of political gender equality, and thirteen indicators of legal gender equality. Using this index allows researchers to discover the extent to which women have the same access to economic resources, legal rights, or positions of political power as men in each of the 50 states.[262]

Across the United States, the rate of female labor force participation is between three fourths and four fifths the male rate. But in over two thirds of the states, the rate of employment for women is at or above that for men. This includes part-time employment, so that only one third of all full-time workers are female. Furthermore, women are far more often employed in low paying jobs than are held by men, a feature of women's economic condition called the ghettoization of women's labor.

A valid indicator of women's participation in the business world is their share of all Small Business Administration loans. In fact, women received less than half of Small Business Administration loans. Loans to women are only 25% of such loans awarded to men.

Women are more likely to be poor than men. This is to some extent caused by the greater chance that children are living in female-headed households than single male-headed households. Childcare expenses increase the economic burden of female householders. For working single mothers, the added expense of child care in addition to the continuing wage gap makes women extremely vulnerable to poverty.

Political equality is another aspect of women's liberation from their traditional non-involved role. The number of women holding membership in state legislatures is one measure of gender equality in the political sphere. In 2016, there were 1,805 or 24.2% women members in state legislatures nationwide. In that same year, 84 or 19.3% of all members of the US House of Representatives were women and there were 20 women among the 100 members of the United States Senate. Since women are a majority of Americans, it is evident women are far from being represented adequately in our legislatures. In 2016, there were only six women governors among the 50 states.[263]

For many years there has been a considerable discrepancy among the regions of the country with respect to female participation in the legislative process. Evidently the Northeast leads the Midwest and West and South in political gender equality, with the South allowing women fewer political opportunities than the other regions of the country. Thus, in 2015 in Nevada,

33.3% of statehouse members were female. In Alabama in 2015, only 14.3% of statehouse members were female.

Externally Imposed Standards of Appearance

Although women have undoubtedly achieved a great deal during the last half-century, they are still far from attaining true gender equality. This can be demonstrated by recognizing that even now, in 2017, women are more likely to be judged by their appearance than by their achievements. Because that is true, women, and particularly young women, suffer all kinds of eating disorders which are the product of self-destructive behavior. Best known of these disorders are anorexia nervosa and bulimia. These disorders do not come from some virus or bacterial infection. Instead these disorders come from unrealistic body images, as taught by the media and particularly television, which dictate the nature of female attractiveness. [264]

Naomi Wolf in her study *The Beauty Myth* calls the beliefs about female beauty in America a modern hallucination. She further shows that the number of anorexics has increased immensely since the 1970s. Likewise, Kim Chernin writes in *The Hungry Self* that half the women in United States colleges have had experiences with anorexia and bulimia.[265]

The imposition of appearance over achievement leads to a homogenized look, as can readily be seen by observing that almost all female television announcers have long dyed blonde hair and a body which resembles as closely as possible the models who appear on the covers of fashion magazines.

There are therefore numerous women and some men who seek to reshape their body parts by the use of plastic surgery. Plastic surgery is painful and is in fact a form of body mutilation. Plastic surgeons divide women's bodies into subsections such as "upper neck," "eyes and brows," "nose," "mouth," "skin," "breasts," "abdomen," and "hips and thighs." These body part procedures are quite costly. They are advertised by the plastic surgery industry as if surgery were no different than buying a new dress. Yet the fact is that silicone implants can move around the body or leak and create serious hazards. Nevertheless, more than 80,000 women have their breasts made larger each year at the cost of at least $9,000 per person. It is evident that the advertisements concerning acceptable female appearance lead women to tolerate the pain and expense of this kind of surgery.[266]

Effects of Pornography

It can hardly be denied that pornography (Greek= writings of a whore) demeans women. It is therefore not surprising that feminists denounce such entertainment as sexual discrimination and contend that it inspires men to rape, to disrespect women and to treat them as objects rather than sensitive and intelligent beings.[267]

It is further argued that pornography diminishes equal opportunities for women in employment, education, and politics, and encourages men to treat women as second-class citizens. This appears to be a reasonable conclusion, yet the pornography industry is so popular in the United States that it earns about $11 billion each year.

According to the anti-pornography feminists, pornography lies about the nature of women and therefore promotes sexist attitudes. According to these critics of pornography, pornography instills the erroneous belief that women are inferior to men and do not deserve equal rights. It is further argued that pornography teaches men to treat women as sex objects, having no other work or importance apart from their capacity to provide sexual gratification to men. As a result of this indoctrination, men supposedly learn to devalue and exploit women as a class. These beliefs have led to the argument that pornography "is the un-diluted essence of anti-female propaganda."[268]

A number of studies concerning the effect of exposure to nonviolent pornography failed to find a significant relationship between pornography and the tendency to view women as sex objects or the belief in traditional sex roles.[269]

Influenced by feminist beliefs concerning pornography, a number of city legislatures passed ordinances prohibiting the sale of such materials. In Minneapolis such legislation was vetoed by the mayor. In Indianapolis a similar ordinance was passed by the city council but was almost immediately challenged on constitutional grounds. Consequently, Judge Sarah Evans of the US District Court for the Southern District of Indiana held that the ordinance violated the First Amendment right of free speech. This was affirmed by the Seventh Circuit Court of Appeals, who said that an approved view of women is a form of thought control. Subsequently, the Supreme Court affirmed the Court of Appeals decision.[270]

The California Coalition Against Sexual Assault has published two articles concerning the influence of pornography on rape. Accordingly, Ferguson and Hartley argued in the journal *Aggression and Violent Behavior* in 2009 that "it is time to discard the hypothesis that pornography contributes to increased sexual assault behavior." In that same year, Michael Flood concluded in *Child Abuse Review*: "that especially among boys and young men who are frequent consumers of pornography, including violent materials, consumption intensifies attitudes supportive of sexual coercion, and increases the likelihood of perpetrating assault." We conclude from these conflicting views that pornography does not necessarily promote violence against women. It is, however, known to sociologists that men already prone to commit violence against women may find violent pornography a catalyst for taking such action.[271]

Violent Abuse and Rape

The legal protection of women refers to laws prohibiting sex discrimination and defending women against domestic violence. All states of the union have such laws, including the prohibition of sexual harassment . Domestic violence refers primarily to physical abuse, beatings, and/or psychological abuse of women by men. If democracy means anything, it should at least mean respect for the rights of others, and particularly the physical safety of every American. Nothing is more egregious than an assault on women and children by a boyfriends, husbands, or so-called significant others. A society which includes brutality against one's closest relatives is undermining the very idea of democratic living. Yet we must unfortunately record that a good deal of domestic violence persists in this country. The facts are these: Women between the ages of 18 and 24 are most likely to experience abuse from their current or former partner or spouse. Women who live with violent men have a greater risk of contracting HIV infection from a perpetrator. Furthermore, men and women who experience intimate violence are more likely to engage in risky behavior like injecting drugs or having sex without a condom. Domestic violence is likely to cause women to suffer from depression and suicidal behavior and has a negative impact on the victim's ability to perform well at work. Without adequate financial means, victims often find themselves trapped in an abusive relationship without enough money to leave. The victims of such abuse often do not reveal their victimization to the authorities. Only about a third of victims injured in intimate partner violence receive medical care. Between 2001 and 2012, 6,488 American troops were killed in Afghanistan and Iraq. During that same time, 11,766 women were murdered by current or ex-male partners. Women with disabilities are 40% more likely to experience intimate partner violence than women without disabilities.

Every year numerous women experience physical violence by an intimate partner, and of these women, 926 were killed and 264 of those were killed by an intimate partner during an argument. One in four women will be victims of severe violence by an intimate partner in their lifetime and one in seven men will be victims of severe violence by an intimate partner. In their lifetime, eight million paid work days are lost by women every year because of abuse perpetrated against them by male partners. This loss is equivalent to 32,000 full-time jobs. One woman is being beaten every nine seconds in the United States and intimate partner violence often leads to female homicide and injury related deaths during pregnancy. 81% of women who are harassed by a current or former male partner are also physically abused by that partner. Black women experience intimate partner violence and rates 35% higher than white women. Violence is the third leading cause of homelessness among families, and 15.5 million children are exposed to domestic violence every year.[272]

The Young Women's Christian Association has published a fact sheet concerning firearms related domestic violence homicides. Accordingly, a woman living in the United States is 11 times more likely to die from gun violence than in any other developed nation in the world. Guns are the deadly weapon of choice for most perpetrators of domestic violence. Intimate partner homicides account for nearly half of all women killed each year in the United States. Perpetrators with access to firearms are 5 to 8 times more likely to kill their partners than those without firearms. Nearly 50% of intimate partner homicide were committed by a current or former dating partner.[273]

Women who have left their violent male partner are often the victims of stalking. This means that the man who beat them and threatened to kill them follows them wherever they go. Such a man will often sit in his car outside the home of his victim. The woman, afraid of the stalker, is therefore frequently absent from work and is so distraught that her work suffers. Then if she is dismissed from her job because of absenteeism, she may even be unable to collect unemployment compensation when her ex-employer succeeds in blaming her for poor performance on the job.[274]

Stalking is not confined to the activities of violent men whose victims have finally left them. There are in addition so-called celebrity stalkers. These are people who feel compelled to harass movie actors and others whom they do not know but whose attention they seek. The vast majority of such celebrity stalkers are men, although a few women are also involved. For example, Diana Napolis threatened to violently confront Steven Spielberg, a movie producer. She believed that Spielberg and his wife were part of a satanic cult and that they were soul catchers trying to kill her. Such extremes may be rare. More common was the behavior of Dante Soiu, a 51-year-old pizza deliveryman who stalked the actress Gwyneth Paltrow by sending her five letters a day as well as pornography, flowers, candy, and pizza, and showed up at her parents' house multiple times. The actress Halle Berry was stalked by Greg Broussard because God told him to marry the actress. He therefore sent her an engagement ring. Likewise a stalker targeted the singer Janet Jackson. He came to a Saturday Night Live rehearsal with a knife and a box cutter. John Hinckley stalked the actress Jody Foster by slipping messages under her door. When he gained no attention from Foster, he decided to kill the President of the United States. That led him to fire six shots at President

Ronald Reagan, one of which wounded the president. This and other such violent behavior indicates that stalkers are not merely bizarre deviants but they can be dangerous, as proved by the murder of a 21-year-old actress, Rebecca Schaeffer, who was shot to death at the door of her Los Angeles apartment in 1989 by Robert Bardo, who had tracked her down and even hired a private investigator to obtain her home address.

Perhaps the most peculiar incidents of stalking occurred in 1992 when the chief judge of the New York State Court of Appeals, Sol Wachtler, was charged and convicted of stalking, blackmailing, and harassing his former girlfriend, Joy Silverman, with whom the married Wachtler had a long time "affair." Wachtler sent her threatening messages, made obscene phone calls to his victim, and sent Silverman's 14-year-old daughter a lewd letter that included a wrapped condom.

Since Wachtler was considered one of America's leading jurists because he had written numerous important decisions and had been connected to some of the most prominent politicians in the country, it seemed particularly egregious to discover this peculiar behavior on his part. Wachtler was jailed for a brief time after having resigned his position as judge.

Children are also the frequent victims of domestic violence. Studies have documented the significant overlap between domestic violence and child abuse. Between 30% and 60% of men who batter their female partners also abuse their children. Children who witness domestic violence are greatly disturbed for that reason. Moreover, sociologists know that 85% of men incarcerated for violent crime came from a violent home. This means that domestic violence is largely responsible for violence in the next generation.[275]

Domestic violence is a hidden crime which receives far less attention in the media than most other crimes. The exception to that rule occurs when prominent men are the offenders. When well-known sports figures are involved in domestic violence, they and their victim received a good deal of publicity. An example of this interest in the misconduct by professional athletes was the considerable publicity given New York Giants kicker Josh Brown. Brown admitted that he was physically, emotionally, and verbally abusive to his wife. In May 2015, Brown was arrested for a fourth assault. He was charged with physically, emotionally, and verbally assaulting his wife. Brown admitted to aggressive conduct towards his wife and abused her emotionally and verbally. It is possible that he was able to do this so many times because of his prominence. There are numerous instances in which important sports figures are excused or barely penalized for violence committed against their own families.[276]

The victimization of women is aggravated by evidence that police are themselves often involved in domestic violence. Moreover, the record shows that police have been largely unsympathetic to the complaints of women who have been abused by men, and that even rape statistics are most unreliable because many women who have been raped are unwilling to report this to the police because they are justifiably afraid of gaining no sympathy from law enforcement. Prior to 2008, a number of states, including Georgia and California, applied the death penalty to some of those convicted of rape. In that year, however, the Supreme Court of the United States ruled in *Coker v. Georgia* that the death penalty could not be applied to someone convicted of rape on the grounds that the victim did not die and that therefore the death penalty is unconstitutional under those circumstances and constitutes cruel and unusual punishment prohibited by the eighth amendment to the Constitution.

In 1974, Ehrlich Anthony Coker was serving several life sentences in a Georgia prison when he escaped. After his escape, Coker broke into the home of Allen and Elnita Carver. He raped Elnita and stole the family's car. Apprehended shortly thereafter, Coker was convicted of rape, armed robbery, and other offenses. He was sentenced to death on the rape charge after the jury found two of the aggravating circumstances present for imposing that sentence. The rape was committed by a person with prior convictions for capital felonies, and the rape was committed in the course of committing another capital felony, the armed robbery. The Supreme Court of Georgia upheld the sentence. The Supreme Court of the United States voided this penalty in part on the grounds that only three states, Georgia, North Carolina, and Louisiana, retained the death penalty for the rape of an adult woman. Shortly thereafter, North Carolina and Louisiana also did not retain the death penalty for rape, so that Georgia was the only state maintaining the death penalty for rape. Coker was re-sentenced to life in prison, a sentence which he was already serving for all his previous crimes.[277]

In 2008, in *Kennedy v. Louisiana*, the Supreme Court justices declared unconstitutional the death penalty as punishment for the rape of a child.

This decision was again based on the argument that the victim did not die.[278] The victim of that rape was Kennedy's eight-year-old stepdaughter. This brutal rape was so horrible that journalists could not adequately describe the cruelty and the hurt and the horror inflicted on the victim. Yet, what was known to the public led to revulsion on the part of all who read about this. Kennedy had assaulted the child with such violence that she was bleeding profusely from the frontal area. She was transported to a Children's Hospital where an expert in pediatric forensic medicine found that her injuries were the most severe he had seen from sexual assault in his four years of practice. A laceration to the left wall of the vagina had separated her cervix from the back of her vagina, causing her rectum to protrude into the vaginal structure.

Her entire perineum was torn from the posterior fourchette (a mucous membrane) to the anus. The injuries required emergency surgery.

According to the FBI's *Uniform Crime Report*, the estimated number of rapes in 2015 in the United States was 90,185.[279] That number is far from the real number of rapes in this country, which criminologists estimate to be six times greater than the number of rapes reported by police departments to the FBI's *Uniform Crime Report*. The reason this crime statistic is so insecure is that traditionally rape victims have been badly abused by our criminal justice system. Indeed, women were often degraded, insulted, and humiliated by lawyers for the accused man, particularly if they had been drinking, had had numerous sexual experiences, were dressed provocatively, or were divorced. These proceedings in the courts reflected total male superiority and gender inequality. There were indeed rapes which were punished by the full force of the law if the victim lived the life of a traditional housewife and was viewed as a man's woman, that is, his property.[280]

Traditionally also, the law exempted husbands from being charged with the rape of the wife if the husband and wife were legally living together. This meant that marriage was a legal defense against a charge of rape, a defense which has been abolished in all 50 states, although it is extremely difficult to prove rape between married partners.[281]

Rape victims are frequently distrusted. The complaining woman is often closely questioned as to her character, sexual history, and nature of the event. Lawyers for the defense accuse the victim and protect the violent male. Lawyers will also attempt to picture the complaining woman as a person of poor moral character so as to cast doubt on the claim of non-consent to the sexual intercourse. There were even some states which required a third party as a corroborating witness to a rape. This was seldom available. These aspects of the common law shifted the attention from the offender to the victim. This caused rape victims to repeatedly complain that they felt as if they were on trial and that they were responsible for the rape because of how they acted or because they didn't resist strongly enough.[282]

One of the results of this system has been that jurors convicted defendants of rape in a small minority of cases. This means that unless there are aggravating circumstances, juries are more critical of the victim than the perpetrator, inferring that the victim placed herself in a hazardous situation and therefore had to take the blame for the consequences. This kind of reasoning is disputed by criminologists, who insist that it is the offender and never the victim or the target of the offense who must be held responsible. Such activities as drinking or hitchhiking leads many juries to the conclusion that nice girls are not raped and bad girls shouldn't complain.[283]

In the 1970s, violent crime in the United States increased to such an extent that the criminal justice system was hardly able to deal with all the offenders. Feminists at that time found the rates of conviction for rape unacceptable, since a rape that was reported to the police had approximately one chance in eight of resulting in conviction.[284]

After the 1970s, feminists succeeded in bringing about a number of changes in rape legislation. One of these was the abolition of capital punishment. Other changes were a graduated form of penalties for rape, the reformulation of rape statutes to a sex neutral definition of rape, and the change in terminology from rape to sexual assault or criminal sexual conduct. The abolition of capital punishment for rape led to the inevitable conclusion that the crime of rape is less horrible than it was in the past. In New Jersey and several other states, the maximum penalty for rape or criminal sexual assault was reduced from a mandatory 30 years to a maximum of 20 years in prison. This reduction in penalty for rape means a lesser amount of social condemnation for this offense. A number of legislatures also recognized various degrees of rape based on such factors as amount of intimidation, force, or injury resulting from the attack. The purpose of this change was that juries were more likely to convict the rapist to one of these alternatives without feeling excessively punitive. In the past, rape had no degrees. A woman was either raped or she was not raped. Because there were only these two alternatives, many a jury voted that the defendant was innocent and did so because they did not want to apply the death penalty nor send the accused to prison for 30 years.[285]

Although rape is largely an offense against women, there are also men who are raped. This kind of victimization of men occurs in almost all American prisons, not only because some prisoners are homosexuals, but also because hetero sex is largely unavailable. Even such conjugal visits are limited to a few prisoners on the grounds of good behavior or because they are well liked by the guards or administrators of the prison.

Furthermore, rape in prison is largely an expression of power by physically large strong men over weaker men. Since prisons value physical violence and domination, rape is just one expression of values which contradict the expectations of civil society. While rape involves penetration with consequences for the victim such as injury and major psychological trauma, it turns out that the attempted rape victims did not differ significantly in the immediate and long-term response to the sexual assault.

Chapter 9. The Assault on Ethnicity: The Fate of Native Americans

"We hold these truths to be self-evident, that all men are created equal, that they are endowed by their Creator with certain unalienable Rights, that among these are Life, Liberty, and the Pursuit of Happiness." — The Declaration of Independence.

The cruelties inflicted on Native Americans in this country directly contradict this magnificent declaration. There can be no question that Native Americans have been deprived of the "unalienable rights" promised in 1776 to all men.

Long before the United States was founded, at a time of the arrival of Europeans to the North American continent, there were about 500 Native American nations here. The population of North America, it has been estimated, was approximately 1 million in the 16th century. Then the Europeans systematically drove the natives from their lands, destroying their way of life and a destroying their various tribal cultures.

This deliberate cruelty was augmented by the diseases Europeans imported into North America, so that the native population suffered such a great decline that Europeans believed that the American Indian would soon be extinct. In fact, by the year 1800, the number of Native Americans had been reduced to only 600,000. 50 years later, the wars of extermination against the Indians had reduced that population by another half to 300,000. In 1834 alone, 4000 Indians died on a forced march from their homeland in Georgia to reservations in Oklahoma and Arkansas, a distance of nearly 800 miles. The reason for removing Indians from Georgia was greed, because gold had been discovered in the North Georgia mountains. For that reason, Congress passed the Indian Removal Act in 1830, and

President Andrew Jackson quickly signed the bill into law. That law was challenged in the Supreme Court, which ruled that the Cherokee nation was sovereign and would therefore have to agree to be removed. Nevertheless, Pres. Jackson ordered Gen. Winfield Scott and the United States Army to invade Cherokee nation land so as to remove them. Therefore, men, women, and children were taken from their land, herded into makeshift forts with minimal facilities and food, and then forced to march 1000 miles. As a result, 4000 Cherokees died on the route, which became known as the Trail Of Tears.[286]

Likewise, the Sioux were forced off their land in the northern United States and southern Canada, and delivered to a reservation because of the discovery of gold in the Black Hills of the Dakotas in 1889. This was followed by the Wounded Knee Massacre in South Dakota. This occurred on December 29, 1890, when the Seventh US Cavalry slaughtered 300 men, women, and children without provocation. The victims were members of the Sioux nation who had left their reservation to seek refuge in the "badlands".[287]

From then until the middle of the 20th century, an effort was made by anthropologists and ethnographers to assure the survival of Indian culture, followed by a resurgence in Indian self-awareness, cultural differentiation, and self-assertion at the end of the 20th century.[288]

Dispossessing the Locals

Immediately after the American War for Independence, George Washington, our first president, wrote to a congressional committee that it should draw a boundary line where Native Americans, labeled Indians, were to live and beyond which "we will endeavor to restrain our people from hunting and settling." Subsequently, such boundary lines described ever narrower spaces and the land behind them smaller, until finally Indians were forcibly settled on some land generally called reservations. Evidently, Washington's belief that the Indian "barbarians" should be isolated was also supported by most other Americans, including later presidents such as Andrew Jackson who demanded that all Indians be removed to an Indian territory.[289]

Consequently, the United States made a number of efforts to not only isolate the Indian population, but also to cause their disappearance by rejecting the idea of communal ownership of land, which is the very heart of Indian culture and survival. Therefore, despite a number of treaties between the United States and several Indian nations, Congress included in the appropriations act of 1871 a rider to the effect that "Indians should no longer be acknowledged or recognized as an independent tribe or power with whom the United States may contract by treaty." Furthermore it was proposed that all Indian landholdings be broken up and given to private individuals, so that they could eventually be bought by non-Indians as the Indians assimilated into the Euro-American population and disappeared altogether. This view was further underscored in 1878 when Congress passed the Allotment Act , once more seeking to break up all mutually held Indian lands. In 1895, the Supreme Court ruled that the Indian nations were indeed sovereign governments. Then finally in 1934, Congress enacted The Indian Reorganization Act, which has brought the loss of tribal lands to an end.[290]

According to the United States Census, there are approximately 2,375,000 Indians in the United States, including the natives of Alaska. Of these Native Americans, about 219,000 live on the 10 largest reservations, and another 219,000 live on smaller reservations; all others live on privately held land. Since 1934, Congress has repeatedly dealt with Indian concerns, including The Indian Self-Determination and Education Assistance Act of 1975 and the 1989 US Senate report of the Select Committee on Indian Affairs. That report sought a reduction in federal programs supporting Indians living on a reservation, although tribal leaders called that report a blueprint for disaster.[291]

Reservations about Reservations

That disaster has been the abject poverty in which most Native Americans have lived for all the centuries since the coming of the Europeans. It continues today. American Indians are the poorest ethnic minority in the United States. The United States Census reported in 2014 that the real median household income for Native Americans was $36,641. This was 69% of the national average of $55,515.[292] This means that in Arizona, Utah, and New Mexico, a large number of Native Americans live in houses without running water, sewage facilities, or electricity services. As a result, Native Americans have significantly lower life expectancy and higher infant mortality rates than other Americans. If ever the stigma directed at Native Americans had real consequences, a shorter lifespan and more childhood deaths are the most significant.

Unemployment rates on the reservations are approximately 50%, which is due in part to the lack of education among Native Americans. Native Americans also suffer from a considerable amount of alcoholism.

Alcoholism, according to the Institute of psychiatry at the Stanford School of Medicine, comes about in four stages. These are: craving a strong need to drink, loss of control in that one cannot stop drinking once drinking has started, physical dependence consisting of withdrawal symptoms, such as nausea, sweating, shakiness, and anxiety after a time of heavy drinking, and tolerance which, is a need to drink greater amounts of alcohol in order to get high.

All this affects Native Americans, whose youth become socialized into the culture of alcohol at an early age. Approximately 20% of Indian youth between the seventh and 12th grades belong in that category. Many Native American youth exhibit an experimental pattern of drinking through adolescence and that becomes one of the biggest identifiers of binge drinking later in life. Reservations have high rates of alcohol and substance abuse, which leads to academic failure, delinquency, violent criminal behavior, suicide, and alcohol related mortality among Native Americans which is far greater than the rest of the United States population. As a result, American Indian populations are much more susceptible to alcoholism and related diseases and deaths. In fact, the mortality due to alcohol was as much as 5.6 times higher among the Indian population than among the US population in general. Alcohol-related fatal car accidents are three times more prevalent among Indians than the general population and alcohol was shown to be a factor in 69% of all suicides of American Indians. In addition, domestic violence is highly prevalent among Native Americans, with devastating effects on individuals, families, and communities. Usually substance abuse and the excessive use of alcohol are characteristics of the offender and the victim of domestic violence.[293]

There are those who seek to attribute the poverty, lack of education, and alcoholism of Native Americans to some kind of genetic factor or inherited condition. There is no evidence for this. Instead, the manner in which Native Americans have been treated in this country is responsible for these difficulties. There can be little doubt that anyone having been so abused would not also develop such problems or difficulties of a similar nature.

Reclaiming Some Rights

In more recent years, despite all these handicaps, many Indians have continued to retain a sense of significance for their own culture in order to avoid subjugation and remain sovereign nations within their reservations. It is important to remember that American Indian culture is of course diverse, because there are about 500 different Indian tribes and other groupings in this country.[294]

Native Americans differ from all other minorities in this country in that no one else has legal standing to negotiate with the United States government on a government-to-government basis. To ensure these rights, the American Indian Movement was founded in 1968. This movement augmented the National Congress of American Indians, but has more radical aims than the old organization. The American Indian Movement made a considerable effort to conclude some 600 treaties between the United States government and various Indian nations.

Furthermore, they sought the return of Indian lands taken from the native population by demanding the enlargement of reservations now in existence. That demand has been consistently denied and has led to some unfortunate and violent confrontations. The worst example of such a confrontation occurred in June 1975. At that time events took place on the Pine Ridge Reservation in South Dakota which led Democratic Senator Frank Church of Idaho to declare that the FBI had "engaged in lawless conduct and responded to deep-seated social problems by creating violence and unrest."[295]

Sen. Church referred to a firefight between the FBI and Native Americans. As a result of that firefight, Leonard Peltier, a leader in the American Indian Movement, was convicted of killing two FBI agents and was therefore sentenced to life in prison. Numerous appeals in that case give rise to the strong possibility that Peltier is not guilty. In any event, that encounter and so many other grievances on the part of the Indian nations against the government have made Native Americans suspicious of the Bureau of Indian Affairs and other government agencies assigned to deal with them.[296]

Because of the abject poverty of American Indians both on reservations and in the cities, another demand has been the increase in federal dollars to remedy poverty and unemployment. That request has been granted to Native Americans by the introduction of a number of federal programs supporting various benefits. First there is the United States Indian Health Service, which provides healthcare of every kind without co-payment for Indians living on a reservation. The Department of Education also provides Native Americans with a number of impact aid programs. This means that school districts with a large number of Indians receive a large amount of aid designed to help with the operating budget of the school or provide Indian language instruction or support numerous other functions. The Department of Education also supports tribal colleges, which are two-year community programs. Furthermore, "treaty money" has been given to numerous Indians in lump sums of $10,000 at the age of their maturity.

It should also be noted that Indians who live and work on reservations are exempt from a number of taxes. This pertains particularly to gambling casinos, which have grown in number on reservations and have provided an income for many who live there. Child care is also federally funded on Indian reservations. Labeled Head Start, this program does not apply only to Indians. It includes funding of meals, healthcare, and education for children on reservations. Welfare regulations in several states exempt Indians from the welfare reform laws, particularly the work requirement. All of this applies to anyone who is 1/8 Indian, so that a good number of people benefit from this program who are not truly associated with Indian culture and heritage.[297]

There are those who view with envy all these efforts to help the natives of North America. The truth is, however, that these programs create a stigma of helplessness and dependency for those who take advantage of them. These programs have not aided the Indian community as they were designed to do. There are those who have left their jobs and abandoned their ambitions because those programs have crippled their initiative. Worse, these programs have left the impression that all Indians are lazy, dependent, and incompetent and therefore stigmatized. The truth is that there are Indian businessmen, ranchers, doctors, scholarship students, farmers, and many others who do not use any of these government programs and do not exhibit any of the characteristics that dependency and lack of initiative invariably produce.

Origins of Stereotypes

Native Americans are plagued with being portrayed in a manner unrelated to their real lives. This is because there is a mythical so-called Indian was invented by novelists and later by the entertainment industry. One of the first to write about Indians without reference to the facts concerning them was Charles Brockton Brown, who wrote a novel called *Edgar Huntley*. This was followed in short order by Washington Irving's *Sketchbook*, which includes "Traits of the Indian character" and which launch the "noble savage" stereotype into American literature, emphasizing the defeat of the Indians but also their "fierce satisfaction and draining the last dregs of bitterness" from bed defeat.[298]

James Fenimore Cooper (1789–1851) did more than any other American author to fix stereotypes upon the reputation of the American Indian. He did this with the publication of several novels between 1823 and 1841. Born in Burlington, New Jersey, he spent his adult life in Cooperstown, New York. He wrote *The Pioneer, The Last of the Mohicans, The Deer Slayer, The Prairie*, and *The Path Finder*. None of these novels had any relationship to the native culture he claimed to portray. The message of these novels was that the "red man" was being extinguished by the inexorable advance of Western civilization. Of course, Native Americans are not red, nor are they the natives of India — and therefore are not Indians. All that didn't bother Cooper, whose inventions entered into popular beliefs concerning Native Americans. Cooper did not know any "Indians" but admired traits that his imagination attributed to them. Cooper also recognized the cruelties and victimization of the Native Americans by the European invaders of their land.[299]

Not so Samuel Langhorne Clemens (1835–1910), who called himself Mark Twain. An inveterate bigot, Twain attacked Jews, Catholics, blacks, and Native Americans alike, showing a particular animosity to so-called Indians in his twin novels *Tom Sawyer* and *Huckleberry Finn*. Twain also wrote an essay called "Fenimore Cooper's Literary Offenses" in which he was evidently motivated to savage Cooper because the latter had some admiration for his, albeit fictional, Indians.

French authors also contributed in creating mythical Indians. The explorer Jacques Cartier wrote that giants were populating the area north of Jamestown in Virginia and dog headed natives were shown on 16th century maps of North America. Cannibalism was attributed to various Indian tribes, but in fact seemed only to be true of some South American Indians, but not Eskimos, who were nevertheless included in that practice by European writers.

In 1855, Henry W. Longfellow published *The Song of Hiawatha*, a lengthy poem which ends in the absurd command by the Indian hero to his people instructing them to welcome the Jesuits who had come from Europe to bring the good life to the natives. Longfellow did not hesitate to label "the Jews the tribe accursed" even as he fed his Christian audience the myth that the Indians were "waiting to behold the strangers" waiting to receive the message "of Christian and Western superiority, truth and the good life."[300]

Numerous other American authors added to the list of nonsense written about the American Indian, including John Greenleaf Whittier, Mayne Reed, and Alfred Riggs. In addition to these American authors, the German author Karl May added a great deal to the mythological Indian when he published his novel *Winnetou* in 1892. That book and other stories by May predicted the total extinction of the Indian on the grounds that he stood in the way of inevitable progress. May's novel has been so popular in Europe that it has repeatedly been made into various movies in which actors of every European nationality have been featured. May's books contain absurd descriptions of Indians and adventures utterly foreign to Indian experience. In *Winnetou*, Germans read about the love of the Indian for his German white brother. Since May wanted all Indians to become extinct, his hero Winnnetou does not marry. May's heroes are utterly indifferent to material wealth and have no income whatever. How they survive this lack of funds is never mentioned, even as May deplores Yankees and other greedy business types.

All told, May introduced Europeans to an American Indian who never existed but whom many German visitors still seek to see on coming to this country, more than a century after May invented him. German speaking travelers frequently visit American Indian reservations expecting to see the spiritually superior but materially uninterested "pure red men," only to find reality to be quite otherwise.[301]

There can be little doubt that the entertainment industry has contributed greatly to the stigma associated with Indian life in this country. Numerous movies shown in theaters and on television have portrayed Indians as absolute barbarians. *Dances with Wolves,* produced in 1990, is at least willing to let the Lakota tribe have normal human emotions, even as the Pawnees are portrayed as utter barbarians. The movie does not mention that the Lakota tribe was forced onto reservations in the 1880s. Even more astounding is *The Last of the Mohicans,* written by James Fenimore Cooper. This book leaves the impression that the Mohicans have died out. That must come as a tremendous surprise to the Mohegans, who live in Connecticut to this day. Yet even more unrealistic is the Disney production of Pocahontas. Here children are taught that Indians sing with forest animals and that Indian women wear provocative clothes and have the figure of a Barbie doll. The truth is that Pocahontas was only 12 years old when she met John Smith, he never married her, and died in England at the age of twenty-two. Furthermore, the Powhatan Confederacy was nearly slaughtered by English colonists while most died of disease. None of this is found in the Hollywood version of events.

Today the mythical Indian continues to exist on the television screen. Innumerable Western movies depict the Indian that has been drawn by the novelists of the previous century. He is a savage but nevertheless an admirable, always truthful, honest warrior. He is the loser in the battle for control of his land but he is morally superior to the evil white manipulators who never speak the truth. Nevertheless, the depiction of Indians in movies and on television is racist throughout. According to this form of entertainment, Indians are endlessly fighting either for themselves or as allies of one or another white faction. As Ward Churchill has phrased it: "The public perception of the historical existence of Native Americans is of beings who spend their time serving as little other than figurative pop-up targets for non-Indian guns." In the overwhelming number of stories about Indians written by whites, the Indian was conquered for his own good and to effect betterment and to continue progress. All of these narratives are cultural fictions and fabrications which suit the writers and their allies in explaining the past and the present without dealing with the facts concerning Indian stigmatization and genocide on this continent.[302]

Even more gross and unreal are many television cartoons about Indians electronically fed to small children every day. These cartoons portray Indians as savages with the result that all over the television world, in Europe, America, and other areas, children play such games as "Cowboys and Indians," even though it was the United States Army, not cowboys, who fought the Indians. In such portrayals, Indians do not speak like normal human beings but grunt "ugh," with the result that there are millions of Americans and other television viewers who really believe that Indians, if they speak at all, speak in monosyllabic burps. Then there is the expression "Indian givers," which implies that the Indians took back what they once gave. The truth is exactly the opposite. It is the United States government that has so often violated treaties with numerous Indian nations that the phrase "US Government givers" would be far more appropriate.[303]

Those who have reviewed American history books concerning Indians have alleged that many of these books fail to include anything whatsoever about the natives of this country or that they include a kind of "feel-good" history that pretends that all the native people of the Western Hemisphere are content with their fate, namely, subjugation and loss of their culture and civilization. In fact, it is alleged that many historians teach that Indians were just an obstacle to be overcome by Christians who came from Europe to civilize the continent and rescue the natives from themselves.

Then there is a different stereotype. This is the belief that all Indians are "noble savages" who were generous, nature loving, and pure in heart, only to be seduced into cruelty and savagery by the evils of European civilization. That stereotype always includes the introduction of "firewater," i.e., alcohol, to the Indians, which according to legend makes Indians far more violent and bizarre than European drunks, giving rise to the meme of the "drunken Indians."

There are also many drunken fraternity brothers in every college. Overall, American adults who are not Indians drink 2.5 gallons of wine, 32 gallons of beer, and 1.8 gallons of liquor a year. This means that alcohol is more popular than either coffee or milk, which are consumed at a rate of 21.1 and 24.7 gallons respectively. In view of this popularity of alcoholic beverages in the United States and the large number of known and hidden alcoholics in the Euro-American population, it is evident that the stigma of the "drunken Indian" is a product of prejudice.[304] There can be no question that there are Americans of European descent who drink as much as any Indian.

A number of researchers report that Native Americans have a higher rate of mortality from alcoholism than the United States population generally,[305] but this does not mean that Native Americans drink more than all other Americans, since alcoholism is widespread in American society. It may mean that alcohol kills Native Americans sooner and more often than others because Native Americans do not eat as well and are more often ill than other Americans.

There are numerous other beliefs about Native Americans common in the general population. Included is the belief that Indians had no civilization until the Europeans arrived here; are treacherous; that Indians had no religion until converted to Christianity; it is even believed that Indians are Stoics who feel no pain. In addition, many people believe that all Indians are alike in that there is only one Indian nation or community. Such a belief would be rejected outright if applied to Europeans. In fact, diversity among American Indians is as great as it is among Europeans.

One belief concerning Native Americans which is not a myth is that Native Americans suffer from a far higher violent crime rate than the average American community. That is a fact. Using the FBI's violent crime rate classification of crimes including homicide, rape, assault, and robbery, it turns out that Native Americans in 2015 had a violent crime rate of 101 per 1000 in the population. The overall crime rate for all Americans is only 41 per 1000 in the population.[306]

It is well-known to criminologists that the poor commit more homicides and other violent crimes than those generally labeled middle-class or upper-class. The reason for this discrepancy is the product of the subculture in which the lives of people in different social classes take place. The poor, who have gained very little from American culture and who have few expectations of success, are far more likely to blame others for their problems and therefore commit more violence against others. Likewise, people with large incomes and rewarding occupations and social honor are more likely to blame themselves for failure and therefore commit more suicide. These findings were already known to Emile Durkheim, one of the fathers of sociology, who discovered these social facts while studying homicide and suicide in the 1890s.[307]

Digging In

In December 2016, the United States Army halted construction of the Dakota Access pipeline after the Sioux Indian tribe demonstrated against the routing of the pipeline across the Missouri River ½ mile from the Rock Sioux reservation border. Those who objected did so because they feared that the pipeline could threaten the drinking water supplies. Furthermore, others were concerned that the pipeline would desecrate sacred land, with particular reference to Indian burial grounds. Such burial grounds attract non-Indian archaeologists, curiosity seekers, and tourists. Although the numerous Indian nations on this continent differ in their various cultures, all become concerned when their burial sites are exposed and turned into museums or treated like a sideshow in the circus. One example is the Dixon Mound in Illinois, first discovered by chiropractor Dr. Don Dixon on his family farm in 1927. Unlike previous discoverers of Indian resting places who removed the bones they discovered. Dixon left the bones in place and covered 234 burial sites with a tent. That tent was later replaced by building, which he operated as a private museum. It attracted professional archaeologists, as well as 49,000 visitors a year. During the 1940s, Dixon sold the site to the state of Illinois, which operated it until 1992. In that year, Governor Jim Edgar decided to cover up the 1000 year old Native American burial ground after a number of Indians protested what they considered a racist display.[308]

Said a Pawnee attorney living in Kansas: "If you desecrate a white grave you go to jail — but if you desecrate an Indian grave you get a Ph.D."[309]

Over the years, a number of states have closed Indian burial grounds, although the remains of thousands of Native Americans lie in museums such as the Smithsonian in Washington, DC, which has 19,000 skeletons or specimens. It is to be noticed that archaeologists do not open up the graves of Euro-Americans but only those of the stigmatized Native Americans. In 1990, the president signed the Native American Grave Protection and Creation Act. This law has led to the development of inventories of American Indian artifacts and remains and the repatriation of those items to Native American nations.

In more recent years and today, the effort to eradicate Indian culture has ceased. Now the Bureau of Indian Affairs attempts to promote a more positive policy toward Indian needs. Furthermore, the courts have ruled in favor of Indian demands concerning the return of land and resources assigned to them by treaties. Nevertheless, a good deal must yet be done to eradicate the kind of racism and prejudice from which the natives of this continent have suffered since the coming of the Europeans more than 400 years ago.

Chapter 10. "That government is best, that governs the least." —Thomas Jefferson

Corruption, and More Corruption: Politics as Usual

Defining Our Terms — What's a Real Scandal

Anyone acquainted with American history cannot overlook that, in every administration of the 44 men who have been President, there has always been some malfeasance in office and in some instances major scandals. There are also politicians who have been involved in so-called sex scandals, which are not included here, as such conduct does not defraud the taxpayer, however unethical it may be considered.

Since politics involves a great deal of controversy, it is inevitable that some points of view are unpopular and its proponents rejected. Lack of popularity is not a scandal; violations of the law are scandals.

There are politicians and officeholders who may violate ethics on occasion or who have been accused of illegal behavior because of a misunderstanding or a political vendetta. Therefore, it is safest to only consider persons who have been found in violation of law by a court, including lobbyists, or by an Inspector General, as in the case of the Veterans' Administration. In the case of a President of the United States, the House of Representatives of the United States and the Senate are empowered to impeach and convict. This definition also applies to other officeholders whose appointments needed Senate confirmation.

Because of the number of elected and appointed officials who engage in multiple illegal schemes to gain illegitimate wealth is so great, it appears difficult to understand their motives.

This is particularly true because evidently numerous such officials have been convicted and imprisoned. Yet, the misuse of power and influence on the part of officeholders seems to continue year in and year out.

A number of explanations for this kind of conduct have been advanced. In 1912, the Columbia professor Thorstein Veblen published his influential book *The Theory of the Leisure Class*. The third chapter of this volume, labeled "Conspicuous Consumption," refers to consumption of goods and services "beyond the minimum required for subsistence and physical efficiency." Veblen refers to "food, drink, narcotics, shelter, services, ornaments, apparel, weapons and accoutrements, amusements, amulets, and idols or divinities. Since the consumption of these more excellent goods is an evidence of wealth, it becomes honorific; and conversely, the failure to consume in due quantity and quality becomes a mark of inferiority and demerit."[310]

According to Veblen, then, American culture pressures people to exhibit wealth or the illusion of wealth as a measure of the worth of a citizen. No doubt, many of those convicted of acquiring illegal gains are motivated by this belief.

Relative deprivation is yet another motivation for seeking money by any means. In 1938, the sociologist Robert K. Merton (Meyer Schkolnik) published his seminal article "Social Structure and Anomie," which sought to explain crime and deviance. Merton wrote: "...tension generated by the desire to win...is relieved when the cult of success has become completely dominant. Further, said Merton, "...the emotional supports of the rules are largely vitiated by cultural exaggeration of the success goal." This means that willingness to break the rules in order to make as much money as possible is not a psychiatric issue but is the consequence of cultural imperatives which devolve upon the person in the same manner as accommodating all the other cultural conditions which American society provides.[311]

Edwin H. Sutherland, sometimes called the father of American criminology, provided the Theory of Differential Association as an explanation for criminal conduct. In sum, Sutherland wrote:

> Criminal behavior is learned behavior by interacting with other people in small groups. Learning about crime includes learning the techniques of committing crimes as well as learning the motivation and attitudes towards crime. The law expresses what is right and wrong to an offender. Therefore offenders know what they're doing is wrong, however a person becomes criminal because of frequent exposition to repeated criminal scenarios through association with others by means

of frequency, duration, priority, and intensity. Therefore any person of any background can become a criminal.[312]

It is also important to remember that both appointed and elected officials have the power and the influence to help many a citizen achieve their ambitions, whatever they may be. Therefore, political operatives are far more subject to the temptation of accepting a bribe than the vast majority of Americans, who have no such power and are therefore not the targets of those seeking to corrupt them.

The Scandal is Appointed and Elected Officials Who Bilk Us All

No doubt the resignation of this 37th President of the United States, Richard M. Nixon, is the most widely known and documented political scandal ever to occur in the United States. It is not possible to recite here at length all the events surrounding the so-called Watergate Scandal, as the media have called these occurrences. Therefore it is best to recite here only the articles of impeachment against Richard Nixon which were adopted by the house judiciary committee on June 27, 1974.

Nixon was impeached for "high crimes and misdemeanors." Article 1 of this impeachment holds that the president has prevented, obstructed, and impeded the administration of justice. Here Richard Nixon is accused of making false and misleading statements to authorized investigative officers of the United States. Further he is accused of withholding relevant evidence from such investigative officers and condoning and counseling witnesses to give false and misleading statements to such officers. He is further accused of paying substantial sums to silence or influence the testimony of witnesses concerning unlawful entry and other illegal activities. In article 2 of the impeachment, President Nixon is accused of initiating discriminatory audits and income tax investigations in violation of the rights of American citizens. He was further accused of using the Federal Bureau of Investigation and the Secret Service to conduct electronic surveillance of citizens which had nothing to do with security of the United States. Nixon was also accused of encouraging and knowingly supporting unlawful entry into the headquarters of the Democratic National Committee and of "willfully disobeying subpoenas issued by the committee of the Judiciary of the House of Representatives."[313]

Because four governors of Illinois have been sent to jail for various kinds of corruption, it is safe to say that that state has seen more malfeasance in political office than any other state in the union. The most recent such conviction was that of Rod Blagojevich, who had won two terms as Illinois governor before being sentenced to 14 years in prison for a host of crimes as alleged by the prosecution. Blagojevich and his wife had an income of $286,920 in 2005 and even more one year earlier. Nevertheless, Blagojevich was convicted of seeking to sell the United States Senate seat vacated by Barack Obama on his election to President of the United States. Blagojevich solicited a number of persons in an effort to gain money for himself in return for appointing someone to the Senate seat until another election would come around. He was also convicted of demanding a $50,000 campaign contribution from an executive of Children's Memorial Hospital in exchange for $8 million in state healthcare funding. He also was convicted of demanding money from a person before signing a bill that benefited him. He was further charged with extortion in connection with funding for a school. In sum, a jury found Blagojevich guilty of 17 counts of corruption.[314]

In September 2006, George Ryan, former governor of Illinois, was sentenced to 6½ years in federal prison for racketeering and fraud. He was convicted of using taxpayers' money towards his campaign, lying to federal agents, and handing out contracts and leases to his friends in exchange for gifts, including island vacations for himself and his family. Ryan was applauded all over the world after he abolished the death penalty in Illinois. Unlike most politicians, he was not a lawyer, but a pharmacist who rose from one political office to another until he became governor. He was released in 2013.[315]

In December 1972, Otto Kerner, then a Judge of the United States Court of Appeals, was indicted for conspiracy, mail fraud, income tax evasion, and lying to a grand jury. All these charges related to the time when Kerner was governor of Illinois from 1960 to 1968. A federal jury found Otto Kerner guilty of arranging favorable racing dates for horse racing association owners in return for Racing Association stock sold to him at prices far below their market value. He was also found guilty of concealing his racing stock profits on his income tax returns and lying about this to a grand jury. Kerner served in the US Army during the Second World War and rose to the rank of Major General. Until his death in 1976, Kerner insisted that he was an innocent man who had been the victim of a politically ambitious prosecutor acting on behalf of President Nixon and Attorney General John Mitchell. Kerner was sentenced to three years in prison but served only seven months because he was found to have lung cancer. He died in May 1976.[316]

In August 1987, former governor Daniel Walker of Illinois pleaded guilty to fraud and perjury charges. Walker had borrowed the limit allowed him from the First American Savings and Loan Association, of which he was chairman and executive officer. After he had reached the limit allowed under federal banking regulations, he asked his son and a close friend to seek loans from First American. He then used about two thirds of the more than

$205,000 they had borrowed to meet personal obligations, which led to the charge of the misapplication of bank funds. Walker was also charged for fraud involving $1.1 million in loans from five banks in Illinois Florida and Arkansas. Walker was also charged with failing to include the $3 million in liabilities on a loan application and overstating his income. He was sentenced to three years in prison on charges of bribery, tax evasion, and perjury, but released in 1975 because of ill health.[317]

It Is indeed remarkable that several governors of Illinois were all imprisoned for illegitimate financial dealings, which may be summarized as greed. It is peculiar that former Governor Blagojevich did not recognize that his predecessor was in jail for financial miscreancy, and that that was also true of two other former governors.

From 1977 to 1980, the F.B.I. entrapped a number of public officials willing to accept money and in return use their government influence on behalf of the contributors. The scheme which the FBI invented in order to entrap their targets consisted of creating a fictitious corporation called "Abdul Enterprises." This nonexistent corporation appeared to be headed by Sheikh Yassir Habib of Abu Dhabi. In fact this so-called sheikh was an F.B.I. Informant named Melvin Weinberg. The so-called sheikh reputedly wanted to invest and immigrate to the United States. The investment was to be an Atlantic City casino. The mayor of Camden New Jersey, Angelo Errichetti, agreed to use his political resources to find a public official willing to exchange political influence for money. Errichetti knew almost all important politicians in New Jersey. He therefore introduced the FBI agent posing as an Arab sheikh to New Jersey Senator Harrison Williams.[318] Despite his prestigious and highly paid position, Williams was willing to involve himself in a dubious enterprise reputedly financed by an Arab sheikh.

Weinberg posed as fabulously wealthy and willing to bribe American officials with immigration problems and investment projects. In fact, Weinberg surreptitiously videotaped or tape recorded his meetings and conversations with officials and their co-conspirators. Sen. Williams was charge with interceding with a New Jersey official to gain a decision from the state's Casino Control Commission that would have saved a casino developer $30 million. The company which had a controlling interest in the casino employed the senator's wife. Sen. Williams and his wife also received shares in a carpet recycling enterprise and used his influence to get a government contract for a titanium mine for the benefit of an Arab sheikh in which Williams had a concealed interest. Sen. Williams conspired to sell the titanium enterprise to a second group for $70 million profit, of which Williams would get 18% or $12.6 million in the end. Sen. Williams was convicted of bribery and conspiracy and receiving an unlawful gratuity as well as conflict of interest and aiding a racketeering enterprise.

In addition to Sen. Williams, a number of other politicians were also jailed as a consequence of the Abscam investigations. Richard Kelly, a Florida politician and Congressman who had been a prosecutor and judge himself, was convicted of accepting a $25,000 bribe. Likewise, Florida representative John Jenrette and Camden Mayor Errichetti were convicted and served time in prison on similar charges.

Not only elected officials but also appointed officials have violated the trust of the American people by truly criminal behavior while in office. This pertains particularly to the treatment of veterans by the Veterans' Administration hospitals across the country. There is absolute evidence that hospital administrators and others have committed deliberate fraud in order to cheat sick veterans of the opportunity to be treated for wounds and illnesses. An example of this kind of fraudulent conduct was the fate of 71-year-old U.S. Navy veteran Thomas Breen, who rushed to the Phoenix VA hospital on September 28, 2013, with blood in his urine and a history of cancer. His family said that he was sent home with instructions that he was to be seen within one week by a primary care doctor or urologist, and a note on his patient chart said that the situation was urgent. After being sent home, his family said that they were told that there was a seven-month waiting list in that there were other critical patients. Thomas Breen died on November 30, 2013. The VA called a week later, on December 6, to make an appointment — after Breen had died.[319]

Appointed politicians are not immune to violating the trust placed in them. An example is Felipe Sixto, who pleaded guilty to theft from a federally aid program. He had been Special Assistant for Intergovernmental Affairs to President George W. Bush. Sixto admitted to stealing $579,274 by overcharging The Center for a Free Cuba, of which he was the administrator. The United States Agency for International Development gives the Center for Free Cuba millions of dollars a year for rent, travel, and equipment such as shortwave radios and laptops. Sixto was also assigned to deal with state legislators, Native American groups, and Hispanic officials in connection with health, labor, transportation, the environment, and energy. He was sentenced to 30 months in prison for stealing nearly $600,000 for personal use.[320]

In 2003, James W. Treffinger, the Essex County executive in New Jersey, was the leading Republican candidate for the United States Senate. However, in May of that year he pleaded guilty in Federal District Court to obstruction of justice and mail fraud. He had solicited an illegal $15,000 campaign contribution from a company in exchange for a county contract.

He had also hired two people in county jobs who instead worked exclusively on his political campaign. It is notable that Treffinger was first elected county executive in 1995 on a promise to clean up its government. He was sentenced to go to prison for 10 to 16 months.[321]

In January 2007, Ohio Republican Congressman Robert W. Ney was sentenced to 30 months in prison because he traded luxury vacation trips, skybox seats at sporting events, campaign contributions, and expensive meals for inserting amendments to benefit the clients of the lobbyist Jack Abramoff. Ney accepted gifts worth more than $170,000. Ney also helped the client of Abramoff to win a multibillion-dollar contract to provide wireless communication services to the US Capitol. In addition, the Congressman inserted in the Congressional Record comments bolstering Abramoff, who sought to take ownership of a Florida casino company. Ney also stayed at a luxury hotel in Lake George, New York, at the expense of Abramoff because he used his congressional influence to gain a passport for the daughter of an Abramoff client who wished to take a trip to Russia.[322]

Not only Congressman Ney but a number of other elected and appointed government officials were corrupted by the activities of Jack Abramoff, who amassed a fortune by showering gifts on congressional and executive branch officials. Abramoff and other lobbyists associated with him defrauded Indian tribes of $66 million. These activities came to an end when Jack Abramoff was sentenced to six years in jail.[323]

In 2013, United States representative Rick Renzi agreed to sponsor legislation authorizing an ad exchange that would allow the Resolution Copper Mining Corporation to excavate a huge ore deposit in Arizona in return for a land swap measure that would benefit Renzi and his business associates. Renzi was convicted of 32 counts of extortion, conspiracy and fraud over numerous years. Renzi evidently siphoned money from clients of his insurance company to pay for his congressional campaign. After having been elected Renzi used his political power in an extortion conspiracy. Renzi was convicted and sentenced to a three-year prison term.[324]

One of the most publicized cases of criminal conduct by a United States congressman was the conviction of William J. Jefferson on bribery, racketeering, money laundering, and other charges in 2009. Jefferson represented New Orleans, Louisiana, when a jury found him guilty on 11 charged counts, including wire fraud and conspiracy. Jefferson used his position as an elected member of the House of Representatives to corruptly seek, solicit, and direct that things of value were to be paid to himself and his family members in exchange for his performance of official acts to advance the interests of people and businesses who offered him bribes. He accepted hundreds of thousands of dollars' worth of bribes in the form of payments from monthly fees or retainers, consulting fees, percentage shares of revenues and profits, flat fees for items sold, and stock ownership in the companies seeking his official assistance. Jefferson also utilized congressional staff members to promote businesses and business persons. This included telecommunications in Nigeria, Ghana, and elsewhere; oil concessions in Equatorial Guinea; satellite transmission contracts in Botswana, Equatorial Guinea, and the Republic of the Congo. Jefferson was sentenced to 13 years in prison on November 13, 2009.[325]

Americans were indeed astonished when in April 1996 Representative Dan Rostenkowski pleaded guilty to charges of mail fraud and was sentenced to 17 months in prison. Rostenkowski, an Illinois Democrat, was the most prominent lawmaker ever to go to prison for corruption. Rostenkowski had served in Congress for 36 years and was chairman of the Ways and Means Committee. He was found guilty of sending official payroll checks from his office in Washington to his office in Chicago to pay employees who didn't do official work but performed personal services for him. He was also charged with embezzlement from the house post office and using his official expense account to buy cars for his personal use.[326]

Melvin Paisley, assistant secretary of the Navy during the Reagan administration, was found to have accepted hundreds of thousands of dollars in bribes. He was found guilty of bribery and served four years in prison. Nine government officials were also convicted, as were 42 Washington consultants and corporate heads and seven military contractors. Paisley admitted accepting hundreds of thousands of dollars in bribes from Navy contractors he helped while he was the senior Navy official responsible for research, engineering, and systems. Paisley helped a military manufacturer of pilotless reconnaissance planes with several contracts in return for cash sent to a Swiss bank , and also provided confidential information to the Sperry Corporation to win a bid for the Aegis weapons system. Paisley had been a member of the Army Air Corps in World War II, where he received the Distinguished Service Cross and the Silver Star. After the Second World War, Melvin Paisley was employed by the Boeing Corporation, where he became international sales manager. On leaving Boeing and going to the Defense Department, he received a severance package worth hundred and $183,000 from Boeing. Nevertheless he accepted bribes.

Peter Voss, Vice Chairman of the Board of Governors of the United States Postal Service, was sentenced to four years in prison and fined $11,000 for his scheme to defraud the Postal Service of millions of dollars. Voss pleaded guilty to three federal counts of fraud and embezzlement. He had taken $20,000 in kickbacks to help a Texas company win a $250 million Postal Service equipment contract. Voss also admitted embezzling $1,180 of Postal

Service funds by submitting vouchers for first-class airline tickets he did not use.

Few members of the House of Representatives have ever achieved the popularity of Mario Biaggi. Biaggi was a highly decorated New York City police officer and later a 10 term Democratic congressman from the Bronx. Biaggi began his working life as a shoe shiner and later carried the mail before becoming a police officer. In 23 years on the force, he was wounded 11 times, killed two suspects in self-defense, and became a law enforcement legend, winning dozens of citations for valor and international recognition. He had saved a woman on a runaway horse, shot and killed a man who tried to stab him with an ice pick, and also shot and killed a man who tried to rob him at gunpoint. He was wounded in the shootout but won the Medal of Honor, the Police Department's highest award. Consequently, he was also honored by national police organizations.

Despite all this success, Biaggi accepted free vacations from former Brooklyn Democratic leader Meade Esposito in exchange for using his influence to help a ship repair company that was a main client of Esposito's insurance agency. He was convicted of accepting an illegal gratuity and obstructing justice, sentenced to 2 ½ years in prison and fined $500,000. The House ethics committee recommended that Biaggi be expelled - the most severe penalty. In 1988, Biaggi was charged in the Wedtech scandal of having accepted bribes for assisting Wedtech in getting federal procurement contracts. He was convicted of 15 counts of obstructing justice and accepting illegal gratuities. He was sentenced to eight years imprisonment but was ordered released in 1991 on the grounds of ill health.

The career of Mario Biaggi may appear bizarre, considering his great success, his popularity, and his rise from immigrant poverty to national recognition. Therefore, it is necessary to consider that the United States is a stratified society. This means that Americans are daily confronted within enormous differences between billionaires and homeless people. Because the ladder of income inequality is so great, those who seek to climb it will find that that at every rung there is someone who has yet more money and yet more social honor. With the exceptions of those at the very top, all those on the lower level may well be tempted to use any means at all, including illegal means, to increase their incomes.

There have been politicians who were so popular that they were reelected despite being convicted of various crimes. That was certainly true of James Michael Curley, who was elected mayor of Boston five times. He was convicted of mail fraud and served five months in prison. He was later fined $30,000 for another legal infraction, but his followers donated the money so he could pay the fine. He was imprisoned a second time when he took a civil service examination for a friend. Curley won his first election for mayor in 1913. He then served as Mayor of Boston for 16 years even though he had been jailed twice in his political career. He also served one term in Congress and then won a fourth term as mayor in 1945. After Harry Truman became president of the United States, he pardoned Curley for all his various offenses.[327]

In April of 2002, Representative James Traficant was convicted of racketeering and corruption by a jury that found that he used his office to extract bribes and kickbacks from business executives. He was also convicted of filing false tax returns, racketeering, and forcing his aides to perform chores at his farm in Ohio and houseboat in Washington, DC. He received a sentence of seven years in prison.

In 1983, Traficant acted as his own lawyer at a criminal trial in which he was accused of accepting bribes. Although he did not have a law degree, he was the only defendant representing himself who was ever acquitted of charges based on the Racketeer Influenced and Corrupt Organizations Act.

Traficant was elected to the House of Representatives as a Democrat in the 17th District in Ohio and was reelected eight times.[328]

A Fine History of Scandals — And Fines

We can review American history and find that in every generation there have been those who used their political power illegitimately for private gain. Among those who did so, Albert B. Fall will always be remembered in connection with what finally was called the Teapot Dome Scandal. Teapot Dome is a geological structure in Wyoming which at one time housed the government oil reserves needed by the United States Navy to power its ships. These reserves had at one time been under the control of the Navy Department. However, President Warren Harding assigned control over these reserves to the Department of the Interior. This occurred during the tenure of Albert B. Fall, who was secretary of the interior from 1921 to 1923. Fall had been one of the first two Senators from New Mexico. In 1922, Fall secretly granted the company of oil executive Harry F. Sinclair leases to work the oil reserves for their profit. Fall accepted $100,000 from Sinclair and another $300,000 from Edward Doheny, Sinclair's partner. Four hundred thousand dollars in 1921 was worth about $5 million in 2016. As a consequence of a congressional investigation, Fall was removed from office and imprisoned for one year.[329]

Members of Congress have been convicted of various crimes for so long that we can go back all the way to 1926, when Calvin Coolidge was President, and find that that John Wesley Langley, a representative from Kentucky's 10th congressional district, was convicted of conspiracy to violate the Volstead Act. He had been caught trying to bribe a Prohibition Officer and sent to the federal penitentiary in Atlanta, Georgia. While in prison, he asked his constituents to elect his wife to vindicate his name. Thereupon his wife Catherine Langley campaigned by delivering over 100 speeches, each time glorifying the name of her husband and promising to carry out his goals. Because Prohibition was unpopular in Kentucky and because Catherine Langley had been an active member of the Republican Party, she won the next election and was subsequently reelected in 1928 with 56% of the vote. John Langley was paroled after serving 11 months of his two-year sentence.[330]

Early in the 20th century, in 1905, a major land fraud scandal occurred in Oregon. Speculators and timber companies had illegally obtained large portions of the public lands with the assistance of public officials. Oregon's congressional delegation, including John N. Williamson, a Republican congressman from Oregon, as well as second District and US court commissioner Marion R. Biggs, illegally obtained land claims under the Timber and Stone Act of 1878. This law was designed to allow settlers to claim up to 160 acres of timber and mining land that was unfit for agriculture. Williamson and Biggs subverted the act by paying local residents to take up about 16,000 acres in claims and then immediately selling the land to Dr. Van Gessner, who ran a sheep operation and wanted to use the land for that purpose. After two juries were deadlocked, a third jewelry found Gessner, Williamson, and Gibbs guilty. All three were sentenced to a fine and sent to jail between five and 10 months. Williamson appealed his case to the United States Supreme Court, which overturned the original verdict in 1908. Gessner and Gibbs served their sentences, although President William Taft pardoned both of them four years later.[331]

Professor Domenec Mele has published a list of 10 possible causes of corruption. Mele is professor emeritus of business ethics at the University of Navarra. According to Mele, personal greed and unfettered desire for money and power without regard to moral boundaries is the first cause of corruption. Second, he lists decline of personal ethical sensitivity, due mainly to the lack of education or negative learning experiences. Thirdly, he mentions no sense of service when working in public or private institutions. Here he indicts those who use politics for selfish interests instead of serving the community. Fourth, there are people who are aware of corruption and stay quiet because they lack the courage to denounce corrupt behavior. Fifth, a cultural environment that defends and even admires excuses such as the arguments that everyone does it or that life is short. Sixth, lack of transparency at institutional levels. Seventh, regulations and inefficient controls. Eighth is a slow judicial process involving endless appeals, so that by the time a sentence comes the crime is already forgotten. Ninth, lack of moral criteria in promotion and promotions simply because of loyalty to whoever is in charge or those in control of a party without reference to moral character. Tenth, downplaying or reacting mildly to corruption charges.[332]

Chapter 11. The Fourth Estate: The Failure of American Journalism

Before the French Revolution of 1789, the kings of France and the governments of all other states in Christendom divided the population in their countries into segments called estates. In France, the first estate were the clergy, the second estate the nobility and the third estate everybody else.[333]

The Role of Journalism

This feudal system disappeared with the rise of democracy. Nevertheless, the term "Fourth Estate" entered into the English language to designate journalists, whose role has been to hold those in power accountable to the public who elected them. To that end journalists were considered to be employed to inform the readers of newspapers, and later the listening and viewing audience of radio and television, for what is commonly called "the news". It was assumed that journalists would present the facts without taking sides or becoming partisans to political disputes. This ideal was never really achieved, not only because no one can be absolutely objective in reporting anything but also because during the many years when print journalism was in the ascendancy, competing newspapers would promote the interests of either the Democrat or Republican point of view. That absolute objectivity is really impossible and that final truth can never be achieved is true of journalism as well as all other human endeavors. Even mathematics has been subject to change so that final truth cannot be found anywhere. For example, after centuries of considering Euclid's geometry as the last word, Gauss, Riemann, and Lobachevsky invented non-Euclidean geometry and Georgia Boole created Boolean algebra.

American journalism was at one time thought to be quite reliable, so that Walter Cronkite was considered "the most trusted man in America." Cronkite was, for 19 years from 1960 to 1981, the NBC "anchor" television reporter of the news of the day. Cronkite was called a celebrity so that even in 1995, 14 years after he retired from CBS Evening News, a TV Guide poll ranked Cronkite number one among reporters for being trustworthy and honest.[334]

Cronkite was not the only television reporter who achieved recognition among American television viewers. Both ABC and NBC increased their audiences as newspapers declined so that before the 21st century NBC employed such luminaries as news anchors as John Chancellor, David Brinkley, Tom Brokaw and Roger Mudd. [335]

Cronkite's popularity depended largely on the ever increasing television audience (which grew at the expense of print journalism, so that a considerable number of newspapers failed and were forced to close), in almost all American cities. There was at one time a morning newspaper and an afternoon newspaper. However as television became more and more popular, only the largest cities such as New York, Chicago and Los Angeles, could sustain several print publications. Consequently, by the end of the 1970s most American cities supported only one daily paper. For example, in Cleveland, Ohio, The Cleveland News "folded" in 1960 in favor of the morning Plain Dealer and in Buffalo, New York, The Courier Express, a morning publication, closed in 1985, leaving only the Buffalo News.

As television news and to a lesser extent the radio expanded more and more at the expense of the print media, new television networks developed. In October 1996, Rupert, the owner of News Corporation initiated a new television channel called Fox News. Murdoch claimed that his new channel would be fair and balanced and he also complained that all the other channels exhibited a liberal bias in television news. He therefore championed a conservative alternative on the grounds that most television viewers agreed with him. Subsequently Fox News bureaus were established in Washington, Miami, Chicago, Denver, Los Angeles, San Francisco and in Hong Kong, Jerusalem and London. Twenty years later there can be little doubt that Fox News is highly successful and without question promotes a conservative agenda.[336]

Also in 1996 MSNBC was founded. There are those who claim that MSNBC is devoted to what has been labeled "liberal propaganda." MSNBC was created by NBC News and Microsoft and features commentators and news reporters who without doubt promote a liberal or progressive agenda.[337]

Politicization of the News

With Fox News on one side and MSNBC on the other, 1996 became the opening year for the politicization of news broadcasting on television. Indeed, newspapers, radio and even early television did not always agree on everything and had tendencies to value one point of view over another. However, the proliferation of numerous new television channels at the end of the 1990s was at least one reason for the decline in public support for television news generally, because large numbers of Americans came to believe that they were not given objective facts but propaganda on both sides of the political spectrum. Indeed, there are also true believers on both sides of American political debates who view anyone with an opinion other than their own as undoubtedly belonging to "the flat earth society."

In addition to television, radio has also played its part in promoting different political views. Among radio personalities who have attracted large audiences over the years are Howard Stern and Rush Limbaugh (Leimbach). While Stern is mainly concerned with entertaining the audience by means of sexual innuendo and gross jokes, Rush Limbaugh advances a conservative political agenda which reaches 15 million listeners each week. Together with other radio personalities, Limbaugh is without doubt influential in molding public opinion[338]

Peace Journalism vs. War Journalism

The introduction of several new television channels with different political agendas weakened the neutrality of news reporting considerably. It was however the introduction of peace journalism in the 1970s which created an entirely new relationship between journalists and their readers or audiences. It was at this time that American journalism began to waver in its commitment to report events objectively and to hold those in power accountable. Evidently, journalists who have become partisans to one point of view or another can hardly be expected to report the shortcomings of their favorites to the public. This became particularly evident with the development of peace journalism which is now taught at some schools of journalism such as Park University in Missouri, Regent in Virginia and Quinnipiac (Algonquin for 'original people') University in Connecticut.

In the 1970s, Johan Galtung, a Norwegian scholar, first began using the term "peace journalism" as opposed to "war journalism," by which he meant reporting of the endless wars to which mankind has been subject throughout its entire history. Galtung objected to the common focus on "winning is the only thing". [339] Since absolute objectivity cannot exist, peace journalists believe that they contribute to peace in the world. It is without doubt one of the greatest hopes of mankind to live in peace. Although we have been able to walk on the moon and develop atomic energy we have been unable to learn how to live peaceably together. Christians pray to the Prince of Peace. Jews ask God three times a day for peace on earth and Muslims call their religion the religion of peace. Yet, the whole history of mankind is one of war and killing. Therefore peace journalism is most attractive. Hence Galtung suggests that peace journalism is similar to health journalism and that a good health correspondent helps patients battle against disease while peace journalists helps mankind to avoid war. Thus peace journalism is defined as a more accurate way of framing stories by drawing on the insights of conflict analysis. Jake Lynch and Annabelle McGoldrick, the authors of *Peace Journalism*, claim that peace journalism provides a new road map tracing the connection between journalists, their sources, the stories they cover and the consequences of their reporting. They call this the ethics of journalistic intervention.[340]

Peace Journalism has also been called new journalism, post-realist journalism, solutions journalism, conflict analysis journalism, change journalism, holistic journalism, big picture journalism, open society journalism, developmental journalism, reflective journalism and constructive journalism. By whatever name it may be known, peace journalism seeks to respect and acknowledge all sides of a conflict while keeping in mind that the suffering of all sides is not a substitute for analyzing the conflict. It is essential to peace journalists to establish the real formation or map of the conflict. This means that journalists have to decide that journalists must be part of the solution and not part of the problem.[341]

Peace journalists also seek to report on the invisible effects of the conflict such as psychological trauma or the chances that those involved may become violent in the future. Peace journalism seeks to discover the cause and process of conflict in the effort and initiatives from all sides to encourage peace building. Therefore peace journalists avoid focusing entirely on what divides the parties involved. Hoping to have a more positive influence on conflict situations, peace journalists try to find common ground between conflicting parties and make suggestions of shared or even compatible values.[342] Peace journalists also are weary of the assistance of propaganda from all parties involved and try to be more analytical and history oriented in their reporting [343]

According to Lynch and McGoldrick, peace journalism maps a conflict as a roundtable, consisting of many parties, many issues. A complex, interlocking pattern of fears, inequities and resentments which can only be overcome by seeking, devising, and implementing complex, interlocking solutions. Media should be careful about this information which occurs a great deal in wartime because war is suitable to false and incorrect reports. From the point of view of peace journalism, journalism must be against war and must support peace. Of course, in war conditions exist that can force journalists to take sides. This is particularly unavoidable if the journalists own country enters the war. Journalists must be careful lest they risk being called traitors to the motherland if they tell the truth about a war from both sides. Also, argue Lynch and McGoldrick, from the peace journalists' point of view journalists should avoid making stark distinctions between self and others. It is argued by peace journalists that the accusation that another party is a threat or beyond the pale of civilized behavior leads to justification for violence. Peace journalists are also encouraged to trace the links and consequences for people in other places now and in the future by treating a conflict as if it is only going on in one place and only at the time that violence is occurring.

Peace journalists should report on how people are affected by the conflicts in everyday life. Peace journalists can also help to empower parties to a conflict to articulate their goals. Furthermore peace journalists should not concentrate on what divides the parties but should ask what common grounds there are between warring parties. Furthermore, say Lynch and McGoldrick, peace journalists should avoid the reporting of violent acts and the describing of the horrors of war. It is best to suggest that the explanation for violence is previous violence such as revenge. Peace journalists ought to show how people have been blocked and frustrated or deprived in everyday life as a way of explaining violence. Peace journalists should avoid blaming one side for starting the violence or dividing the parties into villains and victims. Instead peace journalists should treat as equally newsworthy the sufferings, fears and grievances of all sides. Peace journalists are also asked to avoid using victimizing language such as "destitute," "devastated," "defenseless," "pathetic" or "tragedy," which only tell what has been done to and could be done *to* a group of people. Instead peace journalists should report what has been done and could be done *by* the people. Ask how people are coping and what do they think and if they know any solutions. Lynch and McGoldrick even go so far as to recommend that peace journalists not use such words as genocide, tragedy, assassination or massacre since many of such terms are hearsay and their truth cannot be objectively verified. Lynch and McGoldrick want peace journalists to report only what they really know, since extremist language escalates violence. Such words as vicious and cruel, brutal or barbaric, always describe only what the other party has done. Therefore the use of such words, according to Lynch and McGoldrick, justifies the escalation of violence. Peace journalists should not use demonizing labels like terrorist, extremist, fanatic or fundamentalist, since the individuals in question do not think of themselves that way, but have act according to the logic that they are only defending, or counter-attacking, or resisting another side's extremism — and using such labels means the journalist is promoting one side over the other. And if one side has been so designated, it seems unreasonable to negotiate with them.

Peace journalists are also encouraged by Lynch and McGoldrick not to focus only on one side's human rights abuses, misdemeanors and wrongdoings. Instead peace journalists should try to name all wrongdoers and treat equally seriously allegations made by all sides to a conflict. Furthermore, peace journalists are told to avoid making an opinion or claim seem like an established fact and should also avoid praising the signing of documents by leaders, which bring about military victory or cease-fire, as necessarily creating peace. Instead peace journalists should report on the issues which remain and which may still lead people to commit further acts of violence in the future. Finally, peace journalists should ask ideas for solutions from grass roots organizations and not from leaders on either side of a conflict.[344]

Anyone who has become acquainted with the claims of peace journalism would want to know whether peace journalism works in practice, but it has never been tried fully. It appears unreasonable to call all journalists not associated with the peace journalists' movement war journalists. One could hypothesize that if the peace journalism approach had been preferred, the outcome of the Second World War, the fighting in Northern Ireland, the wars in Kosovo and Rwanda could have been worse. For example in Northern Ireland the peace journalism principle of transparency would have made the secret negotiations between the parties impossible. And in Yugoslavia some suggest that military intervention by NATO forces was the only realistic solution to stop atrocities towards the civilian population.[345]

But we will never know whether a different approach to news coverage would have forestalled the development of these crises in the first place, as each of them was set up by secret pacts, subterfuges and betrayals all along. Meanwhile, peace journalism has become an advocacy form of journalism which leads directly to a form of public relations or propaganda which is the direct opposite of what will be expected by those who want journalists to be trusted and believed.[346]

Advocates of peace journalism make the reporter a participant and thereby deceive the audience who believes that the reporter is at least making an attempt to be an objective observer. Journalists can report on conflicts in which people seek to kill one another but journalists cannot make peace between them. Peace journalists also label all others as war journalists which seems to imply that journalism as usually practiced promotes war because the journalists report on it.

Journalism and the 2016 Election

It is commonly assumed that journalism has two obligations. One is to hold accountable those in power and to report on their activities for voters. The second is to report the facts as far as that is possible.

Yet, on November 9, 2016, during the night following the presidential election of November 8, history will record that there were two winners and two losers. The two winners were the Republican candidate Donald J Trump and democracy. The two losers were the Democrat candidate, Hillary Clinton and journalism.

Throughout June and July 2016 during the primary campaign the media demonized Donald Trump and predicted an overwhelming victory for Hillary Clinton. Many people were absolutely astonished when Republican voters gave Trump the nomination on the Republican ticket with 1,447 pledged delegates. The media immediately predicted Trump's defeat and success for Hillary Clinton in the coming presidential election. Trump was depicted as a buffoon whose insulting and uncontrolled speeches during the primary debates seemed to make him totally unacceptable to the American people. Yet, the American voters decided to give the presidency to Donald Trump despite all the contrary predictions by the nation's journalists.

A review of the predictions by journalists concerning the upcoming presidential election reveals an almost universal certainty that Clinton would win the presidency with an overwhelming majority. It is true that Clinton did win the popular vote. However the 12th amendment to the U.S. Constitution requires that the candidate for the presidency must win the *electoral* vote which consists of a number equal to the members of Congress. Each state is represented by two Senators. In addition every state is also represented by a number of members of the House of Representatives which reflect the size of that state's population. The reason for the inclusion of the 12th amendment is to allow even the smallest states to have some impact on the results.[347]

It is hard to believe that journalists did not know or had forgotten that presidential elections are decided by the electoral vote, although undoubtedly many a citizen did not know or did not understand this requirement. In any case, journalists led the American people to believe that Donald Trump didn't have a chance and that Hillary Clinton was certain to become the first female President of the United States.

On November 5, 2016, Willie Brown, a columnist for the San Francisco Chronicle predicted that Hillary Clinton would win because Democrats are better organized and more disciplined at getting out the vote than Donald Trump and his supporters.[348]

On October 18, 2016, Ed Kilgore published an article in New York Magazine entitled: "some people are now 100% sure Hillary Clinton will win." Kilgore wrote that Trump could not possibly win Pennsylvania, Michigan and Wisconsin and that he would also lose North Carolina.[349]

A publication called Work Leaders published a map under the heading," Map that proves Donald Trump will lose." The map published August 17, 2016, claim that Clinton had already achieved 273 Electoral Votes at that time. It takes 270 electoral votes to win the presidency.[350]

Vicki Needham, writing in The Hill, on July 1, 2016, said, "Hillary Clinton, Democratic nominee, will easily win the presidency with 332 electoral votes."[351]

The Huffington Post published a forecast on October 3, 2016, concerning the coming presidential election which predicted Clinton had a 98% chance of winning.

On the day of the election, November 8, 2016, the New York printed a headline "Hillary Clinton has an 85% chance to win". This story, not credited to any author, included this paragraph: "The Upshot's election model suggests that Hillary Clinton is favored to win the presidency, based on the latest state and national polls. A victory by Mr. Trump remains possible: Mrs. Clinton's chance of losing is about the same as the probability that an NFL kicker misses a 37-yard field goal." There follows a comparison to other forecasts including nine such estimates all of which agreed that Hillary Clinton would win.[352]

On August 15, 2016 Allan Smith, writing in *Business Insider*, headlined his analysis of the coming election NBC's electoral map shows Hillary Clinton with enough electoral votes to win the presidency." According to Smith, NBC News said the Democratic nominee would earn 288 electoral votes while the Republican nominee , Trump would secure just 174.[353]

The television network CBS predicted on September 6, 2016, that Hillary Clinton will gain 341 electoral votes in what was described as a blowout. Scott Whitlock, wrote in MRC News Busters: "The journalists at *CBS* effectively declared the presidential race over, predicting 341 electoral votes for Hillary Clinton in a likely blowout."[354]

It would be easy to cite innumerable other print and television journalists who predicted a Clinton victory. The fact is that journalists, with very few exceptions were wrong in their predictions concerning the election of 2016. Even on election day November 8, 2016, so many journalists predicted a Clinton victory that Americans were not only surprised but shocked by the actual results. Clinton supporters had already prepared for a great victory party at the Javits Convention Center in Manhattan when it became evident during the evening that Clinton was falling behind in Florida and Wisconsin. By 2 AM of November 9, Clinton's campaign chairman, John Podesta, told the crowd that things might not work out the way they had anticipated. At 2:40 AM it was announced that Hillary Clinton had called Donald Trump to concede the race. Democrats were devastated at this news. For a year and a half they had been told by journalists that a Clinton victory was inevitable only to find that the American people and not the journalists, and not the professional politicians, are the boss. Whatever one may think of either Trump or Clinton, this reversal of fortune was a major victory for American democracy because the people rule this country.

It needs therefore to be explained why the journalists were so wrong in their predictions. It should have been known to them that Donald Trump is the fifth president to lose the popular vote while winning the electoral vote. In 1825 the election was decided by the House of Representatives who elected John Quincy Adams because no candidate secured the required number of electoral votes. Andrew Jackson had received the majority of popular votes. His supporters were so disappointed that they founded the Democratic Party. In 1876 Samuel Tilden of New York outpolled Republican Rutherford B. Hayes of Ohio. Tilden had 184 electoral votes compared to a Hayes 165. However, the House of Representatives handed Hayes 20 disputed electoral votes so that he gained the presidency by one vote. In 1888, Benjamin Harrison achieved a majority of the electoral vote over Grover running for a second term. In 2000, George W. Bush lost the popular vote to Al Gore but was awarded Florida's electoral votes by a Supreme Court decision thereby giving Bush the presidency.

For years to come, political scientists, historians and most certainly journalists, will attempt to discover why Trump won. The most obvious reason is that journalists permitted they were wishful thinking to defeat a rational analysis. Someone once exhibited a map of the United States which showed that 45% of the country consisted of New York and another 45% consisted of California with only 10% in the middle. This sarcastic effort sought to display the attitude of so many journalists who simply ignored for years that a large contingent of the population lives in "Middle America." Included among those ignored are a considerable number of people living in small towns or on farms. Many who are designated as working-class were given no credence by journalists and simply forgotten. Yet, these many millions have a vote which they exercised on November 8, 2016 to the shock and surprise of the graduates of our schools of journalism. Some "Monday morning quarterbacks" called this surprise ending a populist explosion. This phrase means that many people who voted looked upon Clinton as part of the corruption of American politics. Trump was viewed as an outsider despite his gross behavior during the primaries. It may be said that Trumps victory was a revolt against "Washington" whose politicians many voters distrust even as they also view journalists with disdain. It needs also to be noticed, that Republicans achieved victory in the Senate and in the House and gained three more governorships leading Democrats by 33 to 14.

For the profession of journalism, the Trump victory should not mean the end of progressive politics. It should mean that the American people want to be told the facts and are not interested in peace journalism or other efforts to make journalists partisans in political disputes. This raises the question whether the failure of journalists to accurately report the opinions of those Americans favoring the election of Trump was a deliberate effort to deceive the American people or whether that huge majority of journalists who predicted Trumps defeat didn't know any better. It is instructive to remember that *The Society* has adopted a code of ethics in 1996 which includes in its preamble the sentence: "Professional integrity is the cornerstone of a journalist's credibility." The code also includes a section entitled: "Seek Truth and Report It," and further reminds the members of the profession that: "Delivering deliberate distortion is never permissible." The code of ethics also demands that all human beings are deserving of respect and reminds journalists to be accountable.[355]

Ethics, What Ethics?

In view of this code of ethics and the professional obligations accruing to journalists, it may well be unjust that so many Americans view that profession with so much suspicion. Unfortunately, such negative views of Turner journalism are bolstered by those who betray their calling and fuel the negative stereotypes which the media have engendered among so many Americans.

One example of this kind of journalistic deceit was committed by Mitch Albom who writes a sports column for the Detroit Free Press. Albom is also a nationally syndicated radio host, and regularly appears on television. Albom is constantly preaching ethics in journalism and has had a great deal to say about such offenders as Jason Blair who had fabricated and plagiarized 73 articles written for the New York Times. In April 2006 Albom wrote a column in the Sunday edition of the Detroit Free Press about Jason Richardson and Mateen Cleever, who had both played basketball at Michigan State University. According to Albom, both men had attended the NCAA semi-final game in St. Louis on a Saturday night. Albom wrote: "In attendance were two former stars for Michigan State, Mateen Cleever and

Jason Richardson." This story continues as Albom describes how the two buddies fly in to root for their former team.

All this was entertaining reading. However, it was not true. Neither Cleever nor Richardson attended that game and Albom was not in St. Louis that night. Albom wrote this column on Friday night before the game took place and had it published on Saturday morning. This was in face of the ethics policy of the Detroit Free Press which states in part: "We do not mislead our readers. We do not publish made up material. Presently, Albom continues to write for the Detroit Free Press.[356]

The Columbia Journalism Review has published an article entitled: "Plagiarize, Plagiarize, Plagiarize — only be sure to call it research." The article discusses a number of well-known journalists who have gone on to fame and fortune despite having stolen the work of others. Included is Nina Totenberg, one of the most celebrated journalists and winner of numerous prizes for her reporting. Totenberg was fired when she worked for the National Observer because she took several paragraphs and verbatim quotes from a Washington Post report about the Speaker of the House. The Columbia Journalism Review article enumerated many other instances of journalistic transgressions. Mark Hornung, editorial page editor for the Chicago Sun-Times, copied 12 paragraphs from a Washington Post editorial. Michael Kramer of Time Magazine used material copied from the Los Angeles Times. Edwin Chen, a reporter for the Los Angeles Times, lifted 40 passages from a story that had appeared in Vanity Fair and included them in a book he wrote. Fox Butterfield, Boston bureau chief for the New York Times, took five paragraphs from a Boston Globe story and published them as is own. Bob Morris, at one time a columnist for the Orlando Sentinel, "borrowed" from the Columbus, Ohio, Citizen Journal and Gregory Freeman, a columnist for The St. Louis Post-Dispatch, copied three sentences from a column written by a Boston Globe writer. Laura Parker was fired from her job as Miami bureau chief for the Washington Post because she quoted people she had never interviewed. It is of interest that those who engage in this kind of plagiarism are competent writers who had no need to do so.[357]

Christopher Newton wrote an article for the Associated Press in which he claimed to have interviewed two professors concerning criminal justice statistics. Neither of these people, whom Newton called "Ralph Myers" and "Bruce Fenimore," existed. An investigation into Newton's work revealed that he had quoted 45 other sources in earlier stories that did not exist.[358]

CHAPTER 12. THE ASSAULT ON DEMOCRACY BY HATE AND VIOLENCE

Democracy vs. Mob Rule

One of the most important American traditions has been the peaceful turnover of power consequent to the election of a new President of the United States. Because American presidents are elected by the people, refusal to accept the outcome of such an election undermines democracy and promotes the intentions of those who seek to turn the United States into a police state. The Constitution of the United States does indeed support "the right of the people peaceably to assemble..." Unfortunately there are some Americans who were provoked to violence because the candidate they supported did not win the latest election.

The New York Times reported on November 9, 2016, that in California, several hundred protesters ran through the streets of Berkeley and Oakland early in the morning venting their anger at the election of Donald J. Trump as President of the United States. Such demonstrations were also conducted in Pittsburgh, Seattle, and Portland, Oregon. The demonstrators smashed car windows, set fires, broke store windows, and forced a delay in train service. Some of the protesters stood in the middle-of-the-road to block traffic. They burned the American flag and shouted, "That's not my president."

Car owners and business owners whose windows were smashed and whose property was damaged lived in neighborhoods which had in fact supported the candidate of the Democratic Party. Therefore those who committed this violence attacked the very people who had voted for their cause.[359]

Likewise in Los Angeles and San Francisco, students left their high school and college classes and ran out into the streets. School officials accompanied the students as they marched.[360] In Los Angeles, they burned a giant Trump head in effigy and blocked traffic on downtown streets. Such events also occurred in Portland, Oregon, Boston, Massachusetts, and Philadelphia, Pennsylvania. In New York City thousands assembled in front of the Trump Tower, building shouting slogans and denouncing the President-Elect.

Refusal to accept the outcome of an election undermines democracy and seeks to void the will of the people and their right to govern themselves. Yet these protests generally dissipate shortly after the cares of daily life overtake those who vented their anger in the streets.

Hate Crimes

There are, however, others in this country whose assault on American democracy is not occasional but a permanent feature of their lives. These are people who belong to so-called hate groups, which the Federal Bureau of Investigation defines as "a traditional offense like murder, assault and vandalism with an added element of bias," or "a criminal offense against a person or property motivated in whole or in part by an offender's bias against a race, religion, disability, sexual orientation, ethnicity, gender, or gender identity." Hate itself is not a crime, as expressions of hate are protected by the First Amendment's requirement that freedom of speech cannot be curtailed.[361]

In 2015, The Southern Poverty Law Center identified 892 active hate groups in the United States. One year earlier, in 2014, 784 groups were listed as hate groups by the SPLC.[362]

In part, hate groups are related to low income. The evidence is that hate groups are more likely to be present when the percent of households below the poverty line increases. Yet, welfare payments do not reduce the likelihood that a hate group is present. On the contrary, it increases it. This is because a stigma is attached to receiving welfare payments. Hence, a link exists between poor economic conditions and racial harassment.[363]

It has also been found that tradition and history have a considerable impact on the presence of hate groups. Where resentments have been fueled by long-simmering tensions along ethnic, race and class lines, hate groups are more likely to form.

Other reasons for hate group formation include boredom, frustration concerning innumerable defeated hopes and wishes, scapegoating, which consists of blaming an outgroup for one's own perceived shortcomings, and validation. Validation refers to the wish to assert one's importance and meaning at the expense of targeted people, who are perceived as outgroups and hence inferior and probably dangerous. Thus, hate groups validate themselves, enhancing their internal image with a peer group, and, in their opinion, with society at large.[364]

Hate groups may also develop when people regarded as an outgroup by reason of religion, race, or ethnicity move into a previously segregated neighborhood. Such changes may well lead to the formation of hate groups who also enjoy victimizing others. Such hate groups resemble gangs who are held together by shared incapacity and the need to identify with someone or something. Such gangs as well as such hate groups are also a social safety net. Their associations give the membership protection from violence imposed by other groups, and in time of need help the membership to survive, particularly by becoming a source of employment among people with limited skills. Hate groups may well serve to give its members financial security, or at least some financial support through unemployment. Members of such hate groups, like all groups, seek to be in good terms with their fellow members and therefore provide help. A good number of hate group members have the feeling that they have been wronged and that therefore they can compensate for their grievances by targeting outsiders. There are also parents of schoolchildren who dislike the curricula taught in the public schools. As members of such extremist organizations as the neo-Nazis or Christian Identity members, such parents dislike the teaching of diversity and all-inclusiveness taught in almost all public schools in America.

There are among adherents to these extremist hate groups some who are willing to assault and kill those they dislike. The targets of these violent extremists are usually members of some minority or someone who behaves in a matter that does not meet the approval of the haters.

On December 24, 1985, David Lewis Rice, posing as a taxi driver, delivered a package to the home of Charles Goldmark, a Seattle, Washington attorney. Having gained entrance to the house, he attacked the Goldmark family with a knife and killed Charles Goldmark, his wife Annie, and their two children, Colin, 10, and Derek, 12. Rice was a member of an extremist group called The Duck Club, which believed that the Goldmarks were Jewish and Communists and therefore deserve to die. At his trial, Rice said repeatedly, "I knew what I was doing." Rice had punctured the victims' heads with a kitchen knife after hitting them with a laundry iron. Rice was sentenced to life imprisonment.[365]

In 2004, Daniel Romano was walking on the street in Queens, New York, when he was attacked by two teenagers, Paul Rotondi and Frank Scarpinito. The two men pulled up in a car as Romano was walking on 73rd St. in New York. Romano was wearing a crucifix upside down and black clothing to indicate that he was a Satanist. The two attackers shouted at Romano and called him, "baby sacrificer," "hooker killer," and "Satan worshiper." They then attacked Romano with a metal club and an ice scraper. Romano was taken to the Elmhurst Hospital, where he received 12 stitches.

In September 2001, Frank Roque, a member of an extremist hate group, fatally shot the Sikh owner of a Chevron gas station in Mesa, Arizona. Twenty minutes later, Roque shot but missed a clerk of Lebanese descent at a Mobile station. Then, after that, Roque fired several shots into the home of a family of Afghan descent, but hit no one. Roque kept shouting "I stand for America all the way" as he was handcuffed upon being apprehended by the police. Roque was sentenced to life in prison without the possibility of parole.[366]

In June 2009, *The Denver Post* published a recollection of the 25th anniversary of the murder of Denver talk radio host Alan Berg at the hands of the white supremacist group.

Those who attack someone by reason of his religious beliefs or ethnicity do not only attack one person but an entire religion or set of beliefs or a whole community. Hate crimes are equivalent to terrorism because the attack sends a message to all who belong to that same group that they too will be attacked later. In addition, hate crimes against any ethnic group may well set off retaliatory violence, leading to cyclical acts of violence against Americans of different beliefs.

Recently, the FBI's Hate Crimes Report indicated that in 2015 there were 6,727 victims of hate crime incidents known to the police. 47% of these hate crimes targeted racial minorities, 18.6% were directed against religious minorities, mainly Jews, another 18.6% of hate crimes were motivated by hatred concerning sexual orientation, ethnicity was the target of 11.9% of hate crimes, and, disability, gender, and gender identity together accounted for 3.9% of hate crimes.[367]

A number of those who commit hate crimes belong to organizations which seek to justify their crimes by interpreting the Bible or other tracts as supportive of their hatred. One such organization is the Aryan Nations, founded by Richard G. Butler, who preached that Jews descend from apes and black people are subhuman. Butler lived in a house containing books about Adolf Hitler and Holocaust denial. Butler had about 200 followers in 17 chapters nationwide. Butler lived in Hayden, Idaho, where he ran unsuccessfully for mayor in order to "keep it white." The Aryan Nations seeks to segregate the Northwestern states as a refuge for whites. Every year Butler holds a world Congress at his compound, where he sets up his silver bust of Hitler, stained-glass swastikas, Nazi flags, and a sign reading "whites only" at the front gate.

Followers of Butler were responsible for the murder of Alan Berg, the Denver talk show host. They also bombed a synagogue in Boise, and held up an armored car and bombed the home of a Roman Catholic priest in Coeur d'Alene, Idaho.[368]

The West Pearl Baptist Church is based in Topeka, Kansas, and is known nationwide for its hate speech and protests against members of LGBTQ. That abbreviation refers to lesbians, gays, bisexuals, transgenders, and "queers." The members of the church regularly picket the funerals of homosexuals and of military personnel on the grounds that God hates homosexuals. The members of this church engage in harassment and assault. They lured a 21-year-old gay youth, Matthew W Shepard, from a Wyoming bar, tied him to a fence, pistol whipped him, severely wounded him in the head, and left him to die in near freezing temperatures. In 2009, the United States Senate passed the Matthew Shepard Act. It provides funding to state and local authorities to prosecute a number of hate crimes motivated by race, religion, national origin, gender, sexual orientation, and disability. It authorizes the federal government to prosecute these crimes when the states fail to do so. [369]

An example of the kind of hate crime affected by this legislation pertains to the murder of a federal employee, Joseph Santos Ilero, a citizen of Filipino descent, who was gunned down by Buford O. Furrow, Jr. on August 10, 1999.

Furrow also shot five people who survived but were severely wounded. Because Furrow had a previous felony assault conviction, he was also charged with illegal possession of a firearm. Furrow drove to Los Angeles from Washington State in a van filled with weapons, ammunition, and even hand grenades. Having reached the Granada Hills neighborhood of Los Angeles, he walked into an area where there were summer camps and opened fire. He used an Uzi submachine gun to fire 70 bullets, which hit five people, including three children.

For several years prior to this shooting, Furrow had lived with Debbie Matthews, widow of Robert J. Matthews, the white supremacist leader and the founder of an neo-Nazi group, The Order. The Order had carried out a campaign of assassinations, bombings, and robberies. Matthews was killed in a shootout with the FBI in 1994.[370]

In July 1998, security guards at the Aryan Nations compound in Idaho shot at Victoria Keenan and her son after their car backfired nearby. The Keenans were returning from a wedding and stopped briefly in the Aryan Nations compound to look for a wallet that had fallen out of the car.

Bullets struck the car several times before the vehicle careened into a ditch. Members of the Aryan Nations then held the Keenans at gunpoint.

The compound was heavily guarded and consisted of the home of Aryan Nations leader Richard Butler and of several other structures. It was the meeting place for violent white supremacists. The Southern Poverty Law Center then sued the Aryan Nations and Butler on behalf of the Keenans.

In September 2000 they were awarded $6.3 million. The judgment forced Richard Butler to turn over the 20 acre compound to the Keenans. The Keenans in turn sold the property to a philanthropist, who later donated it to a local college.[371]

One of the most bizarre belief systems in the United States is the Christian Identity Movement. This movement teaches its followers the very opposite of Christian teachings as understood by Catholics and Protestants alike. Instead of relying on the most basic Judeo-Christian doctrine, that is, "to love your neighbor as yourself," the Christian Identity movement promotes acts of violence against others. The movement is particularly willing to commit violence against government and its officials, ethnic and other minorities, black churches, all Jewish establishments, and law enforcement agencies.[372]

Resisting Violence

There are in this country numerous groups who preach violence against those perceived as outsiders. Included are the Aryan Nations, The Order, The Covenant Sword and Arm of the Lord, and neo-Nazis who call themselves The National Socialist White People's Party and the Ku Klux Klan.[373]

It has been estimated that in 2016 there were 892 hate groups in the United States. This means that hatred is on the rise in the United States. These hate groups promote animosity and hatred and sometimes violence towards people belonging to a particular ethnic group or religion, and target people with minority sexual orientations. These groups organize demonstrations, write publications, and harass those they do not like.

According to The Southern Poverty Law Center, Arkansas has the highest concentration of hate groups in the nation, along with most other Southern states. This is due to the success of the civil rights movement, which directly assaulted some of the core values of the white population. States with high numbers of hate groups also have larger shares of black residents than other states. In addition to racial minorities, religious minorities are also targeted by these hate groups. The principal targets of religious bigots are Jews and Muslims. It should be noted, however, that American Muslims are themselves guilty of spreading hatred against the Jewish population in this country. Of course, poverty is somewhat related to hate behavior, as is lack of education.[374]

Attacks or Counter-Attacks

Race hate and religious bigotry are not confined to people of European descent. There are also those of African descent who make every effort to denounce whites. One of the leaders in this endeavor is Louis Farrakhan, who was born Louis Eugene Wolcott in 1933. As leader of The Nation of Islam, Farrakhan preached recently that white people deserve to die. He also said that God will send a UFO to rescue his followers, and will carry out justice if a race war began.[375]

In 1955, Louis Walcott met Elijah Moore, the leader of the Nation of Islam. Elijah Moore (Mohammed) was responsible for the growth of the Nation of Islam. He called whites "devils" and prohibited his followers from smoking, drinking, fighting, eating pork, or engaging in destructive behavior. After Elijah Mohammed's death, his son became the leader of the renamed American Society of Muslims. This led Farrakhan to organize the Nation of Islam, using the old name. He visited Libya and accepted an interest-free loan from the then dictator Muammar al-Qaddafi. In 2000, he organized The Million Man March, which gave him a great deal of publicity. Farrakhan said that he was an admirer of Adolf Hitler, calling him a very great man. He recently praised Donald Trump for not taking campaign money from Jews. Farrakhan is obsessed with blaming Jews for all the ills of this world.[376]

Psychiatric Underpinnings

Our understanding of the phenomenon of hate-obsessed Americans needs to be expressed by seeking psychiatric information concerning such aberrant conduct. The Constitution of the United States and all that flows from it defeats ethnic, religious and gender hatred, and makes such beliefs and attitudes appear un-American.

Some people have no compunction in engaging in behavior which they know to be harmful or hurtful to others. Such people, according to the American Psychiatric Association, have feelings of grandiosity, the need for admiration, lack of empathy, and the need to control others. Such individuals see themselves as special and unique and deserving of special treatment, attention, and resources.[377]

Recent research suggests that serial aggressors have elevated or high self-esteem. Such aggressors engage in bullying behavior and seek to exploit and domineer and manipulate others in their effort for social dominance. There are others who claim that those who exhibit domineering bullying behavior possess low beliefs in their abilities and use aggression as a defense mechanism to protect low self-esteem.[378]

Whatever the reason for hate crimes, in October 2009, Congress passed The Matthew Shepard and James Byrd Jr. Hate Crimes Prevention Act. This law, signed by President Obama on October 28, 2009, was named after Matthew Shepard, who was murdered because he was a homosexual, and James Byrd who was murdered because he was black.

This law provides $5 million per year in funding to help state and local agencies pay for investigating and prosecuting hate crimes. The law also requires The Federal Bureau of Investigation to track statistics on hate crimes. Accordingly, the 2015 hate crime statistics depict the following: Bias Motivation Crimes: 6,885. 734 of these targeted whites and 2,125 targeted African Americans. The others were distributed among victims of various ethnic origins, including American Indians, Asian Pacific Islanders, Arabs, Hispanics, and people of multiple race origins.

Since 1965, some 52 years ago, the Catholic Church and all Protestant denominations have denounced and condemned all discrimination against others on account of race or religion.[379] This came about when Pope John XXIII called an Ecumenical Council to the Vatican for the purpose of renewing the Church. That council met for three years, from 1962 to 1965. Some 2,800 bishops from 116 countries produced 16 documents including *Nostra Aetate* (In our age, etc.), which dealt with the relation of the Church to non-Christians.[380] *Nostra Aetate* proclaims, in part: "the church reproves as foreign to the mind of Christ any discrimination against people or any harassment of them on the basis of their race, color, condition in life, or religion."[381]

One thousand three hundred and fifty four (1,354) crimes targeted people of various religions. Of these, 695 were anti-Jewish, 301 targeted Muslims, and the others were directed against Catholics, Protestants, Mormons, Jehovah's Witnesses, Eastern Orthodox, Christians, Buddhists, and Hindus.

Sexual orientation also led to a good deal of aggression, with 1,219 Americans victims of violence by reason of their sexual orientation. 758 of these crimes were directed at homosexual men, 235 at bisexual or transgender people and lesbians, and the others at heterosexual persons.[382]

It is indeed unfortunate that hate crimes continue to be a feature of American life. Nevertheless, we need to place this problem in perspective and recognize that things are far worse with reference to ethnic and religious bigotry in certain other parts of the world. It speaks for American democracy that special concern is given to crimes motivated by hate.

POST SCRIPT. THE SOCIOLOGY OF DEVIANT BEHAVIOR

Whether or not behavior is considered deviant depends largely on the culture in which it is observed. Culture is the man-made environment, consisting of physical culture such as the chair we sit on or the atomic bomb, ideological culture, such as the belief in democracy, and behavioral culture, such as shaking hands on greeting someone or paying income tax.

Every culture includes expected behavior called norms. Cultures also exhibit subcultures, consisting of minorities whose conduct is derived from subcultural norms, which may very well conflict with the behavior and beliefs of the majority.

This book demonstrates that there is a good deal of pressure in American culture today which leads numerous Americans to conduct themselves in a manner which the law prohibits but which large numbers of Americans do not condemn. This means that deviant behavior is literally created by American culture. The best example of this is the effort on the part of so many to increase their incomes by illegal means. For example, income tax evasion, bribery, and selling one's political office are common practices and are supported by a good number of Americans who believe that money and that which money will buy is more important than any ethics.

The deviance of subcultures is supported by norms or expected behavior in a particular group that is opposed to the expectations of the majority. Good examples are terrorists who, in the name of their religious beliefs or political views, will murder people with the approval of their in group, thereby neutralizing their consciences. Politicians, antiabortion fanatics, religious believers of all kinds, white supremacists, and a host of others are enabled by the support of the reference to steal, maim and kill.

It is, of course, only a small minority who constantly violate the law as well as the norms of the society in which they live. Moreover, there are many people who will deviate from the norms some occasions while usually obeying the rules.

BIBLIOGRAPHY

"12th Amendment." Constitution of the United States. n.d.

"15 United States Congress I, 1221." 1964.

Abeles, Schwartz, Haeckel and Silverblatt. *The Chinese Garment Industry Study*. New York: International Ladies Garment Workers' Union, 1983.

Adair v. United States. 208 US 161 (1908).

Alatas, Syed Hussein. *Corruption: Its Nature, Causes and Consequences*. Aldershot, England: Avebury Publishers, 1990.

Alder, Madison. "Vehicle Plows into Phoenix Officers Standing at Quick Trip Convenience Store." *The Arizona Republic*, September 11, 2016.

"All in the Family." *The Progressive Review*. 2015. http://prorev.com/family.htm (accessed October 18, 2016).

Aloisi, James. "For Better or For Worse, James Michael Curley Defined Boston in the Early Half of the 20th Century." *CommonWealth*. September 23, 2013. http://commonwealthmagazine.org/politics/005-the-mayor-of-the-poor/ (accessed January 5, 2017).

American Bar Association. *A Current Glance at Women in the Law*. Chicago: American Bar Association, 2013.

American Booksellers Assocation v. Hudnut. 771 F.2d 323 (7th Cir., August 27, 1985).

American Indian Historical Society. *The American Indian Reader: Literature*. San Francisco: American Indian Historical Society, 1973.

American Psychiatric Association. *Diagnostic and Statistical Manual Of Mental Disorders*. Washington, DC: APA, 2013.

American Steel Foundries v. Tri-City Central Trades Council. 257 U.S. 184 (U.S. Supreme Court, December 5, 1921).

Amoruso, David. "How the Sicilian Mafia Flooded the U.S. with Heroin." *Mob Magazine*, October 4, 2008.

Ang, R.P., O.E.L. Ong, and I.C.Y. Lim. "From narcissistic exploitativeness to bullying behavior." *Social Development*, 2010: 1-26.

Archibald, Randall C. "Ex-Congressman Gets Eight-Year Term in Bribery Case." *The New York Times*, March 4, 2006.

Associated Press. "Ex-Bush aide Pleads Guilty to Stealing from Federally Aided Center." *Washington Post*, December 20, 2008.

Baleman, Robert. "Wounded Knee." *Military History*, 2008: 62-67.

Bandler, Aaron. "Seven Statistics You Need to Know about Black on Black Crime." *The Daily Wire*, July 13, 2016: 1-7.

—. "The Alton Sterling and Philando Castille Shootings." *The Daily Wire*, July 7, 2016.

Barnes, Robert. "Supreme Court Strikes Down Limits on Federal Campaign Contributions." *Washington Post*, April 2, 2014: 1.

Barringer, Felicity. "A.P. Says It Couldn't Find 45 of Fired Writer's Sources." *The New York Times*, October 22, 2002: A22.

Barry, Susan. "Spousal Rape: The Uncommon Law." *American Bar Association Journal*, 1980: 1088-1091.

Bedard, Paul. "Sanctuary Cities Cross the 300 Mark with Dallas, Philly." *Washington Examiner*, February 2, 2016: 1.

Berger, Thomas R. *A Long and Terrible Shadow*. Seattle: University of Washington Press, 1991.

Berman, Mark. "Number of Law Enforcement Officers Fatally Shot This Year up Significantly Affect Ambush Attacks Report Says." *The Washington Post*, July 27, 2016.

Bethel School District v. Fraser. 478 U.S. 675 (US Supreme Court, 1987).

Binder, John. "Here Are the Shocking Numbers of Crimes Committed by Illegal Immigrants." *The Hayride*. September 2015. http://thehayride.com/2015/09/here-are-the-shocking-numbers-on-crimes-committed-by-illegal-immigrants/ (accessed October 17, 2016).

Binding, Arthur C. *A History of the United States*. New York: Charles Scribner's Sons, 1951.

Blanchard, Dallas. *Religious Violence and Abortion*. Gainesville: University Press of Florida, 1993.

Blanco, Juan Ignacio, Ed. Murderpedia- The Free Online Encyclopedic Dictionary of Murder. n.d. (accessed July 26, 2016).

Brown v. Board of Education. 347 U.S. 483 (US Supreme Court, 1954).

Brown, Tony. "JMU Student Tied to Voter Registration Fraud." *Daily News-Record*, September 16, 2016.

Brown, Willie. "Ground Game Will Put Hillary Clinton in the White House." *The San Francisco Chronicle*, November 5, 2016: 14.

Brownmiller, Susan. *Against Our Will: Men, Women, and Rape.* New York: Simon and Schuster, 1975.

Bruno, Joe. *Mobsters.* Fiskdale, MA: Knickerbocker Publishing Company, 2014.

Buenker, John D. *Urban Liberalism And Progressive Reform.* New York: Scribners, 1971.

Bureau of Justice Statistics. "Violent Crime in the United States." United States Department of Justice, 2015.

Bureau of Labor Statistics. Usual weekly earnings of wage and salary workers second quarter 2016. Bureau of Labor Statistics, 2016.

Burt, Martha and R. Estep. "Who is Victim? Definitional Problems in Sexual Victimization." *Victimology*, 1981: 15-28.

Campbell, J.C. "Cultural Contact and Polynesian Identity in the European Age." *Journal of World History*, 1997: 29-55.

Cannato, Vincent J. *The Ungovernable City.* New York: Basic Books, 2001.

Cassini, Gina. "Muslims Say Fallen US Soldiers Should Not Be Honored On Memorial Day." *Top Right News.* July 26, 2016. http://toprightnews.com/muslims-say-u-s-military-should-not-be-honored-on-memorial-day/ (accessed October 19, 2016).

Catalano, Shannon, Erica Smith, Howard Snyder and Michael Rand. *Female Victims of Violence.* Washington, DC: US Department of Justice, Bureau of Justice Statistics, 2009.

Cavendish, Richard. "The 'Casa de Contratacion'." *History Today*, 2003.

Chapman v. California. 386 US 18,22 (1967).

Chen, Pauline W. "Sharing the Pain of Women in Medicine." *The New York Times*, November 29, 2012: D7.

Chernin, Kim. *The Hungry Self.* New York: Harper, 1994.

Chester, C. Ronald. "Perceived Relative Deprivation as a Cause of Property Crime." *Crime and Delinquency*, 1976: 17-30.

Clark, Roger. "Women's Access to Prestigious Occupations: A Cross National Investigation." *Social Science Quarterly*, 1991: 20-32.

Cleaver, Hannah. "Turkish Workers a Mstake Claims Schmidt." *London Daily Telegraph*, December 30, 2004: 1.

Clifton, James A. "Cultural Fictions." *Society*, 1990: 28.

Clines, Francis X. "Ohio Congressman Guilty in Bribery and Kickbacks." *The New York Times*, April 12, 2002: 1.

Cohen v. California. 403 US 15 (1971).

Coker v. Georgia. 433 U.S. 584 (U.S. Supreme Court, 1977).

Colias, Mike. "Children's Memorial Target of Guy's Shakedown Efforts." *Crain's Chicago Business*, December 9, 2008: 1.

Comerford v. International Harvester. 235 Ala. 376 (1938).

"Comment: Passenger Protection Will Not Sink the Cruise Ship Industry ." *Thomas M. Cooley Law Review*, 2009: 597.

Cook, Jamie. "Hathaway's Fall from Grace Tragic." *Macomb Daily*, May 28, 2013.

Coontz, Stephen. "How Can We Help Men? By Helping Women." *The New York Times*, January 11, 2014.

Cooper, James Fenimore. *The Best Known Works of James Fenimore Cooper.* New York: Book League of America, 1942.

Coppage v. Kansas. 236 US 1 (1915).

A Current Glance at Women in the Law. Chicago: The American Bar Association, 2013.

Davey, Monical. "Ex-Governor of Illinois Gets 6 1/2 Years in Prison." *The New York Times*, September 7, 2006: A19.

Davis, Ethan. "An Administrative Trail of Tears: Indian Removal." *American Journal of Legal History*, 2008: 65-68.

Dawan, Shaila. "Law Lets IRS Seize Accounts on Suspicion, No Crime Required." *The New York Times*, October 26, 2014: A1.

"Declaration of Independence." july 4, 1776.

Dellios, Hugh. "Controversy Laid to Rest as Dickson Mound Closes." *Chicago Tribune*, April 4, 1992: 3.

Deming, Mary and Ali Eppy. "The Sociology of Rape." *Sociology and Social Research*, 1981: 357-379.

D'Encousse, Helene Carrere. *The End of the Soviet Empire.* New York: Basic Books, 1993.

"Department of Justice, Office of Public Affairs." *United States Department of Justice.* August 5, 2009. https://www.justice.gov/opa/pr/former-congressman-william-j-jefferson-convicted-bribery-racketeering-money-laundering-and (accessed January 5, 2017).

Derber, Twila. "Three Convicted Rampart, Police Officers Request New Trial." *Los Angeles Times*, 2000.

Doan, Alesha E. Opposition and Intimidation: The Abortion Wars and Strategies of Political Harassment. Ann Arbor: University of Michigan Press, 2007.

Doe v. University of Michigan. 721 F.Supp. 852 (1989).

Durant, Will. *The Age of Faith.* New York: Simon and Schuster, 1950.

Edleson, John L. "The Overlap Between Child Maltreatment and Woman Battering." *Violence Against Women*, 1999: 134-154.

Efron, Sonni. "Eating Disorders Go Global." *Los Angeles Times*, October 18, 1997: A1,A9.

Elder, Pliny the. *Natural History.* Cambridge, MA: Harvard University Press, Loeb Classical Library, 1989.

Eley, Geoffrey. "The View from the Throne: the Personal Rule of Kaiser Wilhelm II." *The Historical Journal*, 1985: 469-485.

Engel v. Vitale. 370 U.S. 421 (US Supreme Court, 1962).

Erie, Stephen P. Rainbow's End: Irish-Americans and the Dilemmas of Urban Machine Politics 1840 – 1985. Berkeley: University of California Press, 1988.

Fairbanks, Phil. "Ciminelli's Court Appearance Moved to Manhattan." *The Buffalo News*, September 27, 2016.

Falk, Gerhard. *Murder: An Analysis of Its Forms, Conditions, and Causes.* Jefferson, NC: McFarland & Company Inc., 1990.

Farah, Joseph. "Illegal Aliens Murder 12 Americans Daily." *WND*, November 28, 2006: http://www.wnd.com/2006/11/39031/.

Federal Bureau of Investigation. *Crime in the United States 2015.* Washington, DC: United States Department of Justice, 2016.

Federal Bureau of Investigation. *Uniform Crime Report.* Washington, DC: U.S. Department of Justice, 2015.

Federal Bureau of Investigation, Criminal Justice Information Services Division. *Defining a Hate Crime.* Washington, DC: U.S. Department of Justice, n.d.

Federici, Sylvia. *Wages Against Housework.* Bristol, England: The Falling Wall Press, 1998.

Ferguson, C. J. and Hartley, R. D. "The Influence of Pornography of Rape and Sexual Assault." *Aggression and Violent Behavior*, 2009: 323-329.

"Fifth Amendment." United States Constitution. n.d.

Fisher, Jan. "In New York City's Underworld: a Window on Immigrant Crime." *The New York Times*, June 17, 1993.

Fisher, Jim. *Forensics Under Fire.* New Brunswick, NJ: Ruters University Press, 2008.

Flood, Michael. "The Harms of Pornography Exposure Among Children and Young People." *Child Abuse Review*, 2009: 384-400.

Foley, Elizabeth Pryce. "Sovereignty Reclaimed: The Tea Party and Constitutional Amendments." *Tennessee Law Review*, 2011: 751.

Francis, Sam. "AnarchoTyrannay - Where Multiculturalism Leads." *VDARE. com.* December 30, 2004. http://www.vdare.com/articles/anarcho-tyranny-where-multiculturalism-leads (accessed October 17, 2016).

Frank, J.S., R.S. Moore, and G.M. Ames. "Historical and Cultural Roots of Drinking Problems Among American Indians." *American Journal of Public Health*, 2000: 344-351.

Frantz, Douglas. "Vote Fraud in City Outlined at Hearing." *Chicago Tribune*, September 20, 1983.

French, Lawrence A. *The Winds of Injustice.* New York: Garland Publishing Company, 1994.

Friedan, Betty. *The Feminine Mystique.* New York: W. W. Northon and Company, 1963.

Friedesdorf, Conor. "Stripping a Professor of Tenure Over a Blog Post." *The Atlantic*, February 9, 2015.

Friedman, Samuel P. "Drug Arrests and Injection Drug Deterrence." *American Journal of Public Health*, 2011: 2.

Friedrich, Carl J. "Revolution and Ideology in the Late 20th Century." In *Revolution: Yearbook of the American Society for Political and Legal Philosophy*, by Carl J. Friedrich. New York: Atherton Press, 1966.

Fuller, Thomas. "Anti--Trump Demonstrators Take to the Streets in Several US Cities." *The New York Times*, November 9, 2016: A1.

Garrity v. New Jersey. 385 U.S. 493 (U.S. Supreme Court, 1967).

Gates, Henry Louis. "Let Them Talk: Why Civil Liberties Pose No Threat to Civil Rights." *New Republic*, September 20, 1993: 37.

Gianelli, Paul. "The Abuse of Scientific Evidence in Criminal Cases: The Need for Independent Crime Laboratories." *Virginia Journal of Social Policy and the Law*, 1997.

Goldhaber, Dan. "An Endogenous Model of Public School Expenditures And Private School Enrollment." *Journal of Urban Economics*, 1986: 106-128.

Goode, William. "Force and Violence in the Family." *Journal of Marriage and the Family*, 1971: 624-636.

Goss v. Lopez. 419 U.S 565 (US Supreme Court, 1975).

Government Accountability Office. "Elections: Additional Data Could Help State and Local Election Officials Maintain Adequate Vote Registration Lists." Washington, DC, 2005.

Green, Milton. "West Virginia Mine Explosion: Massey Energy Mine had Scores of Safety Citations." *Huffington Post.* June 6, 2010. http://www.huffingtonpost.com/2010/04/06/west-virginia-mine-explos_n_526810.html (accessed October 20, 2016).

Greene, Donald P., Dara Z. Strolovich and Janelle S. Wong. "Defendant Neighborhoods: Integration and Racially Motivated Crime." *American Journal of Sociology,* 1998: 172-403.

Greene, Nancy. Ready-To-Wear, Ready to Work: a Century of Industry and Immigrants in Paris and New York. Durham, NC: Duke University Press, 1997.

Greene, Robert. "Court Appeal Upholds Perrodin Victory over Bradley in Compton." *Metro News Letter,* March 11, 2003.

Greenfield, Daniel. "188,382 Criminal Illegal Aliens Deported in 2011." *Front Page Magazine.* November 12, 2012. http://www.frontpagemag.com/point/164910/188382-criminal-illegal-aliens-deported-2011-daniel-greenfield (accessed October 17, 2017).

Guist, Claudia and Philip S. Cohen. "Headed Toward Equality? Houwork Change in Comparative Perspective." *Journal of Marriage and Family,* 2011: 44.

Hamilton, Matt and Barbara Dimmick. "Trump win sparks student walkouts and protests across the United States." *Los Angeles Times,* November 9, 2016.

Haynes, Danielle. "University of Arizona Fraternity Investigated for Alleged Attack on Jewish Students." *UPI.* November 18, 2014. http://www.upi.com/Top_News/US/2014/11/18/University-of-Arizona-fraternity-investigated-for-alleged-attack-on-Jewish-students/2171416350505/ (accessed October 19, 2016).

Hazelwood v. Kuhlmeier. 484 U.S. 260 (US Supreme Court, 1988).

Hedyx, Martin et. al. "Lung Cancer Mortality is Elevated in Coal Mining Areas of Appalachia." *Lung Cancer,* 2008: 1-8.

Hennessy-Fiske, Molly. "Veteran Swore Times at El Paso VA are Latest to Come under Scrutiny." *Los Angeles Times,* June 4, 2013: 1.

Hensli, John. *Sociology: A Down to Earth Approach.* New York: Allyn and Bacon, 2004.

"Hinkle v. Baker." *The Center for Individual Rights.* n.d. https://www.cir-usa.org/cases/hinkle-v-baker/ (accessed October 20, 2016).

Hoffer, Stephen. "Giants Kicker Josh Brown Admitted to Domestic Abuse, According to Police Documents." *Huffington Post.* October 20, 2016.

http://www.huffingtonpost.com/entry/josh-brown-domestic-abuse_us_5808c328e4b0dd54ce386009 (accessed December 30, 2016).

Hollis, Andre. "Narco-Terrorism." In *Transnational Threats: Smuggling and Trafficking in Arms, Drugs, and Human Life.*, by Kimberly Thachuck, 23. Westport, CT: Prager, 2007.

Hoppe, Hans-Hermann. "My Battle With the Thought Police." *The Mises Institute.* April 12, 2005. https://mises.org/library/my-battle-thought-police (accessed October 20, 2016).

House Judiciary Comittee, The. "Articles of Impeachment." Washington, DC, July 27, 1974.

Huang, X., V. Van and V. Evert. "Breaking the Silence Culture." *Management and Organization Review*, 2005: 740.

Hurdle, John and Richard Perez Peña. "Gunman Said He Shot Philadelphia Officer for ISIS." *The New York Times*, January 9, 2016: A10.

Hymowitz, Carol and Sisam Frier. "IBM's Rometty Breaks Ground as Corporation's First Female Leader." *Bllomberg BusinessWeek*, October 26, 2011.

Islam - the Religion of Peace. n.d. http://www.thereligionofpeace.com/ (accessed July 26, 2016).

"It Turns Out Trump Was Right." *US Message Board.* July 9, 2015. http://www.usmessageboard.com/threads/it-turns-out-trump-was-right.429608/ (accessed October 17, 2016).

Jackson, Abby. "Dis-invitations for College Speakers are on the Rise." *Business Insider*, July 28, 2016.

Jacobs, James P. Mobsters, Unions, and Feds: the Mafia And the American Labor Movement. New York: New York University Press, 2006.

Jacobs, JoAnn. "Indoctrination U: Thought Police at the University of Delaware." *PJ Media.* 2007. https://pjmedia.com/blog/critically_thinking_approved_t/ (accessed October 20, 2016).

Jacobs, Wilbur R. *Dispossessing the American Indian.* New York: Charles Scribner's Sons, 1972.

Johnson, Kirk. "Releases Video Showing Death of Occupier." *The New York Times*, January 29, 2016: A13.

Johnson, Michael P. and Kathleen J. Ferrero. "Research on Domestic Violence: Making Distinctions." *Journal of Marriage and the Family*, 2000: 948-963.

Johnston, David. "Ex-CIA Official Admits Corruption." *The New York Times*, September 29, 2008: A19.

Kaczynski, Alice. "12 Huge Lies About Justice in America." *Annual Review of Criminal Procedure*, 2015.

Kamen, Al. "Caroline Kennedy Poised for Japan." *The Washington Post*, July 13, 2013.

Katz, Deborah. "Injury Toll from Marathon Bombs Reduced to 264." *The New York Times*, April 24, 2013.

Keenan v. Aryan Nations. CV-99-441 (District Court of the First Judicial District, Idaho, Kootenai County, 2000).

Keener, John. "McVeigh's Mind: A Special Report; Oklahoma Bombing Suspect: Unraveling of a Frayed Life." *The New York Times*, December 31, 1995: 1.

Kempff, Wilhelm. "Peace Journalisms: A tightrope walk between advocacy and constructive coverage." *Conflict and Communication Online*, 2007.

Kennedy v. Louisiana. 554 U.S. 407 (U.S. Supreme Court, 2008).

Kernaghan, Charles. "Paying to Lose Our Jobs." In *No Sweat Fashion: Free Trade and the Rights of Garment Workers*, by Andrew Ross, 88. New York: Duke University Press, 1996.

Kilgore, Ed. "Some People Are Now 100% Sure Hillary Clinton Will Win." *New York*, October 18, 2016.

King, Rufus. *Gambling and Organized Crime*. Washington, DC: Public Affairs Press, 1969.

Kirkham, Chris. "War on Undocumented Immigrants Threatens to Swell U.S. Prison Population." *The Huffington Post*. August 23, 2013. http://www.huffingtonpost.com/2013/08/23/undocumented-immigrants-prison_n_3792187.html (accessed October 17, 2016).

Kirkpatrick, Janet. "Introduction: Shelling Out? Solidarity and Choice in the American Feminist Movement." *Perspectives on Politics*, 2010: 241-245.

Klein, Herbert S. & Ben Vinson III. *African Slavery in Latin American and the Caribbean*. New York: Oxford University Press, 1986.

Kleinfeld, E.R. "U.S. Attacked: Hijacked Jets Destroy Twin Towers And Hit Pentagon In Day Of Terror." *The New York Times*, September 12, 2001.

Klepper, David and Larry Neumeister. "New York Gov.'s Ex Top Aide among the Nine Charged in Bribery Case." *Register-Herald*, September 23, 2016.

Kolbert, Elizabeth. "Firebrand Phyllis Schlafly and the Conservative Revolution." *The New Yorker*, November 7, 2005.

Krinsky, Carol H. "Carl May's Western Novels and Aspects Of Their Continuing Influence." *American Indian Culture and Research*, 1999: 53-72.

Kushner, Harvey. *Encyclopedia of Terrorism*. Ann Arbor, MI: University of Michigan Press, 2003.

Laksin, Jacob. "Columbia University's Political Agendas." *Front Page Magazine.* December 1, 2006. http://archive.frontpagemag.com/readArticle. aspx?ARTID=1264 (accessed October 20, 2016).

Landesco, John. *Organized Crime in Chicago.* Chicago: University of Chicago Press, 1968.

Larner, John. "The Certainty of Columbus: Some Recent Studies." *History,* 1988: 3-23.

Latham, Robert. *The Travels of Marco Polo.* New York: Penguin Books, 1958.

Laurentz, Robert. *Racial and Ethnic Conflict in the New York City Garment Industry.* Binghamton, NY: State University of New York, 1980.

LeGrand, Camille E. "Rape and Rape Laws: Sexism in Society." *California Law Review,* 1973: 919.

Leo, John. "Indoctrination in Writing Class." *Minding the Campus.* 2008. http://www.mindingthecampus.org/2008/07/indoctrination_in_writing_clas/ (accessed October 20, 2016).

Levin, Brian. "A Dream Deferred: The Social and Legal Implications Of Hate Crimes." *The Journal of Intergroup Relations,* 1993: 3-27.

Levinthal, Charles F. *Drugs, Behavior, and Modern Society.* Boston: Allyn and Bacon, 1996.

Levitt, Joshua. "Jewish Students Report Intimidation as BDS Battle Ignites at University of Michigan." *Algemeiner.* March 25, 2014. https://www.algemeiner.com/2014/03/25/jewish-students-report-intimidation-as-bds-battle-ignites-at-university-of-michigan/ (accessed October 19, 2016).

Lewin, Tamar. "Sikh Owner of Gas Station is Fatally Shot in Rampage." *The New York Times,* September 17, 2001: 1.

Lewis, Neil A. "Abramoff Gets Four Years in Prison for Corruption." *The New York Times,* 2008.

Lieberman, Trudy. "Plagiarize, Plagiarize, Plagiarize- Only Be Sure to Call it Research." *Columbia Journalism Review,* 1995: 4.

Linz, Daniel, Edward Donnerstein and Steven Penrod. "Effects of Long-Term Exposure to Violent and Sexually Degrading Depictions of Women." *Journal of Personality and Social Psychology,* 1989: 758-768.

Lob, Wallace D. "The impact of common law and rape statutes on prosecution." *Washington Law Review,* 1980: 543-562.

Lockheed Aircraft Coporation v. Superior Court. 28 Cal.2d. 481 (1946).

Longfellow, Henry Wadsworth. *The Song of Hiawatha.* New York: Sloan and Pearce, 1966.

Lopez, German. "These States Let Police Take and Keep Your Stuff Even If You Haven't Committed a Crime." *Vox*, April 21, 2016.

The Los Angeles Times. "San Bernardino Shooting Updates." December 9, 2015.

Loyn, David. "Good Journalism or Peace Journalism." *Conflict and Communication Online*, 2007: 10.

Luna, Kausha. "Palestinians and Syrians Buy Honduran Identities." *Center for Immigration Studies.* May 27, 2016. http://cis.org/luna/palestinians-and-syrians-buy-honduran-identities-make-their-way-us (accessed October 17, 2016).

Lynd, Staughton and Alice Lynd. *The New Rank and File.* Ithaca, NY: Cornell University Press, 2000.

Lynn, Jake and Annabelle McGoldrick. *Peace Journalism.* Gloucestershire, UK: Stroud, 2000.

MacIsaac, Tyra. "Bad Forensic Science And Wrongful Convictions." *Epochal Times*, April 27, 2014.

MacKinnon, Catherine. "Pornography, Civil Rights, and Speech." *Harvard Civil Rights/Civil Liberties Law Review*, 1985.

Maffly, Brian. "LaVoy Finicum's Widow tells Utah Rally Her Hsband was Mrdered." *The Salt Lake Tribune*, March 5, 2016: 1.

Margolis, Max L. and Alexander Marx. *A History of the Jewish People.* New York: Meridian Books, 1958.

Martin, Douglas. "Walter Cronkite, 92, Dies; Trusted Voice of TV News." *The New York Times*, July 7, 2009.

Marx, Gary. "Columbia's Cocoa Diplomacy Promises Aims to Lift Ban." *Chicago Title*, December 6, 1992.

Maslow, Abraham H. *Motivation and Personality.* New York: Harper & Row, 1954.

May, Matthew. "Schadenfreude." *The Washington Post*, April 9, 2005.

McCarthy, Robert J. "Two Parties Jointly Back Four of Five Judgeships." *The Buffalo News*, September 22, 2014.

McClellan, David. *Karl Marx: Selected Writings.* New York: Oxford University Press, 1998.

McCoy, Terrence. "The Self-Destructive Mania of Representative Aaron Schock." *The Washington Post*, March 18, 2015.

McFadden, Robert D. "Explosion At The Twin Towers: Blast Hits Trade Center." *The New York Times*, February 27, 1993.

McKinley, James C. Jr. "Case for New Trial for Johnny Hincapie In Subway Murder Centers on Witnesses." *The New York Times*, July 21, 2015.

McPhate, Mike and Ben Sisario. "4 More Years: Rush Limbaugh Signs a New Radio Contract." *The New York Times*, August 2010.

Mele, Domenec. "Corruption: 10 Possible Causes." *Business Ethics Blog Network.* June 11, 2014. http://blog.iese.edu/ethics/2014/11/06/corruption-10--possible-causes/ (accessed January 5, 2017).

Merton, Robert K. "Social Structure and Anomie." *The American Sociological Review*, 1938: 672-682.

Merton, Robert. *On Theoretical Sociology.* New York: The Free Press, 1967.

Messing, John. "Public Lands, Politics, And Progressives: The Oregon Land Fraud Trials, 1903 – 1910." *Pacific Historical Review*, 1966: 35-66.

Midland Daily News. "Three Killed, Nine Wounded in the Attack on Planned Parenthood." November 27, 2015.

Midland Daily News. "Three Killed, Nine Wounded in the Attack on Planned Parenthood 2015." November 27, 2015.

Mihesuha, Devon A. *American Indian Stereotypes And Realities.* Atlanta: Clarity Press, 1996.

Mills, Hendrik. "American Indians and Welfare Liberalism." *American Enterprise*, 1998: 58.

Miranda v. Arizona. 384 US 436 (US Supreme Court, 1966).

Missouri Synod of the Lutheran Church. "Resolution 309 of the Missouri Synod of the Lutheran Church." 1983.

Missouri Synod of the Lutheran Church. "To Clarify a Position on Anti-Semitism." 1983.

Mitchell, Robert D. *Commercialism and Frontier: Perspectives on the Early Shenandoah Valley.* Charlottesville, VA: University Press of Virginia, 1977.

Moore, Wilbert E. *The Conduct of the Corporation.* New York: Random House, 1962.

Myrdal, Gunnar. *Asian Drama.* New York: Pantheon, 1968.

Nakashima, Ellen. "FBI Reports 27 Cops Were Killed Last Year. But How Many Civilians Were Killed by Officers?" *The Washington Post*, July 27, 2016.

National Abortion Federation. AAF Violence and Disruption Statistics: Incidents of Violence and Disruption Against Abortion Providers. National Abortion Federation, 2015.

National Assembly of France. "Declaration of the Rights of Man." 1789.

National Conference of State Legislatures. *Women in State Legislatures for 2016.* September 20, 2016. http://www.ncsl.org/legislators-staff/legislators/womens-legislative-network/women-in-state-legislatures-for-2016.aspx (accessed December 29, 2016).

National Gang Intelligence Center. "National Gang Report." 2015.

The National Review. "Noncitizens Voting." April 4, 2012.

Needham, Vicki. "Election Model: Clinton Will Win Easily." *The Hill*, July 1, 2016: 2.

Nepa, Francisco L. "Langley, Catherine Gudger ." In *American National Biography*, 156-157. New York: Oxford University Press, 1999.

New Jersey v. T.L.O. 469 U.S. 325 (U.S. Supreme Court, 1985).

The New York Times. "Drifter is Found Guilty of Killing a Seattle Family." June 6, 1986: 1.

The New York Times. "Ex-Illinois Gov. Pleads Guilty in Loan Fraud." August 6, 1987.

The New York Times. "Hillary Clinton Has an 85% Chance to Win ." November 8, 2016.

The New York Times. "Matthew Shepard Act." May 5, 2009.

Newman, Alex. "Amid IRS Abuse, Record Number of Americans Give up US Citizenship." *the New American Magazine*, December 9, 2013.

Nicholas, Vincent. *Magna Carta: The Foundation of Freedom.* London: Third Millennium Press, 2015.

Nielsen, Richard. *The Politics of Ethics.* New York: Oxford University Press, 2003.

Nixon, Richard M. "Address to the Nation on Labor Day." The American Presidency Project, September 6, 1971.

NLRB v. Jones and Laughlin Steel Corporation. 301 US 45 (US Supreme Court, 1937).

"Non-citizens Voting and ID Requirements in US Elections. Hearings before the Committee on House Administration. 109th Congress." 2006.

Nye, Joseph S. "Corruption and Political Development: a Cost-Benefit Analysis." *American Political Science Review*, 1967: 417-427.

O'Connor, Donald J. Puerto Rico's Potential as a Site for Textiel, Apparel, and Other Industries. New Brunswick, New Jersey: Rutgers University, 1949.

Ofshe, Richard J. and Richard A. Leo. "The Decision to Confess Falsely." *Denver University Law Review*, 1997.

Olson, Mancur. "The Political Economy of Growth Rates." In *The Political Economy of Growth*, by Dennis C. Mueller, 7-52. New Haven, CT: Yale University Press, 1983.

O'Malley, John W. "Opening the Church to the World." *The New York Times*, October 10, 2012.

Orwell, George. *1984.* New York: Penguin, 1950.

Ottosen, Rune. *The Dynamics of Medicalization*. Bern: Peter Lang, 2000.

Oxford Univeristy Press. *OED Online*. September 2016. http://www.oed.com/ viewdictionaryentry/Entry/11125 (accessed October 18, 2016).

Packard, Vance. *The Pyramid Climbers*. New York: McGraw Hill, 1962.

Papademetriou, Demetros G., Doris Meissner, and Eleanor Sohnen. *Thinking Regionally to Compete Globally*. Migration Policy Institute, 2013.

Paquette, Danielle. "It's 2016, and Women Still Make Less for Doing the Same Work as Men." *The Washington Post*, March 8, 2016: 20.

Paul VI, Pope. "Declaration of the Church to non-Chirstian Religions. Nostra aetate, proclaimed by his Holiness Pope Paul VI ." October 20, 1965.

Peerman, Dean. "Bare-Bones Imbroglio." *Christian Century*, 1990: 35.

People v. Connell. 879 NE 2nd 315 (2007).

Philpot, Roger. "A Coal Miner's Son in His Own Words." *Coal Miners*. n.d. http://www.coal-miners-in-kentucky.com/WhyaCoalminerswebsite. html (accessed October 20, 2016).

Picarelli, John T. *NIJ Journal*. 2011. http://www.nij.gov/journals/268/pages/ transnational.aspx (accessed October 21, 2016).

Pinckney, David H. "Napoleon III's Transformation of Paris." *Journal of Modern History*, 1955: 125-134.

Pliny the Elder. *Natural History*. Cambridge, MA: Harvard University Press, Loeb Classical Library, 1989.

—. *Natural History*. Cambridge, MA: Harvard University Press, Loeb Classical Library, 1989.

Plumer, Brad. "These 10 Charts Show the Black- White Economic Gap Hasn't Budged in 50 Years." *The Washington Post*, August 28, 2013: 1-5.

Polcyn, Bryan. "Embattled Professor John McAdams Filed Suite Against Marquette University." *Fox6Now*. May 2, 2016. http://fox6now. com/2016/05/02/embattled-professor-john-mcadams-has-filed-suit-against-marquette-university/ (accessed October 20, 2016).

Pope, Whitney. *Durkheim's Suicide*. Chicago: The University of Chicago Press, 1976.

Prescott, Bruce. "An Accurate Look at Timothy McVeigh's Beliefs." *EthicsDaily. com*. January 26, 2010. http://www.ethicsdaily.com/an-accurate-look-at-timothy-mcveighs-beliefs-cms-15532 (accessed January 4, 2017).

Preston, Brian. "Massive Noncitizen Voting Uncovered in Maryland." *PJ Media*, October 20, 2014.

Preston, Julia and Robert Gebeloff. "Some Unlicensed Drivers Risk More Than a Fine." *The New York Times*, December 10, 2010: A1.

"Pro-Israel and Jewish Students Attacked With Machete by Men Yelling in Arabic." *Live/Leak.* July 26, 2016. http://www.liveleak.com/view?i=9a7_1270665393 (accessed October 19, 2016).

Renaud, Jean Paul. "Cal Poly Settles Suit by Student." *The Los Angeles Times*, May 6, 2004.

Report of the National Advisory Commission On Civil Disorders . Washington, DC: United States Government Printing Office, 1968.

"Rev. Farrakhan to Followers: 'White People Deserve to Die'." *Newsmax.* August 15, 2015. http://www.newsmax.com/Newsfront/louis-farrkhan-kill-white/2015/08/15/id/670304/ (accessed January 4, 2017).

Revkin, Andrew C. "Confronting the Oregon Refugee Invasion." *The New York Times*, January 7, 2016: 2016.

Ritchie, Sam B. "Limiting Voters' Choices in South Carolina." *ACLU*, March 12, 2010.

Rodgers, Grant. "Ron Paul Aids Avoid Jail Time In Endorsement." *Des Moines Register*, September 20, 2016.

Roscigno, Vincent. "Social Movement Struggles and Race, Gender and Class Identity." *Race, Sex, and Class*, 1994: 109-126.

Rose-Ackerman, Susan. *Corruption and Government: Causes, Consequences And Reform.* Cambridge: Cambridge University Press, 1999.

Rosenbaum, David. "Rostenkowski Pleads Guilty to Mail Fraud." *The New York Times*, April 10, 1996.

Rude, George. *Revolutionary Europe 1783-1815.* New York: Wiley Publishers, 1964.

Runge, Robin. "Double Jeopardy: Victims of Domestic Violence Suffer Twice the Abuse." *ABA Journal*, 1998: 19-21.

Russell, Jason. "Which Federal Agency do Americans Hate Most?" *The Washington Examiner*, November 23, 2015: 1.

Schaefer, Richard T. *Racial and Ethnic Groups.* New York: Harper Collins, 1993.

Schmidt, Susan and James V. Grimaldi. "Nye Sentenced to 30 Months in Prison for Abramoff Deals ." *The Washington Post*, January 20, 2007: 1.

Schneider, Andrew and JoAnn Martinez. "Medicaid and the Uninsured." In *Native American Health and Welfare Policy in an Age of New Federalism*, by Rober and Stephanie Carroll Rainie, eds. Merideth. Tucson, AZ: Udall Center Publications, 2002.

Schubert, Theodore. "Muslims Attack Church in America Called Home of the Crusaders." *Shoebat.com.* September 2, 2014. http://shoebat.com/2014/09/02/muslims-attack-three-church-america-called-home-crusaders/ (accessed October 19, 2016).

Schuessler, K. *E.H. Sutherland and Analyzing Crime.* Chicago: University of Chicago Press, 1973.

Schulberg, Pete. "FOXNews: Business If Not Artistic Success." *The Oregonian,* July 15, 1994: E1.

Schulkin, Peter A. "The Revolving Door." *Center for Immigration Studeis.* November 8, 2012. http://cis.org/revolving-door-deportations-of-criminal-illegal-immigrants (accessed October 17, 2016).

Schwartz, Stuart. Implicit Understandings: Observing the Encounter Between Europeans & Other Peoples in the Early Modern Era. Cambridge: Cambridge University Press, 1994.

Schwendinger, Julia and Herman Schwendinger. *Rape and Inequality.* Beverly Hills, CA: Sage, 1983.

Schwoerer, Lois G. "Locke, Lockian Ideas and the Glorious Revolution." *Journal of the History of Ideas,* 1990: 531-548.

Seelye, Catherine. "New Alaska Gov. Gives Daughter His Seat in Senate." *The New York Times,* December 21, 2002.

Shanks-Meile, Stephanie and Betty A. Dobratz. " 'Sick' Feminists or Helpless Victims: Images of Women in Ku ." *Humanity and Society,* 1991: 72-93.

Shaw, Jazz. "Alabama Court Upholds Conviction of Woman Guilty of Voter Fraud," ." *Hot Air,* August 10, 2016.

Shire, Emily. "Freeom of Speech? Not at Brown University." *The Daily Beast.* October 15, 2015. http://fox6now.com/2016/05/02/embattled-professor-john-mcadams-has-filed-suit-against-marquette-university/ (accessed October 20, 2016).

Silverglate, Harvey. "The Slow Death of Free Speech at Harvard." *FIRE.* November 3, 2013. https://www.thefire.org/the-slow-death-of-free-speech-at-harvard/ (accessed October 20, 2016).

Skolnik, Jeffrey and James Fife. *Above the Law: Police and the Excessive Use of Force.* New York: The Free Press, 1993.

Smith, Allan. "NBC's Electoral Map Shows Hillary Clinton with Enough Electoral Votes to Win the Presidency." *The New York Times,* November 8, 2016.

Smothers, Ronald. "Treffinger Pleads Guilty to Corruption." *The New York Times,* May 31, 2003.

Snyder v. Phelps. 131 S.CT. 1207 (2011).

Society of Professional Journalists. "Code of Ethics." 1996.

Southall, Ashley. "Jesse Jackson, Jr. Gets 30 Months, and His Wife 12, to be Served at Separate Times." *New York Times,* August 17, 2013.

Southern Poverty Law Center. "David Duke." *SPLC: Southern Poverty Law Center.* n.d. https://www.splcenter.org/fighting-hate/extremist-files/individual/david-duke (accessed January 4, 2017).

Southern Poverty Law Center. *Klanwatch Intelligence Report.* Montgomery, AL: Southern Poverty Law Center, 1999.

Southern Poverty Law Center. "The Year in Hate; intelligence Report." 2007.

Spencer, Robert. "Muslim students Attack Jewish students at University of Wisconsin – Milwaukee." *Jihad Watch.* May 2, 2010. https://www.jihadwatch.org/2010/05/muslim-students-attacks-jewish-students-at-university-of-wisconsin-milwaukee (accessed October 19, 2016).

Spillius, Alex and Tom Leonard. "Suspect in Abortion Doctor Killing had History of Mental Illness." *The Daily Telegraph,* June 1, 2009.

Stana, Richard M. *Information on Certain Illegal Aliens Arrested in the United States.* United States Government Accountability Office, 2005.

Stares, Paul. *The Drug Culture in a Borderless World.* Washington DC: Brookings Institute Press, 1996.

Stebbins, Samuel. "12 States With the Most Hate Groups." *24/7 Wall St.* February 24, 2016. http://247wallst.com/special-report/2016/02/24/12-states-hate-groups/ (accessed January 4, 2017).

Steinhauer, Jennifer. "Senate, for Just the Eighth Time, Votes to Oust a Federal Judge." *The New York Times,* December 8, 2010: A27.

Stelter, Brian. "With Tagline, MSNBC Embraces A Political Identity." *The New York Times,* August 2010.

Sterngold, James. "Supremacist who killed postal worker avoidance death sentence." *The New York Times,* January 24, 2004.

Sugarman, David B. and Marie Straus. "Indicators of Gender Equality for American States and Regions." *Social Indicators Research,* 1987: 229-270.

Sulek, Judy Prolis. "SF Shooting Victim Kate Steinle: She Was About Loving People friends Say." *San Jose Mercury News,* July 9, 2015: 1.

Sun, Ivan and Brian Payne. "Racial Differences in Resolving Conflicts: a Comparison between Black and White Police Officers'." *Crime and Delinquency,* 2004: 516-541.

Susnjar v. United States. 27 F.2nd 223 (6th Circuit, 1928).

Sutherland, Edwin. *Principles of Criminology.* Lanham, MD: Altamira Press, 1992.

Sveen, Emma K. "Highly Decorated LSU Professor Fired for Occasional Profanity." *The Daily Caller.* June 30, 2015. http://dailycaller.com/2015/06/30/highly-decorated-lsu-professor-fired-for-occasional-profanity/ (accessed October 20, 2016).

Tannenbaum, Frank. *A Philosophy of Labor.* New York: Alfred A. Knopf, 1951 and 2011.

Tapsak, Peter. "Voter Fraud Is Real. Here Are Four More Cases ." *The Daily Signal,* August 18, 2016.

Tepfer, Joshua A. and Laura Nirider. "Adjudicated Juveniles and Post Conviction Litigation." *Maine Law Review,* 2012: 11-12.

Think Progress. "How Did the Dispute Start?" January 3, 2016: 4.

Thomas, Judy L. "Suspect Until His Death Supported Killing Abortion Providers Friends Say." *Kansas City Star,* June 4, 2009.

Thomas, William I. *The Child in America.* New York: Knopf, 1929.

Thornton, Russell. "American Indian Fertility Patterns." *American Indian Quarterly,* 1991: 359-367.

Times Record. "Martha Shoffner Sentenced to 30 Months in Prison on Bribery, Extortion Charges." August 29, 2015.

Tolchin, Martin and Susan Tolchin. *To The Victor.* New York: Random, 1971.

U.S. News. "Arizona Representative Rick Renzi Convicted in Federal Corruption Case." January 11, 2013: 3.

"Union Bosses Talk Wage Inequality, Rake In Six-Figure Salaries." *Labor Pains.* July 29, 2016. http://laborpains.org/2016/07/29/union-bosses-talk-wage-inequality-rake-in-six-figure-salaries-2/ (accessed October 20, 2016).

"United Nations World Drug Report." 2009.

United States Department of Commerce, Bureau of Labor Statistics. *New Household Income.* United States Department of Commerce, Bureau of Labor Statistics, 2015.

United States Department of Justice. "Federal Prosecution of Election Offenses, 7th Edition." 2007.

United States Drug Enforcement Agency. "Drug Trafficking in the United States." *Almanac of Policy Issues.* n.d.

United States Mine Rescue Association. "Mine Disasters in the United States." n.d.

United States of America v. Lauren C. Troescher. 55609 (United States Court of Appeals, Ninth Circuit, November 7, 1996).

United States Office of Personnel Management. "Historical Federal Workforce Tables." 1962.

United States v. Alvarez. 617 F.3d 1198 (US Court of Appeals for the 9th Circuit, 2010).

United States v. Williams. 529 F.Supp 1085 (U.S. District Court for the Eastern District of New York, 1981).

US Department of Labor, Bureau of Labor Statistics. *Current Employment Statistics.* US Department of Labor, 2016.

Vaglanos, Alanna. "30 Shocking Domestic Violence Statistics That Remind Us It's an Epidemic." *Huffington Post.* October 23, 2014. http://www. huffingtonpost.com/2014/10/23/domestic-violence-statistics_n_5959776. html (accessed December 29, 2016).

Van Dyne, Leonard, et. al. "Conceptualizing Employees' Silence." *Journal of Management Studies,* 2003: 1361.

Van Oot, Torey. "Report: Assemblywoman Mary Hayashi Arrested for Shoplifting." *The Sacramento Bee,* October 28, 2011.

Veblen, Thorstein. *The Theory of the Leisure Class.* New York: Oxford University Press, 2007, originally 1912.

Vielmetti, Bruce. "Sherwood Man Charged with 13 Counts of Voter Fraud." *The Journal Sentinel,* June 24, 2014.

Vital Statistics. Washington, DC: Center for Union Facts, 2016.

Vlasic, Bill. "New G.M. Chief is Company Woman Born To It." *The New York Times,* December 12, 2013: Business Day:1.

Wakin, Daniel J. "Richard G. Butler, Founder of the Aryan Nation, Dies." *The New York Times,* September 9, 2004.

Walker, Jim. "Crewmember Rights." *Cruise Law News,* August 9, 2016: 15-16.

Walker, Samuel. *Police Accountability.* New York: Wadsworth, 2001.

Warren, Mark. "Democracy and Deceit: Regulating Appearances of Corruption." *American Journal of Political Science,* 2006: 160–174.

Weber, Max. *Die Protestantische Ethik und der Geist des Kapitalismus,* or The Protestant Ethic and the Spirit of Capitalism. Boston: D.C. Heath & Co., 1926.

Weinstein, Miriam. *Yiddish: A Nation of Words.* New York: Ballantine Books, 2001.

West, Delmo. "Christopher Columbus and His Enterprise to the Indies." *William and Mary Quarterly,* 1942.

Whelan, Carmine Teresa. "Labor Migrants or Submissive Wives: Competing Narratives of Puerto Rican Women in the Post World War II Era." In *Puerto Rican Women's History: New Perspectives,* by Linda Delgado and Felix Matos Rodriguez, 206-226. Armonk, NY: M.E. Sharpe Publishers, 1998.

White, John R. "The Road to Armageddon: Religion and Domestic Terrorism." *Quarterly Journal of Ideology,* 1989: 11-21.

Whitlock, Scott. "CBS Predicts 341 Electoral Votes for Hillary Clinton in Likely Blowout." *MRC NewsBusters.* September 6, 2016. http://www.newsbusters.

org/blogs/nb/scott-whitlock/2016/09/06/cbs-predicts-341-electoral-votes-hillary-clinton-possible-blowout (accessed January 8, 2017).

Wilson, Michelle and John Lynxwiler. "Abortion Clinic Violence As Terrorism." *Studies in Conflict and Terrorism*, 1988: 263-273.

Wolf, Naomi. *The Beauty Myth.* New York: Morrow, 1991.

Work Leaders. "Map That Proves Donald Trump Will Lose." August 17, 2016.

Yasgur, Batya Swift. *Compensation Gender Gap in Health Care.* 2016. http://medcareerguide.com/compensation-gender-gap-in-health-care/ (accessed December 29, 2016).

Young Women's Christian Association. *Fact Sheet: Firearms Related Domestic Violence Homicides.* n.d. http://intranet.ywca.org/atf/cf/%7B38F90928-EE78-4CE9-A81E-7298DA01493E%7D/DV%20Guns%20Fact%20Sheet%20FINAL%20March%202015.pdf (accessed December 29, 2016).

Young, T. J. "Violent Hate Groups in Rural America." International Journal Of Offender And Comparative Criminology, 1989.

ENDNOTES

1. Robert Latham, *The Travels of Marco Polo*, (New York: Penguin Books, 1958), p. 16.

2. Stuart Schwartz, *Implicit Understandings: Observing the Encounter between Europeans and Other Peoples in the Early Modern Era*, (Cambridge: Cambridge University Press, 1994), pp. 249-267.

3. J.C. Campbell, "Cultural Contact and Polynesian Identity in the European Age," *Journal of World History*, vol.8, (1997), pp. 29-55.

4. Herbert S. Klein and Ben Vinson III, *African Slavery in Latin America and the Carribbean*, (New York: Oxford University Press, 1986), Ch.8.

5. John Larner, "The Certainty of Columbus: Some recent Studies," *History*, vol 73, (1988), pp. 3-23.

6. Delmo West, "Christopher Columbus and His Enterpise to the Indies," *William and Mary Quarterly*, vol. 49, no.2 (April 1942), N.P.

7. Richard Cavendish, "The 'Casa de Contratacion,'" *History Today*, vol. 53, no. 1, (January 2003), n.p.

8. Will Durant, *The Age of Faith*, (New York: Simon and Schuster, 1950), pp. 586-587.

9. Vincent Nicholas, *Magna Carta: The Foundation of Freedom*, (London: Third Millenium Press, 2015), pp. 45-169.

10. Lois G. Schwoerer, "Locke, Lockian Ideas and the Glorious Revolution," *Journal of the History Of Ideas*, vol. 51, no.4, (October 1990), pp. 531-548.

11. George Rude, *Revolutionary Europe 1783-1815*, (New York: Wiley Publishers, 1964), p. 183.

12. David H. Pinckney, "Napoleon III's Transformation of Paris," *Journal of Modern History*, v. 22., no.2, (1955), pp. 125-134.

13. The National Assembly of France, *Declaration of the Rights of Man*, (1789).

14. Abraham H. Maslow, *Motivation and Personality*, (New York: Harper & Row, 1954).

15. David McClellan, *Karl Marx: Selected Writings*, (New York: Oxford University Press, 1998), pp. 431-432.

16. Vance Packard,*The Pyramid Climbers*, (New York, McGraw Hill, 1962).

17. Max Weber, *Die Protestantische Ethik und der Geist des Kapitalismus*, or *The Protestant Ethic and the Spirit of Capitalism*, (Boston, D.C. Heath & Co., 1926).

18. Ibid. n.p.

19. Mancur Olson, "The Political Economy of Growth Rates," in *The Political Economy of Growth*, Dennis C. Mueller, Editor. (New Haven, CT: Yale University Press, 1983), pp. 7-52.

20. Robert Barnes, "Supreme Court Strikes Down Limits on Federal Campaign Contributions," *The Washington Post* (April 2, 2014), p. 1.

21. Carl C. Friedrich, "Revolution and Ideology in the Late 20th Century," in: *Revolution*, (New York: Atherton Press, 1966).

22. The Declaration of Independence

23. U.S. Office of Personnel Management, "Historical Federal Workforce Tables," *Total Government Employment Since 1962.*

24. No author, "How did the dispute start?" *Think Progress,* January 3, 2016:4.

25. The Fifth Amendment of the United States Constitution

26. Brian Maffly, "LaVoy Finicum's widow tells Utah rally her husband was murdered," *The Salt Lake Tribune*, (March 5, 2016):1.

27. Kirk Johnson et. al. "Releases Video Showing Death of Occupier," *The New York Times* (January 29, 2016 section a page 13).

28. Mark Berman, "Ammon Bundy was acquitted for the Oregon refuge takeover. Now he is facing another federal tril." *The Washington Post*, (October 28, 2016):6.

29. Kevin Sullivan and Leah Sottile, "Acquittal in the Oregon standoff add fuel to the political fire,"*The Buffalo News*, (October 30, 2016):A2.

30. Andrew C. Revkin, "Confronting the Oregon Refugee Invasion," *The New York Times*, (January 7, 2016) : 8.

31. Hannah Cleaver, "Turkish workers: a mistake claims Schmidt," *London Daily Telegraph*, (November 25, 2004):1.

32. Kausha Luna, "Palestinians and Syrians buy Honduran identities,"*Center for Immigration Studies*, (May, 27,2016):1

33. Judy Prolis Sulek, "SF shooting victim Kate Steinle: she was about loving people friends say." *San Jose Mercury News*, (July 9, 2015):1.

34. Paul Bedard, "Century City's cross the 300 mark with Dallas, Philly," *Washington Examiner*. (February 2, 2016),1.

35. John Binder, "Here are the shocking numbers of crimes committed by illegal immigrants" *The Hayride*, (September 2015):1.

36. Ibid., 4

37. Ibid., 5.

38. Julia Preston and Robert Gebeloff, "Some Unlicensed Drivers Risk More Than a Fine," *The New York Times*, (December 0, 2010):A1.

39. Joseph Farah, "Illegal aliens murder 12 Americans daily," www.wnd.com(November 28, 2006,)

40. Peter A. Schulkin, "The Revolving Door," *Center for Immigration Studies*, (November 8. 2012) www.cis.orh/revolving-door-deportations-of-crimnal-illegal-immifrants

41. Chris Kirkham, "War on Undocumented Immigrants Threatens U.S. Prison Population," *The Huffington Post*, (August 23, 2013):2.

42. Daniel Greenfield, "188,382 Criminal Illegal Aliens Deported in 2011," *Front Page Magazine*, (November 12, 2012):1.

43. Demetros G. Papademetriou, Doris Meissner and Eleanor Sohnen, "Thinking Regionally to Compete Globally," *Migration Policy Institute*, (May 2013):4B.

44. Richard M. Stana, "Information on certain illegal aliens arrested in the United States," *United States Government Accountability Office*, (May 9, 2005):1.

45. No author, "It turns out Trump was right," *US Message Board*, (July 9, 2015):1.

46. National Gang Intelligence Center, 2015:29.

47. Jason Russell, "Which federal agency do Americans hate the most?" *The Washington Examiner*, (November 23, 2015):1.

48. United States Court of Appeals, Ninth Circuit. United States of America, Petitioner-Appellee v.. Lauren C Troescher, Respondent-Applicant . No. 55609. Decided November 7, 1996.

49. Shaila Dewan, "Law lets I.R.S. seize accounts on suspicion, no crime required." *The New York Times*, (October 26, 2014):A1.

50. Elizabeth Pryce Foley, "Sovereignty Reclaimed: the tea party and constitutional amendments," *Tennessee Law Review* (August 3, 2011) v.78. p. 751.

51. Alex Newman, "Amid I.R.S. Abuse, Record Number of Americans Give up U.S. Citizenship," *The New American Magazine,* (December 9, 2013):1.

52. The Oxford Dictionary

53. Al Kamen, "Caroline Kennedy poised for Japan," *The Washington Post,* (July 13, 2013):1.

54. Catherine Seelye, "New Alaska Gov. gives daughter His Seat in Senate" *The New York Times* (December 21, 2002):1.

55. No author, "All in the Family," http://prorev.com/family.htm

56. Ibid., 3

57. Ibid., 4.

58. Robert J McCarthy," Two Parties Jointly Back Four of Five Judgeships," *The Buffalo News,* (September 22, 2014):City and Region:1.

59. Sam B Ritchie, "Limiting Voters' Choices in South Carolina," *ACLU,* (March 12, 2010):1.

60. German Lopez. "These states let police take and keep your stuff even if you haven't committed a crime."*Vox* (April 21, 2016):n.p.

61. Michelle Wilson and John Lynxwiler, "Abortion Clinic Violence As Terrorism," *Studies In Conflict and Terrorism,*Vol. 11, no. 4., (1988), pp. 263-273.

62. "AAF Violence and Disruption Statistics: Incidents of Violence and Disruption against abortion providers," National Abortion Federation (September 21, 2015).

63. Harvey Kushner,*Encyclopedia Of Terrorism,* Ann Arbor, Michigan, University of Michigan Press, (2003), p. 154.

64. Alesha E. Doan, *Opposition and Intimidation: The Abortion Wars and Strategies of Political Harassment.* (Ann Arbor: The University of Michigan Press) p. 23.

65. Juan Ignacio Blanco, Editor. *Murderpedia- The Free Online Encyclopedic Dictionary of Murder* (http://murderpedia.org, (July 26, 2016).

66. Judy L Thomas, "Suspect Until His Death Supported Killing Abortion Providers Friends Say," *Kansas City Star,* (June 4, 2009), p. 1.

67. *Spillius, Alex; Leonard, Tom "Suspect in abortion doctor killing had history of mental illness" The Daily Telegraph (UK).n.d.*

68. No author, "Three Killed, nine wounded in the attack on planned parenthood." *Midland Daily News,* (November 27, 2015).1.

69. Dallas Blanchard, *Religious Violence and Abortion,* Gainesville, Florida, University Pres of Florida, (1993), p. 190

70. Ibid. p. 193.

71. No author, "Jewish student attacked with machete by men yelling in Arabic," *Live/Leak*, (no date) http://www.liveleak.com/, (July 26, 2016).

72. John Hurdle and Richard Perez Peña, "Gunman Said He Shot Philadelphia Officer for ISIS," *The New York Times*, (January 9, 2016)," p. A10.

73. Bradford Richardson, "Persecution of Christians is on the rise, Americans say," *The Washington Times*, (April 5, 2016):1.

74. Steve Bittenbender,"Contempt ruling upheld against Kentucky clerk against gay marriage," *The Philadelphia Daily News*, (July 13, 2016)1.

75. John Hawkins, "Seven examples of discrimination against Christians in America," *Townhall*, (September 17, 2013):17.

76. Lori Sanada, "Two Christians prosecuted for reading the Bible in public," *Christian Newswire*, (March 29, 2012) :1

77. Heather Clark, "Christian Air Force veteran relieved of duties for refusing to affirm homosexual marriage," *Christian News*, (August 19, 2013):1.

78. Hawkins, "Seven examples etc.:13.

79. Brittany Smith, "Defend Christians Org: Top 10 anti-Christian Acts"*Christian Post*, (April 30, 2015).1.

80. Christopher Ingraham, "The nonreligious are now the country's largest religious voting block,"*Tthe Washington Post*, (July 14, 2016):1.

81. Richard Yeakley, "Growth stalls, falls for largest U.S. churches". *Religious News Service*, (February 15, 2011)1.

82. Gary Graff, "Love was the word but what was the truth?" *The Day*, (August 13, 1989):D1-D2.

83. Marcus Tullius Cicero, *de Natura Deorum*, New York: Loeb Classical Library, 1932.

84. Benton Johnson, et.al. "Mainline Churches: The Real Reason for Decline," *First Things*, (March 31, 1993): 13 -18.

85. Carlyle Murphy, "Half of U.S. adults raised Catholic have left the church at some point," *Pew Research Center*. (September 15, 2015):1.

86. 1917 Code of Canon Law. Canon Law 614.

87. Leslie Bennetts, "Unholy Alliances," *Vanity Fair*, (December 1991)1:-2.

88. Benton Johnson, Mainline Churches etc.:8-9.

89. Frank Tannenbaum, *A Philosophy of Labor*, (New York: Alfred A. Knopf, 1951 and 2011):9.

90. Washington D.C. ,United States Department of Labor, Bureau of Labor Statistics (August 5, 2016).

91. Ibid. (June 21, 2016).

92. Richard Nixon, Address to the Nation on Labor Day, (*The American Presidency Project.* (September 6, 1971)

93. Huang, X., Van, V. and Evert, V. "Breaking the silence culture etc." *Management and Organization Review,* (2005) vol.3, number 3:740.

94. Richard Nielsen, *The Politics of Ethics.* New York: Oxford University Press, (2003).

95. Leonard van Dyne, et. al., "Conceptualizing Employees Silence," *Journal of Management Studies,* vol 40, no. 6, (2003):1361.

96. J.C. Tait, American Steel Foundries v. Tri-City Central Trades, 257 US 184 209 (1921).

97. Wilbert E Moore, *The Conduct of the Corporations,* (New York: Random House, 1962):28.

98. Garrity v. New Jersey, 385 U.S. 493 (1967).

99. Comerford v. International Harvester, 235 Ala. 376, 170 So. 894 (1938).

100. Susnjar v. United States, 27 F.2nd 223(6th CTR. 1928).

101. Lockheed Aircraft Corporation v. Superior Court, 28 Cal. Sd. 481, 170 1P Sd., 21,25 (1946).

102. 15 United States Congress I, 1221 e (1964).

103. 208 US 161 (1908).

104. 236 U. S. 1 (1915).

105. 301 U.S. At 45 – 46.

106. Joe Bruno, *Mobsters,* Fiskdale, MA, (2014):3.

107. Ibid., 5.

108. James P Jacobs, *Mobsters, Unions, and Feds: the Mafia And the American Labor Movement.* New York: New York University Press, (2006): 49.

109. No author, Center for Union Facts, *Washington,* DC, Vital Statistics, (February 20, 2016):4.

110. Labor Pains.Org Team, "Union Bosses Talk Wage Inequality, Rake In Six-Figure Salaries" *Labor Pains.* (July 29, 2016):1.

111. Sylvia Federici, *Wages against Housework,* Bristol, England (The Falling Wall Press, 1998):2-10.

112. Danielle Paquette, "It's 2016, and women still make less for doing the same work as men," *The Washington Post,* March 8, (2016):20. I

113. No author, "Usual weekly earnings of wage and salary workers second quarter 2016" *Bureau of Labor Statistics,* (July 19, 2016):1.

114. Shannon Catalano, Erica Smith, Howard Snyder and Michael Rand, Washington D.C. United States Department of Justice, Bureau of Justice Statistics, "Female Victims of Violence"(2009):1-7

115. William Goode, "Force and Violence in the Family," *Journal of Marriage and the Family*, vol.33, (1971):624-636.

116. Michael P. Johnson and Kathleen J. Ferrero, "Research on Domestic Violence: Making Distinctions." *Journal of Marriage and the Family*,vol.62, (2000): 948- 963.

117. Roger Clark, "Women's Access to Prestigious Occupations: A Cross National Investigation," *Social Science Quarterly*, vol.72, (1991):20–32.

118. Thomas M. Cooley, "Comment: Passenger Protection Will Not Sink the Cruise Ship Industry ," *Law Review* (February 25, 2009)vol.23: 597.

119. Jim Walker, "Crewmember Rights," *Cruise Law News*, (August 9, 2016):15-16.

120. Milton Green, "West Virginia Mine Explosion: mine had scores of safety citations," *Huffington Post*, (June 6, 2010:1.

121. no author, "Mine disasters in the United States" United States Mine Rescue Association, no date

122. Roger Philpot, "A Coal Miner's Son," (http://www.rogerphilpot.com)

123. Martin Hedyx, et.al., "Lung cancer mortality is elevated in coal mining areas of Appalachia," *Lung Cancer*, v.. 62 (2008): 1-8.

124. Charles Kernaghan. "Paying to lose our jobs, and will "In: No Sweat Fashion, Free Trade at the Rights of Garment Workers," Andrew Ross editor, (New York: Duke University Press, (1996) p. 88.

125. Robert D Mitchell, *Commercialism and Frontier: Perspectives on the Early Shenandoah Valley*, Charlottesville University press of Virginia (1977) pp. 153-155.

126. Ibid. 228-229.

127. Charles Kernaghan. "Paying to lose our jobs, and will "In: No Sweat Fashion, Free Trade at the Rights of Garment Workers," Andrew Ross editor, (New York: Duke University Press, (1996) p. 88.

128. Carmine Teresa Whelan, "Labor Migrants or Submissive Wives Competing Narratives of Puerto Rican Women in the Post World War II Era," In: *Puerto Rican Women's History, New York. Armonk*, (1998) pp. 206–226.

129. Donald J O'Connor, Puerto Rico's Potential As a Site for Textile, Apparel And Other Industries," (New Brunswick New Jersey, Alexander Library, Rutgers University, 1949).

130. Robert Laurentz, *Racial Ethnic Conflict in the New York City Garment Industry*. (Binghamton, New York, State University of New York, 1980) p. 60. 1958

131. United States Department of Labor, Washington D.C., Bureau of Labor Statistics, Occupational Employment and Wages, May 2015.Chart #51-6031.

132. Abeles, Schwartz, Haeckel and Silverblatt, *The Chinese Garment Industry Study*, (New York: International Ladies Garment Workers Union, 1983) p. 45.

133. Ibid. 46.

134. Nancy Greene, *Ready-To-Wear Ready to Work: a Century of Industry and Immigrants in Paris and New York*, (Durham: Duke University Press, 1997) p. p. 161 - 187

135. Staughton Lynd and Alice Lynd, *The New Rank and File,,* (Ithaca, New York, Cornell University Press, 2000).

136. Gerhard Falk, *Murder*: An Analysis of Its Forms, Conditions, and Causes. (Jefferson, North Carolina, McFarland and Company Inc., 1990) p. 34

137. Brad Plumer, "These 10 Charts Show the Black- White Economic Gap Hasn't Budged in 50 Years," *The Washington Post*, (August 28, 2013):1-5.

138. Ibid., 4-5.

139. Aaron Bandler, "Seven Statistics You Need to Know about Black on Black Crime," *The Daily Wire*, (July 13, 2016):1-7.

140. Alice Kaczynsky, "12 Huge Lies About Justice in America," *Annual Review Of Criminal Procedure, Criminal Law* 2,.0 GEO, L. J.xiii (2015).

141. No author, "After 21 years Texas exonerates an area native." *The Buffalo News*, (December 27, 2016):A1.

142. James C McKinley Jr, "Case for New Trial for Johnny Hincapie in Subway Murder Centers on Witnesses." *The New York Times*, (July 21, 2015):1.

143. 768. S. W. 2-d 281; 577 S. W. 2d 717..

144. Douglas Martin "Randall Adams 61, Dies; Freed with Help of Film." *The New York Times*, (June 25, 2011):A7.

145. 512. A. Sd 1056.

146. 781 S. W.2nd 886; 691 S. W.2nd 699

147. 940 S. W.2nd 623; 741 S. W. 2d 928.

148. 1992II ILL. Lexis he 221; 643 N.E. 2nd, 6363nd.

149. 692P. 2-Dd 991.

150. 247 S.E. 2d 57. 561

151. 561 capital So.2d 692

152. 604 A.2nd793.

153. 845 S.W.2d 228 and 874 S.W.2d 602.

154. Tyra MacIsaac, "Bad Forensic Science and Wrongful Convictions," *Epochal Times*, (April 27, 2014):1.

155. Richard J. Ofshe and Richard A. Leo"," The Decision to Confess *Falsely"* *Denver University Law Review*, vol.74

156. 490 US 279 (1991)., (1997) pp. 979-993

157. Chapman vs. California, 386 US18,22 (1967).

158. People vs. Connell, 879 NE 2nd 315 ,319(Ill2007).

159. Joshua A. Tepfer and Laura Nirider, "Adjudicated Juveniles and Post Conviction Litigation," *Maine Law Review*, Vol. 63, (April 2012):11-12.

160. *Jim Fisher, Forensics under Fire*, New Brunswick, N.J. Rutgers University Press, (2008) p. 236.

161. Paul Gianelli," The Abuse of Scientific Evidence in Criminal Cases: The Need for Independent Crime Laboratories," *Virginia Journal of Social Policy and the Law*,vol. 439, (Winter 1997).n.p.

162. United States Supreme Court, Miranda v. Arizona" # 759 (June 13, 1966).

163. Twila Derber, "Three Convicted Rampart Police Officers Request New Trial," *Los Angeles Times*, (December 3, 2000):1.

164. Jeffrey Skolnik and James Fife, *Above the Law: Police and the Excessive Use of Force*, (New York: The Free Press, 1993).

165. Ivan Sun and Brian Payne"," Racial Differences in Resolving Conflicts: a Comparison between Black and White Police Officers'" *Crime and Delinquency*,vol.50, no.4, (October 2004): 516 – 541.

166. Samuel Walker, *Police Accountability*, (New York: Wadsworth, 2001).

167. *Report of the National Advisory Commission On Civil Disorders* .Washington DC, United States Government Printing Office, (1968) p. 93.

168. 168 Madison Alder, "Vehicle Plows into Phoenix Officers Standing at Quick Trip Convenience Store," *The Arizona Republic*, (September 11, 2016):1.

169. 169 Mark Berman, "Number of Law Enforcement Officers Fatally Shot This Year up Significantly Affect Ambush Attacks Report Says," *The Washington Post*, (July 27, 2016):1

170. Ellen Nakashima, "F.B.I. Reports 27 Cops Were Killed Last Year. But how many civilians were killed by officers?" *The Washington Post*, (November 24, 2014):1.

171. Aaron Bandler, "The Alton Sterling and Philando Castille shootings," *The Daily Wire*, (July 7, 2016):1.

172. George Orwell, *1984*, New York, (Penguin) 1950.

173. Abby Jackson, "Dis-invitations for college speakers are on the rise" *Business Insider*, (July 28, 2016):1.

174. Ibid., 3-10.

175. Jacob Laksin, "Columbia University's Political Agendas," *Front Page Magazine,* (December 1, 20060;1.

176. JoAnn Jacobs," Indoctrination U: Thought Police At the University of Delaware" *PJ Media,* (November 6, 2007P:1.

177. John Leo, "Indoctrination in Writing Class," *Minding the Campus.* (2008):2.

178. *Hinkle v. Baker,* Washinton, D.C. The Center for Individual Rights, (no date). See also: Jean Paul Ranaud, "Cal. Poly. Settles Suit by Student" *The Los Angeles Times,* (May 6, 2004):1.

179. Hans Hermann Hope, "My Battle with the .Thought Police," Vienna, Austria, *The Mises Institute,* (April12, 2005).

180. Emma K. Sveen, "Highly Decorated L.S.U. Professor Fired for Occasional Profanity. " *The Daily Caller,* (June 30, 2015):1.

181. United States V. Alvarez, 617 F 3d 1198, 1213 (9th Cir. 2010).

182. Cohen v. California, 403 US 15, 16, 26(1971).

183. Snyder v. Phelps, 131 S. CT. 1207, 1220 (2011).

184. Doe v. Univ. of Mich, 721 F.. Supp. 852, 853-54, 856(E.D. Mich. 1989).

185. Robert H Brom, Bishop of San Diego, (August 10, 2014).

186. Conor Friedesdorf, "Stripping a Professor of Tenure over a Blog Post " *The Atlantic,* (February 9, 2015).2.

187. Bryan Polcyn, "Embattled Professor John McAdams Filed Suit against Marquette University," *Fox6Now,* (May 2, 2016).

188. Emily Shire, Freedom of Speech?: Not at Brown University," *The Daily Beast,* (October, 10, 2015).

189. Harvey Silverglate, "The Slow Death of Free Speech at Harvard" *Fire.* (November 3, 2013).

190. Henry Louis Gates, "Let Them Talk: Why civil liberties pose no threat to civil rights." *New Republic*(September 20, 1993):37.

191. *Cox v. Louisiana,* 379 US 536 (1965).

192. New Jersey v. T. L. All.(1985).

193. Hazelwood v. Kuhlmeir 91988).

194. Goss v. Lopez (1975).

195. Engel v. Vitale 91962)

196. Bethel School district v. Fraser (1987)

197. Brown v. Board of Education (1954).

198. Edwin Sutherland, *Principles of Criminology*, Lanham, MD, Altamira Press, (1992) pp 4-8.

199. Mark Warren," Democracy and Deceit: Regulating Appearances of Corruption," *American Journal Of Political Science*, vol.60, (2006):160–174.

200. Susan Rose-Ackerman, *Corruption and Government: Causes, Consequences And Reform*. Cambridge, Cambridge University Press, (1999) pp. 9-26..

201. Phil Fairbanks, "Ciminelli's Court Appearance Moved to Manhattan," *The Buffalo News* (September 27 2016):1.

202. David Klepper and Larry Neumeister,"New York Gov.'s Ex Top Aide among the Nine Charged in Bribery Case" *Register Harold*, (September 23, 2016):1.

203. Terrence McCoy, "The Self-Destructive Mania of Representative Aaron Schock" *The Washington Post*, (March 18, 2015):20.

204. Grant Rodgers, "Ron Paul aids avoid jail time in endorsement," *Des Moines Register*. (September 20, 2016):1.

205. Ashley Southall, "Jesse Jackson, Jr. Gets 30 Months, and his wife 12, to be served at separate times". *The New York Times*, (August 17, 2013):1.

206. Jennifer Steinhauer," Senate, for Just the Eighth Time, Votes to Oust a Federal Judge." *The New York Times*, (December 8, 2010):A27.

207. David Johnston, "Ex-- CIA Official Admits Corruption," *The New York Times*, (September 29, 2008):A19.

208. Randall C. Archibald, "Ex-Congressman Gets Eight-Year Term in Bribery Case," *The New York Times*, (March 4, 2006):1.

209. No author, "Martha Shoffner sentenced to 30 months in prison on bribery, extortion charges," *Times Record* (August 29, 2015):1.

210. Torey Van Oot, "Report: Assemblywoman Mary Hayashi arrested for shoplifting," *The Sacramento Bee*, (October 28, 2011):1

211. Jamie Cook, "Hathaway's fall from grace tragic," *Macomb Daily*, (May 28 2013):1.

212. Syed Hussein Alatas, *Corruption: Its Nature, Causes and Consequences*, (Aldershot. England Avebury 1990) pp. 3-4.

213. Joseph S. Nye, "Corruption and Political Development: a cost-benefit analysis," *American Political Science Review*, v.61 no. 2. (1967):417.

214. Gunnar Myrdal, *Asian Drama*, New York. Pantheon, (1968) pp. 940–942..

215. J. S. Nye, "Corruption and Political Development: a Cost-Benefit Analysis" *American Political Science Review*, vol.61, (1967):417-427.

216. Martin Tolchin and Susan Tolchin, *To the Victor*, New York: Random House, (1971).

217. C. Ronald Chester, "Perceived Relative Deprivation as a cause of property crime," *Crime and Delinquency*, vol.22 (1976):17-30.

218. No author, "Noncitizens Voting," *The National Review*, (April 4, 2012):1.

219. Brian Preston, "Massive Noncitizen Voting Uncovered in Maryland," *PJ Media*, (October 20, 2014):1.

220. Jazz Shawl, "Alabama Court Upholds Conviction of the Woman Guilty of Voter Fraud," *Hot Air*, (August 10, 2016):1.

221. Tony Brown, "JMU Student Tied to Voter Registration Fraud," *Daily News Record*, (September 16, 2016): 1.

222. Peter Tapsak, "Voter Fraud Is Real. Here Are Four More Cases," *The Daily Signal*, (August 18, 2016): 1-6.

223. Ibid. 4.

224. Ibid. 4.

225. Bruce Vielmetti, "Sherwood Man Charged with 13 Counts of Voter Fraud,," *The Journal Sentinel*, (June 24, 2014):1.

226. Government Accountability Office, Washington, D.C Elections: Additional Data Could Help State and Local Election Officials Maintain Adequate Vote Registration Lists.(2005).

227. US Department of Justice, *Federal Prosecution of Election Offenses*, (7th Edition 2007).

228. Robert Greene, "Court Appeal Upholds Perrodin Victory over Bradley in Compton" *Metro News Letter*, (March 11, 2003).

229. Government Accountability Office. "Additional data etc":60.

230. Douglas Frantz, "Vote Fraud in City Outlined at Hearing," *Chicago Tribune*, (September 20, 1983):A1.

231. Non-citizens Voting and I.D. Requirements in US Elections. Hearings before the Committee on House Administration. 109th Congress(2006). (Statement of Paul Betancourt, Harris County tax assessor and voter registrar).

232. John D Buenker, *Urban Liberalism And Progressive Reform*, New York, Scribners, (1971) p. 3.

233. Stephen P Erie, *Rainbows End: Irish-Americans and the Dilemmas of Urban Machine Politics 1840 – 1985.* Berkeley, University Of California Press, (1988).

234. Larry Engelman, *Intemperance: the Lost War against Liquor*, New York: Free Press, (1979) p. 4.

235. Michael Johnston, *Political Corruption and Public Policy in America*, Monterey California, Brooks -Cole, (1982) p. 46.

236. Rufus King, *Gambling and Organized Crime*, Washington DC. Public Affairs Press, (1969) p. 23.

237. John Landesco, *Organized Crime in Chicago*, Chicago, University of Chicago Press, (1968).

238. Gary Marx, "Colombia's cocoa diplomacy promises aims to lift ban," *Chicago Tribune*. (December 6, 1992) p. 28.

239. Jan Fisher, "In New York City's underworld: a window on immigrant crime," *the New York Times*, (June 17, 1993):13.

240. Robert Merton, *On Theoretical Sociology*, New York: The Free Press, (1967) p. 135.

241. David Amoruso, "How the Sicilian Mafia Flooded to U.S. with Heroin," *Mob Magazine*, (October 4, 2008):1.

242. Andre Hollis, "Narco- Terrorism," In: Kimberly Thachuck, *Transnational Threats: Smuggling and Trafficking in Arms, Drugs, and Human Life.*(Westport, Con. Prager 2007) p. 23.

243. Paul Stares, *The Drug Culture in a Borderless World*, (Washington, D.C. Brookings Institute Press 1996) pP. 15-46.

244. United Nations World Drug Report, (2009) p. 68.

245. US Drug Enforcement Agency, "Drug Trafficking in the United States." *Almanac of Policy Issues.*

246. John T. Picarelli, "Responding to Transnational Organized Crime " *N TJ Journal*, no.368, (2011):6.

247. No author, "Authorities Arrest Six in Drug Trafficking Sting Operation," *Local News*, KHBS.

248. US Department of Justice, Office of Justice Programs, Bureau of Justice Statistics, (Washington DC 2013)

249. Samuel P. Friedman, Drug Arrests and Injection, "*American Journal of Public Health*," (February, 2011):2.

250. Pliny the Elder, (Gaius Plius Secundus) *Natural History* (Cambridge Mass. Harvard University Press, Loeb Classical Library, 1989) Book 28, Chapter 23, pp. 78-80; Book 7, Chapter 65.

251. William I Thomas, *The Child in America*, (New York, Knopf 1929) p. 572.

252. Betty Friedan, *The Feminine Mystique*, (New York, WW Norton and Company 1963).

253. No author, "A Current Glance at Women in the Law," (Chicago, the American Bar Association, 2013): 2-5.

254. Pauline W. Chen, "Sharing the Pain of Women in Medicine," *The New York Times*, (November 29, 2012): D7.

255. Bill Vlasic, "New G.M. Chief Is Company Woman Born to It," *The New York Times*, (December 12, 2013:Business Day:1.; Carol Hymowitz and Susan Frier, "IBM's Rometty breaks ground as corporations first female leader," *Bloomberg BusinessWeek*, (October 26, 2011) :1.

256. Stephen Coontz. "How can we help men? By helping women" *The New York Times*, (January 11 2014): 1 – 5.

257. Elizabeth Kolbert, "Firebrand Phyllis Schlafly and the Conservative Revolution," *The New Yorker*, (November 7,2005): v.81, no.34,p. 134.

258. United States Department of Commerce, Bureau of Labor Statistics." New household income," (October 28,2015),.

259. Batya Yasgur, "Compensation Gender Gap in Health Care," *The Midcareer Guide*, (2016): no page.

260. Claudia Guist and Philip S. Cohen, "Headed toward equality? Housework Change in Comparative Perspective." *Journal of Marriage and Family*,v.73, (2011):44.

261. Janet Kirkpatrick, "Introduction: Shelling out? Solidarity and choice in the American feminist movement," *Perspectives on Politics*, vol.8, (2010):241-245.

262. David B Sugarman and Marie Straus, "Indicators of Gender equality for American states and regions," *Social Indicators Research*, v.20, (1987):229-270.

263. National Conference of State Legislatures," Women in state legislatures for 2016." *Women's Legislative Network*, (September 20, 2016).

264. Sonni Efron, "Eating Disorders Go Global," *Los Angeles Times*, (October 18, 1997): A1, A9.

265. Kim Chernin, *The Hungry Self*, (New York: Harper 1994) and Naomi Wolf, *The Beauty Myth*, (New York: William Morrow, 1991).

266. Wolf, The Beauty Myth,:213.

267. Catherine MacKinnon, "Pornography, civil rights, and speak". *Harvard Civil Rights – Civil Liberties Law Review*, (vol.20, 1985):1-70.

268. Daniel Linz, Edward Donnerstein and Steven Penrod, "Effects of long-term exposure to violent and sexually degrading depictions of women," *Journal of Personality and Social Psychology*, vol.55, (1989):758-768.

269. Susan Brownmiller, Against Our Will: men ,women and rape. (New York: Simon and Schuster, (1975) p. 394.

270. American Booksellers Association v. Hudnut, 1986.

271. CJ Ferguson, RD Hartley, "The Influence of Pornography on rape and sexual assault," *Aggression and Violent Behavior*. Vol.14, no.5 (2009):323-329. See also: Michael Flood, "The Harms Of Pornography Exposure Among

Children And Young People," *Child Abuse Review*, v.18, no.6 (2009): 384 – 400.

272. Alana Vagianos, "Shocking Domestic Violence Statistics Reminders It's an Epidemic." *The Huffington Post*, (February 12, 2015).

273. No author, "Fact Sheet: Firearms Related Domestic Violence Homicides," Washington D.C. Young Women's Christian Association, no date

274. Robin Runge, "Double Jeopardy: Victims of Domestic Violence suffer twice the abuse," *ABA Journal*, vol.22, no.2 (Spring 1998):19-21.

275. John L Edleson, "The Overlap between Child maltreatment and woman battering," *Violence against Women*, (February 1999):vol.5, 134-154.

276. Stephen Hoffer, "Giants kicker Josh Brown admitted to domestic violence according to police documents." *The Huffington Post*, (October 20, 2016).

277. Coker v. Georgia, 433 U.S. 584, 586 – 600.

278. 278 Kennedy v. Louisiana, 554 U.S. 407 (2008) and Coker v. Georgia 433 U.S. 84, (1977).

279. United States Department of Justice, Federal Bureau of investigation. (Washington DC *Crime in the United States 2015.*).

280. Julia Schwendinger and Herman Schwendinger, *Rape and Inequality*, (Beverly Hills. California, Sage, 1983

281. Susan Barry, "Spousal Rape: the uncommon law. *American Bar Association Journal*,v.66 (1980): 1088 – 1091.

282. Mary Deming and Ali Eppy, "The Sociology of Rape," *Sociology and Social Research*,v.65, (1981): 357– 379.

283. Martha Burt and R. Estep, "Who is victim? Definitional problems in sexual victimization." *Victimology*, vol.6, (1981):15-28.

284. Camille E LeGrand, "Rape and Rape Laws: sexism in society," *California Law Review*,v.62 (1973):919.

285. Wallace D. Lob, "The impact of common law and rape statutes on prosecution," *Washington Law Review*, v.55, (1980): 543 – 562

286. Ethan Davis, "An Administrative Trail of Tears: Indian removal" *American Journal of Legal History*, v. 50, no. 1(2008):65-68.

287. Robert Baleman, "Wounded Knee," *Military History*, vol. 24, no. 4, (2008):62-67.

288. Russell Thornton," American Indian fertility patterns, *American Indian Quarterly*, vol.15, (Summer 1991):359-367.

289. *Wilbur R Jacobs, Dispossessing the American Indian.* (New York: Charles Scribner's Sons, 1972) p. 102.

290. Thomas R Berger, *A Long and Terrible Shadow*, (Seattle: University of Washington Press, (1991):104-106)

291. Lawrence A. French, *The Winds of Injustice* , (New York Garland Publishing Company, 1994) p73.

292. Washington D.C. U.S. Department of Commerce, Bureau of the Census,. (2015).

293. J. W. Frank, R.S. Moore and G.M. Ames "Historical and cultural roots of drinking problems among American Indians" *American Journal of Public Health*, v.90, no.3, (2000):344-351.

294. Richard T. Schaefer, *Racial and Ethnic Groups*, (New York: HarperCollins, 1990, P. 32.

295. French, The Winds of Injustice, p. 83.

296. Ibid.p. 90.

297. Hendrik Mills, "American Indians and Welfare Liberalism," *American Enterprise*, no. 6(November – December 1998):58.

298. American Indian Historical Society, *The American Indian Reader:Literature*, (San Francisco: American Indian historical Society, 1973) p. 189.

299. James Fenimore Cooper, *The Best Known Works of James Fenimore Cooper*, (New York: Book League of America,1942).

300. Henry Wadsworth Longfellow, *The Song of Hiawatha*, (New Yok: Duell, Sloan and Pearce, 1966).

301. Carol H. Krinsky, "Carl May's Western Novels and Aspects Of Their Continuing Influence," *American Indian Culture and Research*, v.22, no. 3 (1999):53-72.

302. James A. Clifton, "Cultural Fictions," *Society*, v.2, no.4, (1990):28.

303. Devon a. Mihesuha, *American Indian Stereotypes and Realities*, (Atlanta: Clarity Press,, 1996) p. 10–11.

304. Charles F Leventhal, *Drugs, Behavior and Modern Society*, (Boston: Allyn and Bacon, 1996).

305. Andrew Schneider and JoAnn Martinez, *"Medicaid and the Uninsured"* In: *Native Americans Health and Welfare Policy in an Age of New Federalism*, Robert and Stefanie Carroll Rainie, eds. Meredith, Tuscon, AZ Udall Center Publications, 2003,

306. United States Department of Justice, Bureau of Justice statistics. *Violent Crime in the United States* .(2015).

307. Whitney Pope, *Durkheim's Suicide*, (Chicago: The University of Chicago Press, 1976).

308. Hugh Dellios, "Controversy laid to rest as Dickson Mound closes," *Chicago Tribune*, (April 4, 1992):3.

309. Dean Peerman, "Bare-bones Imbroglio" *Christian Century*, vol.107 (October 17, 1990):35.

310. Thorsten Veblen, *The Theory of the Leisure Class*, New York: Oxford University Press, (2007 originally 1912) pp. 35-.36.

311. Robert K Merton, "Social Structure And Anomie," *The American Sociological Review*, vol.3, no.5, (1938):672-682

312. Edwin H. Sutherland, In: K. Schuessler, *EH Sutherland And Analyzing Crime:* Chicago: University Of Chicago Press(1973) pp13-29.

313. Articles Of Impeachment, The House Judiciary Committee, July 27, 1974.

314. Mike Colias, "Children's Memorial target of guy's shakedown efforts," *Crain's Chicago Business*, (December 9, 2008):1.

315. Monica Davey, "Ex-governor of Illinois gets 6 1/2 years in prison. " *The New York Times*, (September 7, 2006):A19.

316. No author, "Covered a lot of ground and dies convicted while at home."

317. No author, "Ex-Illinois Gov. Pleads Guilty in Loan Fraud," *The New York Times*, (August 6, 1987):A1.

318. United States v. Williams,529 F.Supp 1085.1090 (1090 e.d. N.Y. 1981).

319. Molly Hennessy-Fiske, "Veteran Swore Times at El Paso V.A. Are Latest to Come under Scrutiny," *Los Angeles Times*, (June 4,2013);1.

320. No author, "Ex-Bush aide Pleads Guilty to Stealing from Federally Aided Center", *(December 20, 208).*

321. Ronald Smothers," Treffinger Pleads Guilty to Corruption," *The New York Times*, (May 31, 2003):N.Y. Region.

322. Susan Schmidt and James V. Grimaldi, "Ney sentenced to 30 months in prison for Abramoff Deals." *The Washington Post*, (January 20, 2007)::1.

323. Neil A Lewis, " Abramoff gets four years in prison for corruption"

324. No author, "Arizona Representative Rick Renzi, Convicted in Federal Corruption Case," US News, (January 11, 2013):3.

325. No author. "Former Congressman William J Jefferson Convicted of Bribery, Racketeering, Money Laundering, and Other Related Charges," Washington DC, the FBI Washington Field Office, office of Public affairs(August 5, 2009):1-3.

326. David Rosenbaum, "Rostenkowski Pleads Guilty to Mail Fraud," *The New York Times*, (April 10,1996):A.

327. James Aloisi, "For better or for worse James Michael Curley defined Boston in the early half of the 20th century." *Common Wealth*, (September 23,2013):1.

328. Francis X. Clines, "Ohio Congressman Guilty in Bribery and Kickbacks," *The New York Times*, (April 12, 2002): 1.

329. Arthur C Binding. *A History of the United States*, (New York: Charles Scribner's Sons, 1951) p. 426.

330. Francisco L Nepa, "Langley, Catherine Gudger." *American National Biography*, (New York: Oxford University Press, 1999):156-157.

331. John Messing, "Public Lands, Politics, And Progressives: The Oregon Land Fraud Trials, 1903 – 1910." Pacific *Historical Review*,v.35, (1966):35-66.

332. Domenec Mele, "Corruption:10 Possible Causes," *Business Ethics Network*, http://blo.iese.edu/ethics/2013.

333. John Henslin, *Sociology: A Down to Earth Approach*, (New York: Allyn and Bacon, 20004) p. 225.

334. Douglas Martin, "Walter Cronkite, 92, Dies; Trusted Voice of TV News," *The New York Times* (July 7, 2009): Politics.

335. Pete Schuloberg, "FOXNews: Business If Not Artistic Success," *The Oregonian*, (July 15, 1994):E1.

336. Brian Stelter, "With Tagline, MSNBC Embraces A Political Identity," *The New York Times*, (October 4, 2010):B3.

337. Mike McPhate and Ben Sisario "4 More Years: Rush Limbaugh signs a New Radio Contract," *The New York Times*, (August 2010):Media

338. Jake Lynn and Annabelle McGoldrick, *Peace Journalism*, Stroud, Gloucestershire UK (2000) p. 10.

339. Ibid.p3.

340. ibid.p. 24.

341. Ibid.p. 24.

342. Rune Ottosen, *The Dynamics of Medicalization*, Peter Lang, (2000) pp. 149-164.

343. Lynch and McGoldrick,

344. David Loyn, "Good Journalism or Peace Journalism," In: *Conflict and Communication online*,vol.6, no.2(2007):10.

345. Wilhelm Kempf, "Peace Journalism: A tightrope walk between advocacy and constructive coverage," *Conflict and Communication online* v. 6, no.2,*2007):7. And he must win the electoral vote

346. 347 12th amendment to the Constitution of the United States.

347. Willie Brown, "Ground Game Will Put Hillary Clinton in the White,," *The San Francisco Chronicle*, (November 5, 2016):14.

348. Ed Kilgore, "Some People Are Now 100% sure Hillary Clinton Will Win," *New York* (October 18, 2016):1.

349. No author, "Map That Proves Donald Trump Will Lose," *Work Leaders*, (August 17, 2016):1.

350. Vicki Needham, "Election Model: Clinton will win easily," *The Hill*, (July 1, 2016):2.

351. No Author, "Hillary Clinton Has an 85% Chance to Win," *The New York Times*, (November 8 2016):1.

352. Allan Smith, "NBC's electoral map shows Hillary Clinton with enough electoral votes to win the presidency," *Business Insider* (August 15, 2016):1-3.

353. Scott Whitlock, "CBS predicts 341 electoral votes for Hillary Clinton and likely blowout " MRC *News Busters*, (September 6, 2016):1.

354. Society Of Professional Journalists, *Code of Ethics*, (1996). Semi final game in St. Louis

355. Matthew May, "Schadenfreude" *The Washington Post*, (April 9, 2005).

356. Trudy Lieberman, 'Plagiarize, plagiarize, plagiarize - but be sure to call it research." *Columbia Journalism Review*, (July-August, 1995):4.

357. Felicity Barringer, "A P says it could not find 45 of fired of fired rider sources," *The New York Times*, (October 22, 2002):A22.

358. Thomas Fuller, "Anti--Trump Demonstrators Take to the Streets in Several U.S. Cities," *The New York Times*, (November 9, 2016):;A1.

359. Matt Hamilton and Barbara Dimmick," Trump win sparks student walkouts and protests across the United States," (November 9, 2016):1.

360. United States Department of Justice, Federal Bureau of Investigation. Washington DC Criminal Justice Information Services Division. "Defining a hate crime," (no date):1.

361. The Southern Poverty Law Center, *The Year in Hate; intelligence Report*, Issue 125, (2007):52-58.

362. Donald P Greene, Dara Z. Strolovich and Janelle S. Wong, "Defendant Neighborhoods: Integration and Racially Motivated Crime. *American Journal of Sociology*, vol. 104(1998): 172 – 403.

363. Brian Levin, A Dream Deferred: The Social and Legal Implications Of Hate Crimes" *The Journal of Intergroup Relations*, vol.20, no.3, (1993):3-27.

364. Special to the New York Times, "Drifter is found guilty of killing a Seattle family." *The New York Times*, (June 6 1986):1.

365. Tamar Lewin, "Sikh owner of gas station is fatally shot in rampage," *The New York Times*, (September 17, 2001):1.

366. United States Department of Justice, Federal Bureau of investigation, Washington DC. Uniform Crime Report, cal Latest Hate Crime Statistics. (November 16, 2015).

367. Daniel J. Wakin, "Richard G. Butler, Founder of the Aryan Nation, Dies." *The New York Times*, (September 9, 2004): Obituaries.

368. Opinion Page, "Matthew Shepard Act," *The New York Times*, (May 5, 2009):1.

369. James Sterngold, "Supremacist who killed postal worker avoidance death sentence," *The New York Times*, (January 24, 2004):A1.

370. Southern Poverty Law Ctr., Keenan V. Aryan Nations, First Judicial District, Idaho, Kootenai County.

371. John R White, "The Road to Armageddon: religion and domestic terrorism," *Quarterly Journal of Ideology*,vol.13,no.2, (1989):11-21.

372. Sarah Bullard, *The Ku Klux Klan, Southern Poverty Law Institute : A History of Violence Embraces, Montgomery Alabama.no date.*

373. Samuel Stebbins, "12 States with the Most Hate Groups" *24/7 wall Street.* February 4, 2016):1.

374. No author, "Rev. Farakhan to followers: White people deserve to die." Newsmax, (August 15, 2016.

375. No author, "Louis Farrakhan biography," *New York: World Biography*, 5th *ed.* (1954).

376. American Psychiatric Association, Washington DC. *Diagnostic and Statistical Manual Of Mental Disorders, APA* (2013):DSM-5.

377. R.P. Ang, O.E.L. Ong, I.C.Y. Lim, "From narcissistic exploitativeness to bullying behavior," *Social Development*,vol.19, (2010):1-26. The law also requires the federal Bureau of investigation

378. Resolution 309 of the Missouri Synod of the Lutheran Church (June 1983).

379. John W. O'Malley, "Opening the Church to the World," *The New York Times*, (October 10, 2012):op ed.

380. Declaration of the Church to non-Christian Religions. Nostra aetate, proclaimed by his Holiness Pope Paul VI on October 20, 1965.

381. United States Department of Justice, Federal Bureau of investigation, Washington DC "Latest hate crime statistics released," (November 14, 2016):1-6.

INDEX

Printed in the United States
By Bookmasters